The College History Series

McNeese State University

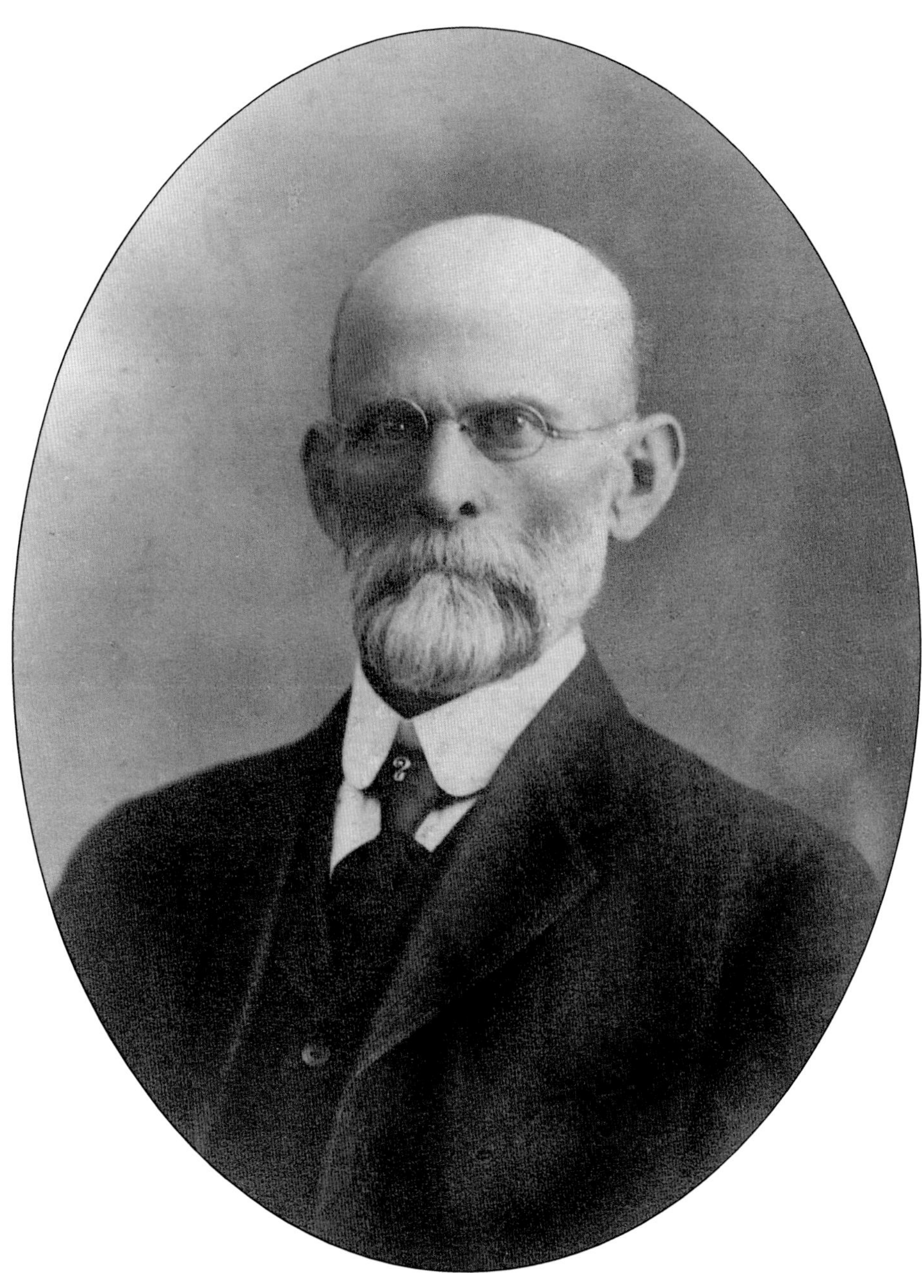

JOHN MCNEESE, 1843–1914. Lake Charles Junior College was established in 1939, but within a year the citizens of Southwest Louisiana renamed it John McNeese Junior College in honor of this pioneer educator. A long-standing argument on campus has been over the correct pronunciation of the name "McNeese"—whether it is "mick" or "mack." The argument was settled in two ways: first, McNeese's son-in-law, L.L. Squires, wrote in his biography of McNeese that his nickname was "Mack." Secondly, this author visited descendants living in Mississippi, North Carolina, and Virginia and was told that the correct pronunciation is, indeed, "Mack" Neese. John McNeese was elected to serve as secretary of the Imperial Calcasieu School Board in 1888 and was named ex-officio parish superintendent. He served six, four-year terms as parish superintendent, retiring in 1913.

The College History Series

McNeese State University

Kathie Bordelon

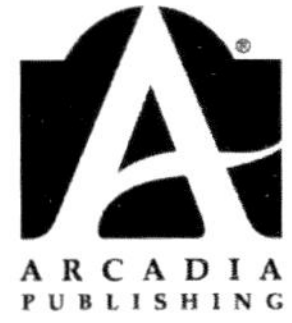

ARCADIA
PUBLISHING

Published by Arcadia Publishing
Charleston, South Carolina

Printed in the United States of America

Library of Congress Catalog Card Number: 2001088279

For all general information contact Arcadia Publishing at:
Telephone 843-853-2070
Fax 843-853-0044
E-Mail sales@arcadiapublishing.com
For customer service and orders:
Toll-Free 1-888-313-2665

Visit us on the Internet at www.arcadiapublishing.com

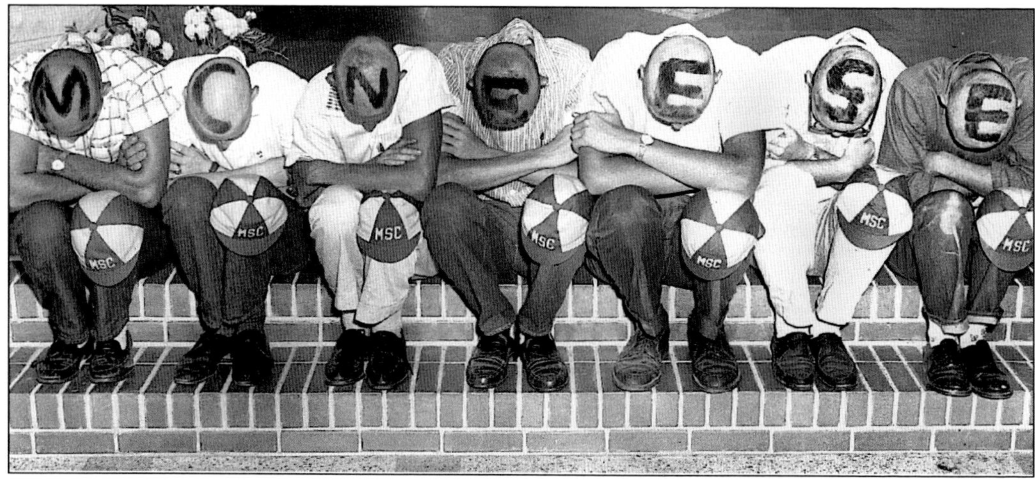

SHAVED HEADS AND BEANIES. An early issue of *The Log* stated that "the accepted method of introducing freshmen to the collegiate way of life consists of making them look and feel as ridiculous as possible for a week or so." Freshman initiation for boys included having their heads shaved, wearing beanies (called doggie caps) and dog tags, and singing the Alma Mater on command. Freshman girls were not allowed to sit in chairs or wear makeup. They were required to wear their hair in braids or in rollers and to wear mismatched shoes and socks. They endured many other humiliations in the spirit of fun. As one reporter said, "In all it's been good, clean fun and it'll do a lot to kindle spirit within you. You'd have mighty drab college memories if you had only the routine of daily classes to recall."

4

Contents

Alma Mater

We hail our Alma Mater,
        with hearts full of gratitude;
Where knowledge dwells with friendship,
        and all that is right and true.
Our mem'ries here will linger,
        with faith in all you do;
McNeese, McNeese, may glory reign here, too-
All Hail! All Hail! McNeese, we are proud of you.

-Kenneth L. Gaburo

ALMA MATER. Kenneth L. Gaburo, instructor in the Department of Music, composed the Alma Mater in 1950. It was first presented to the public on September 22, 1950, in recognition of John McNeese Junior College receiving four-year college status and being renamed McNeese State College.

INTRODUCTION

McNeese State University is located in Lake Charles, Louisiana, in the southwest corner of the state. Situated approximately 30 miles north of the Gulf of Mexico and east of the Texas state line, Lake Charles has a population of about 75,000. It is small enough to retain a friendly, hospitable atmosphere, yet large enough to offer a variety of cultural, educational, and recreational events. According to a Southwest Louisiana Convention and Visitors Bureau brochure, "The area is covered by marshlands and timberlands, prairies and rice fields, rivers and bayous. You'll see alligators and accordions, pirates and pelicans, cowboys and casinos, fiddlers and festivals, beaches and bayous."

McNeese State University and Lake Charles have maintained a mutually beneficial relationship for the last 62 years. Since its inception, McNeese has sought to provide Lake Charles and Southwest Louisiana with teachers, nurses, engineers, and other graduates ready and able to take their place in the community.

In the beginning, Lake Charles Junior College operated under the administration of Louisiana State University. Today, McNeese State University is a member of the University of Louisiana System. Lake Charles Junior College became John McNeese Junior College shortly after its founding in 1939. In 1950, it became McNeese State College when it advanced to four-year status and separated from LSU. The Louisiana Legislature gave the institution its present name in 1970.

The junior college began with a faculty of 13 and 140 registered students. The university now employs over 300 faculty and enrolls close to 8,000 students from 58 Louisiana parishes, 30 states, and over 30 countries around the world.

McNeese offers undergraduate and selected graduate degrees from both the liberal arts and professional programs. The six academic colleges are the College of Business, Burton College of Education, College of Engineering and Technology, College of Liberal Arts, College of Nursing, and College of Science. The slogan "Excellence With A Personal Touch" reflects the university's commitment to academic excellence and personal attention. McNeese is accredited by the Commission on Colleges of the Southern Association of Colleges and Schools.

This photographic history of McNeese State University is intended to complement Dr. Joe Gray Taylor's *McNeese State University 1939–1987: A Chronicle*. Dr. Taylor's chronicle was written to commemorate the university's 50th anniversary that was celebrated in 1989. It was, as the title suggests, a chronicle of the names and deeds of students and faculty members.

The photographs selected for this book illustrate, as much as possible, the information in Dr. Taylor's book.

The photographs selected and the captions written for this photographic history of McNeese cannot possibly convey to the reader the entire picture of the history of the university. Just as Dr. Taylor could not include every student and every faculty member in his book, this book also has its limitations. Many people, important for their contributions to the university, and many events and activities, also of historical significance to the university, must necessarily be excluded in a book with a set format such as this. It was my desire and my intent to include as much of the history of McNeese as possible within the publication boundaries. I sincerely regret having to leave out so many of the wonderful photographs viewed for this project and so much of the additional historical information for which there was no room in the captions.

With these thoughts in mind, I would like to dedicate this book, first of all, to Dr. Joe Gray Taylor's memory, and secondly, to all the faculty, staff, administrators, students, and alumni of McNeese, loyal and devoted as they are and were, who are not mentioned or pictured herein.

One

BEGINNINGS

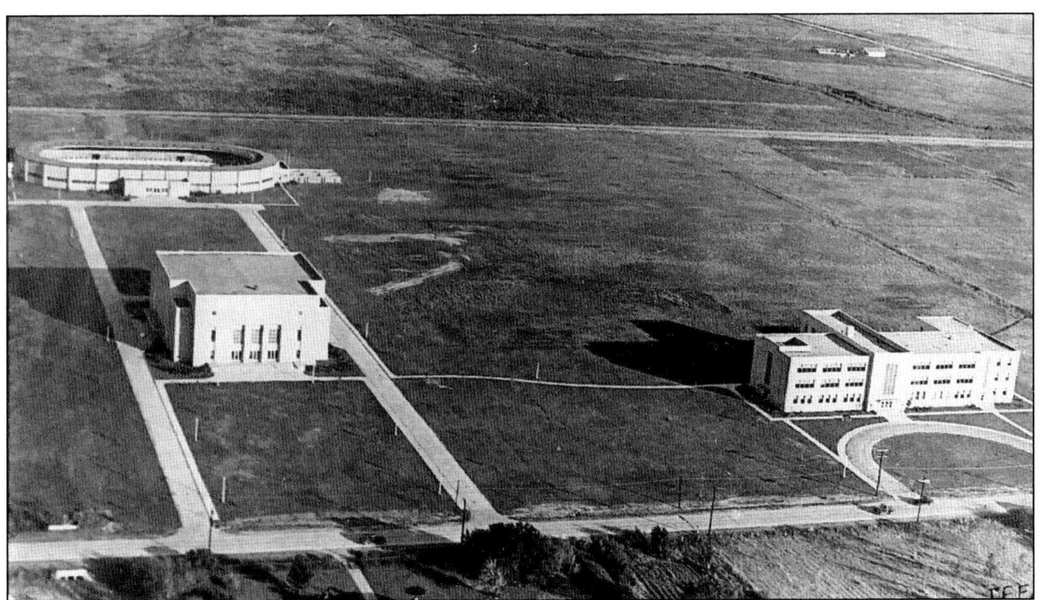

AERIAL VIEW OF CAMPUS, 1939–1940. Lake Charles Junior College was established by the authorization of the Louisiana Legislature in 1938. Three groups working together were responsible for its successful formation. The Southwest Louisiana Cattlemen's Association wanted an arena for livestock shows and rodeos; the Calcasieu Parish Police Jury, representing the people, wanted a college; and the federal government, through the WPA, was making funds available for public facilities such as auditoriums. The first three buildings were the arena, the administration-classroom building, and the auditorium.

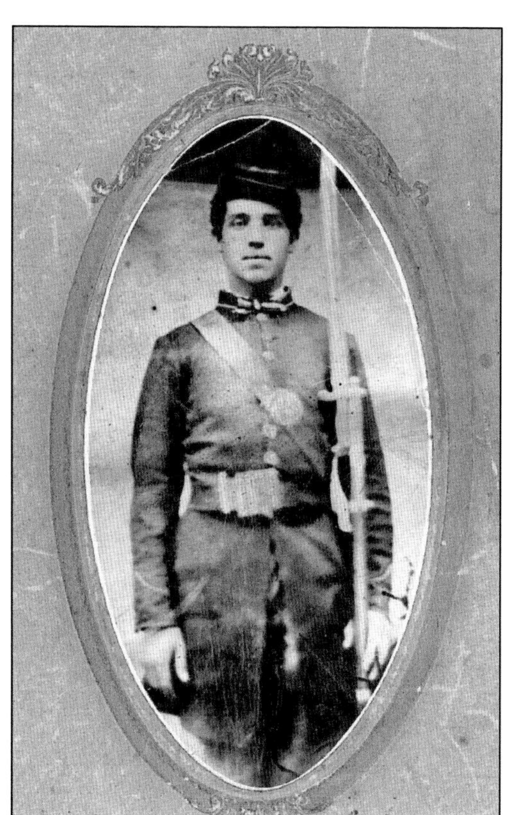

JOHN MCNEESE, UNION SOLDIER, 1862. Originally from Maryland, John McNeese joined the Union Army in 1861 becoming a corporal in Company E, 1st Regiment, Eastern Shore, Maryland Volunteer Infantry. He re-enlisted in 1864 and was assigned to Company B, 2nd Regiment, Maryland Infantry. McNeese is known to have fought at Gettysburg and moved to Texas for his health after the war was over. He served as district clerk for Menard County, Texas, and was also involved in the mercantile and cattle business.

JOHN MCNEESE, BALD AND BEARDED. McNeese settled in Southwest Louisiana in 1873 after a disastrous cattle drive left him stranded on the east side of the Sabine River. He became a teacher of penmanship and singing in Lake Charles, in what was then known as Imperial Calcasieu Parish. He studied law at Tulane University, practicing only briefly, as he became more and more involved in education. In this photograph, McNeese poses with the rest of the faculty on the front steps of one of the area's early schools. The young lady in the white hat is his daughter Emma.

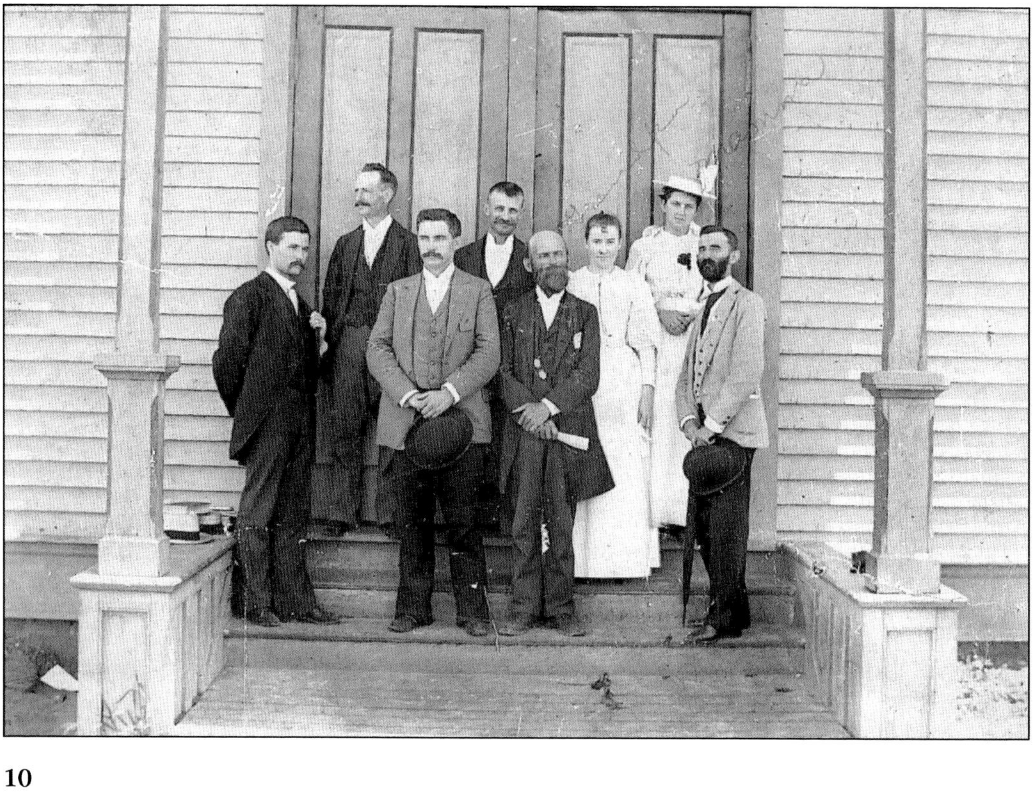

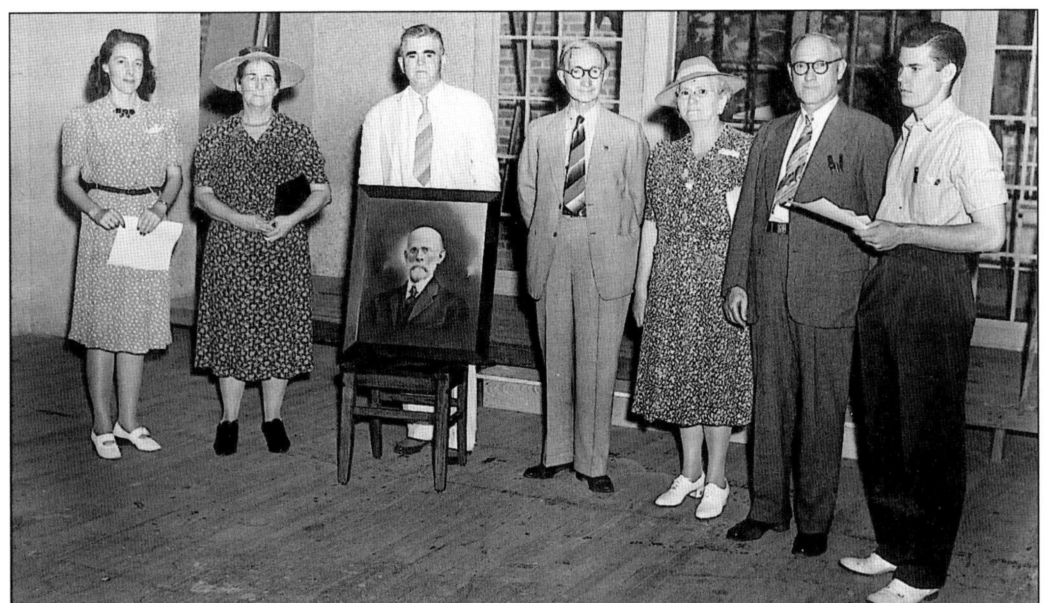

PORTRAIT PRESENTED TO COLLEGE. When this portrait of John McNeese was presented to John McNeese Junior College in 1941, the donor, Dr. M.V. Hargrove, said, "it may be that [McNeese] could visualize through his prophetic eye the location in his beloved Lake Charles and Old Calcasieu this great institution that will perpetuate his name and commemorate his deeds." Pictured are, from left to right, Mrs. Freda Scoggins Thomas, speech instructor; Mrs. L.L Squires, daughter of John McNeese; Dean W.B Hatcher; L.L. Squires, son-in-law of John McNeese; Mrs. M.V. Hargrove; Dr. M.V. Hargrove, Allen Parish Police juror and former principal of Oakdale High School; and G.W. Ford Jr., president of the student body. The portrait still hangs in the university library today.

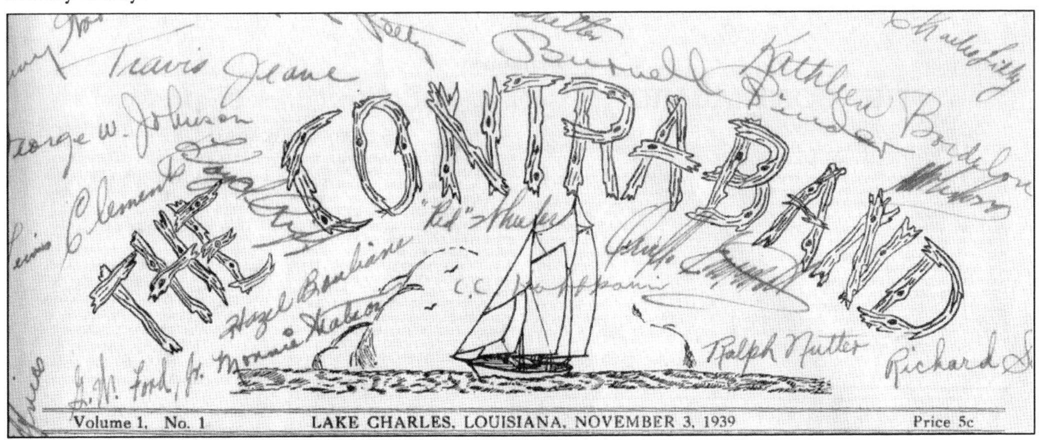

THE CONTRABAND. The student newspaper was named *The Contraband* in 1939 to recognize a popular legend in the Lake Charles area. The legend tells of two swashbuckling pirates, Henry Morgan in 1662 and Jean Lafitte in 1811, who sailed up the Calcasieu River from the Gulf of Mexico in order to evade capture. While taking shelter along the banks of a beautiful bayou, the pirates took the opportunity to bury their treasure where they could come for it another time. Supposedly, their treasure remains buried along the banks of Contraband Bayou, which meanders its way across the south side of the campus. This first issue of *The Contraband* is autographed by the students in the first class. G.W. Ford Jr. was the editor-in-chief.

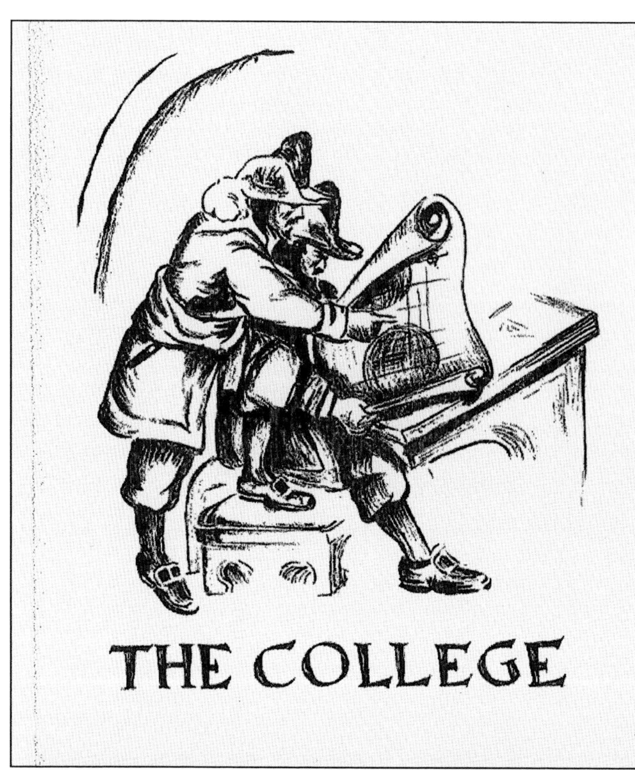

THE LOG. First issued in 1940, the college yearbook, *The Log*, was named to further the nautical theme started by *The Contraband.* As Martha Caldwell, the editor of the 1941 volume wrote, "The bold adventurers who sailed into Grand Lake, thence into Lake Charles and Contraband Bayou, found time from their exploits to keep careful records, or logs, of the daily events, prosaic or exciting, which befell them. These logs remain for us today one of the richest heritages of a bygone day, a heritage that has contributed immeasurably to our tradition. The editors of this book hope that, in a small way, it will serve the same purpose, your *Log* of a successful year spent at John McNeese Junior College."

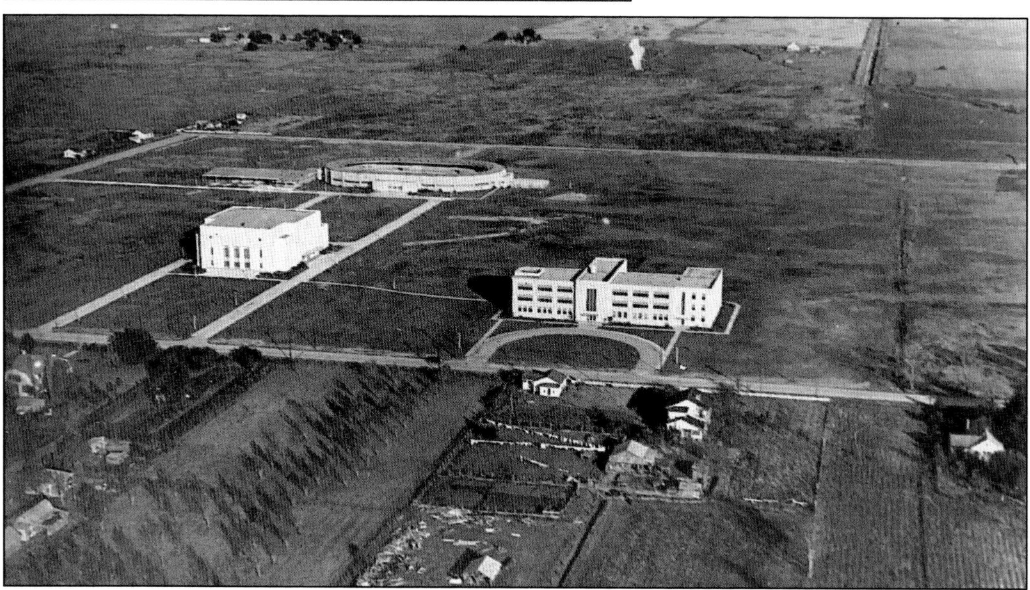

"IT's TOO FAR OUT!" "IT's TOO LARGE!" According to Dr. Harcourt Stebbins, one of the early students, an excited populace voiced these exclamations when the college buildings were under construction. An aerial view of the campus shows how the location chosen was surrounded by prairie land and very much out in the country. The 86-acre tract of land donated by the police jury had been the site of the parish poor farm and cattle-dipping vat. The town of Lake Charles was located several miles northeast of the college. The shell/gravel road from the town to the college was called South Street, today known as Ryan Street.

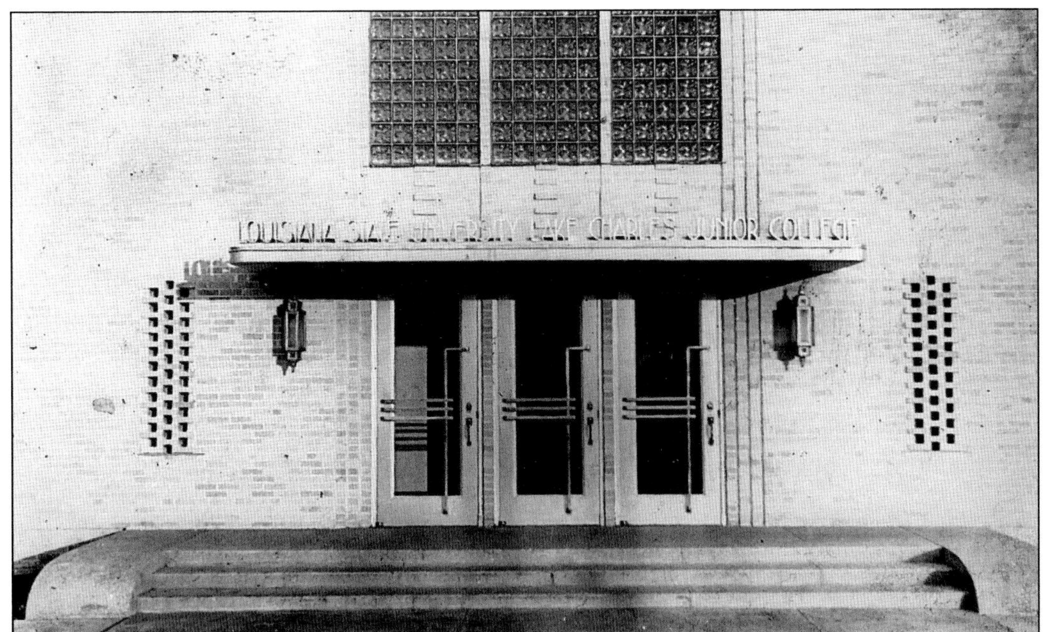

UNDER THE AUSPICES OF LOUISIANA STATE UNIVERSITY. The words "Louisiana State University Lake Charles Junior College" graced the front doorway of the new administration-classroom building in 1939. The name of the school has changed several times: in 1940 to John McNeese Junior College in honor of the pioneer Southwest Louisiana educator, in 1950 to McNeese State College when four-year status and separation from Louisiana State University was achieved, and in 1970 to McNeese State University when university status was granted.

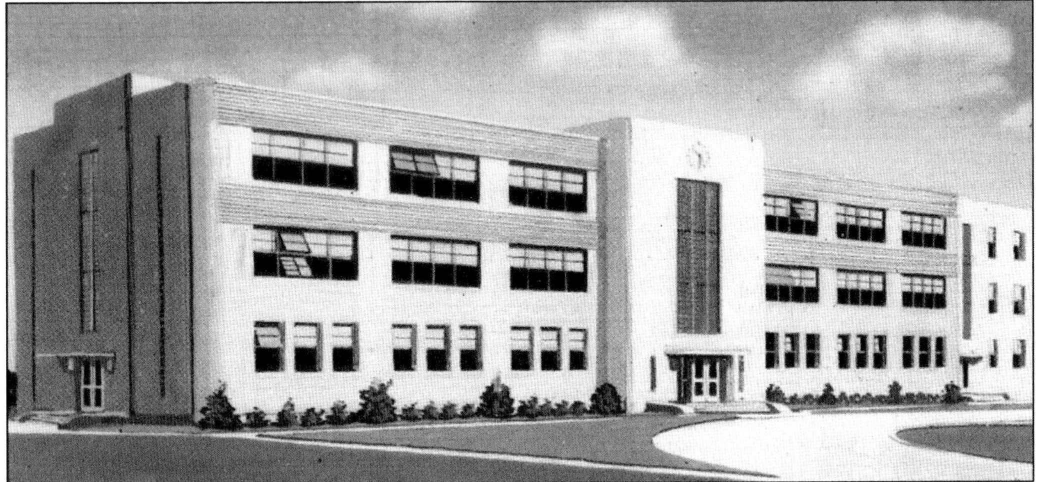

KAUFMAN HALL. The administration-classroom building was named Kaufman Hall in 1965 in honor of Leopold Kaufman, an early merchant, civic leader, philanthropist, and founder of the First National Bank in Lake Charles. His son E.R. Kaufman was one of the local citizens lending his support to the establishment of the college. In 1950, when a Louisiana legislator filed suit to prevent the college from obtaining degree-granting status, Kaufman was one of the outstanding attorneys representing McNeese. The others, former Gov. Sam H. Jones, former Gov. Alvin O. King, Cullen R. Liskow, and Vance Plauche, successfully represented McNeese in the courts. Naming the first building Kaufman Hall honored both father and son.

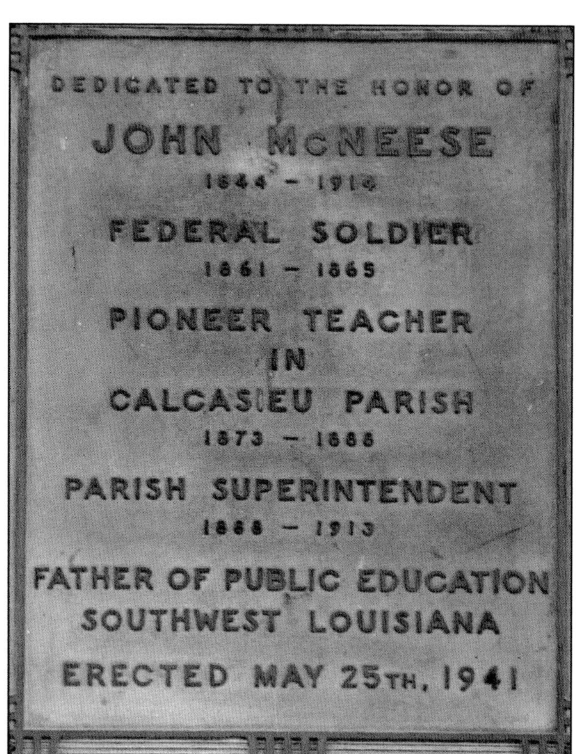

DEDICATION PLAQUE. This plaque, honoring the memory of John McNeese, hangs inside the front doors of Kaufman Hall. McNeese died in 1914 and is buried in Orange Grove Cemetery in Lake Charles.

LAKE CHARLES JUNIOR COLLEGE AUDITORIUM. Constructed in the art deco style in 1939, the auditorium was dedicated in January 1940. During the early days of the school, before additional buildings were constructed, the auditorium served many purposes. School dances and plays were staged, a ring was set up for boxing matches, commencement exercises were conducted, homecoming queens were crowned, and the first basketball games were even played here.

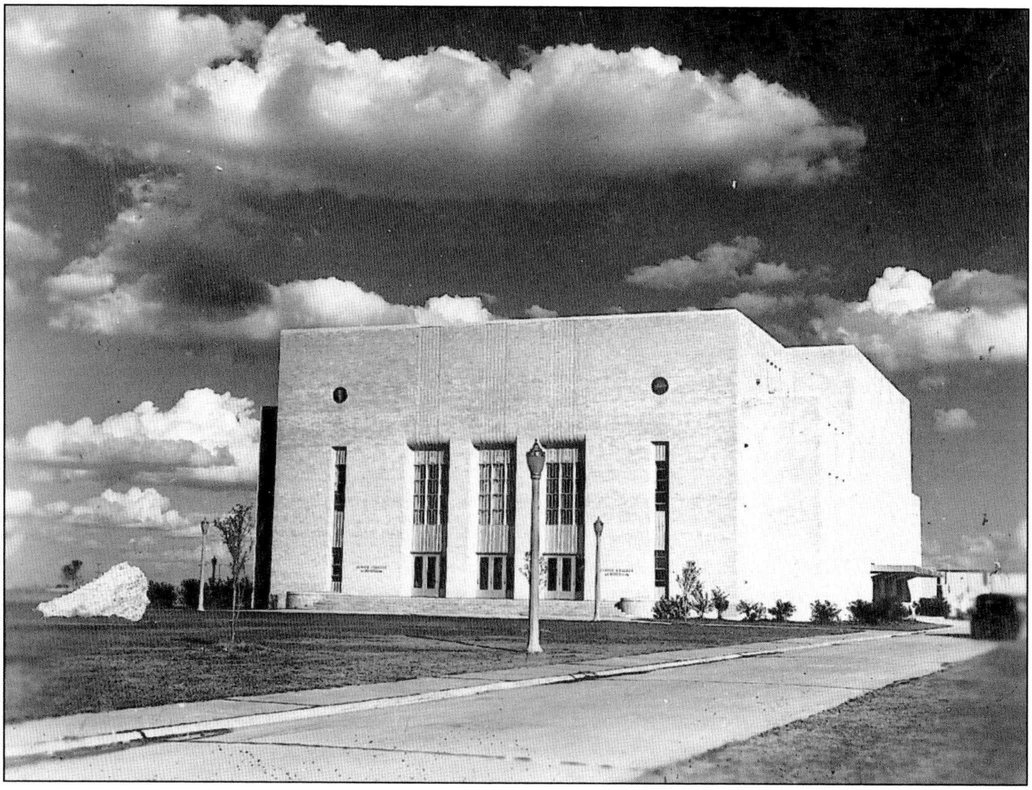

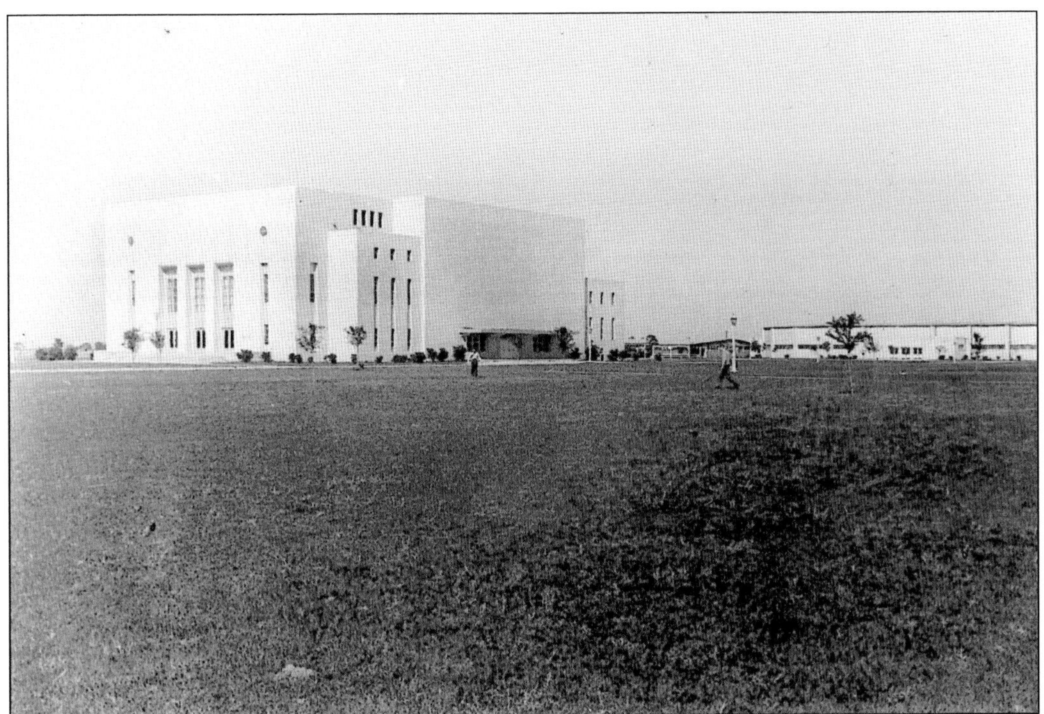

THE AUDITORIUM AND *THE MESSIAH*. On December 15, 1940, Dr. Francis G. Bulber directed McNeese's first annual performance of Handel's *Messiah*, beginning a tradition that continues today. The idea for the performance had existed among local churches and choir directors for a number of years. With the new college providing an appropriate site and a director capable of handling such an event, it seemed that the time had come. *The Messiah* was performed before a packed house that day in 1940. On the first Sunday afternoon in December of each year, the tradition continues. Dr. Bulber came out of retirement to conduct the 50th anniversary celebration of *The Messiah* in 1989.

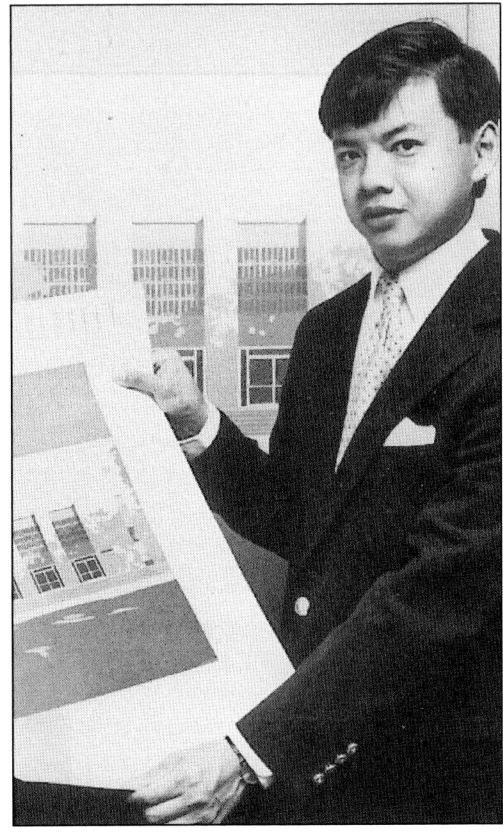

CHARLIE HUANG'S PAINTING OF THE AUDITORIUM. McNeese art student Charlie Huang holds a poster of his painting that commemorated the 50th anniversary of the university in 1989. The painting features the main auditorium, which was placed on the National Register of Historic Places. Numerous festivities, productions, and publications highlighted this anniversary year, including an hour-long documentary produced by one of the local television stations, KPLC-TV.

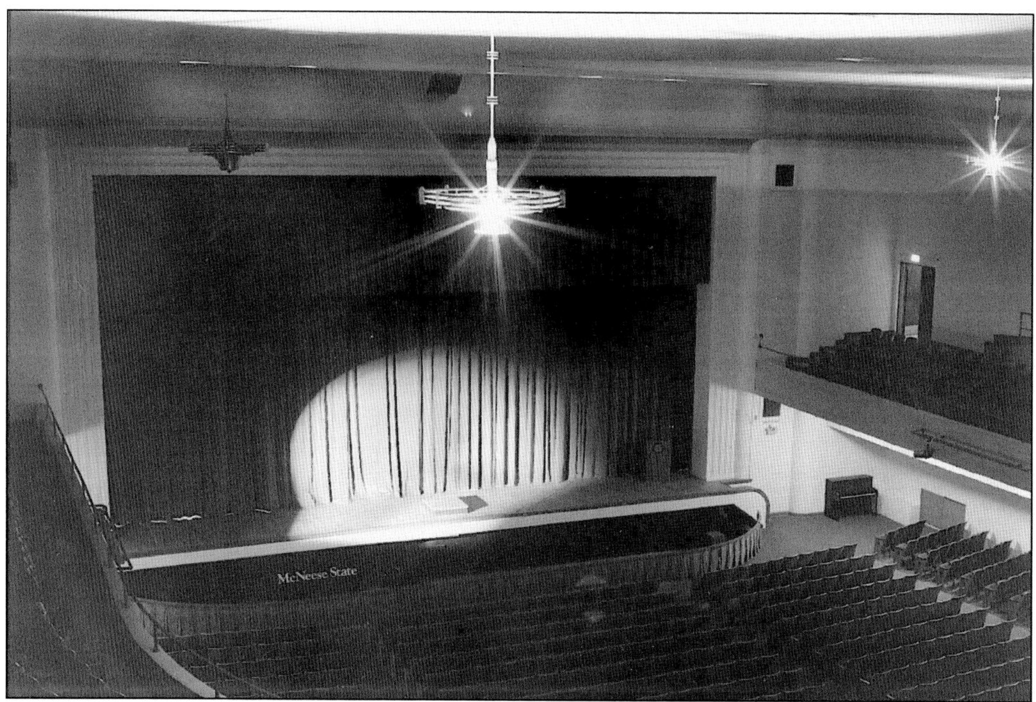

AUDITORIUM STAGE AND LOBBY. The auditorium is a good example of the art deco style of architecture. Its vertical windows, brick patterns, and stylized figures above the entrance openings are art deco features. According to architect M. Jude Benoit, who described the building for the application to the Historic Register, other art deco features include the sunrise medallion on the front facade, the iron grill work at the front windows and ticket booth, and the curved window heads. Interior features include the curved corners, the curved ceiling in the upstairs reception hall, and the step ceiling trim.

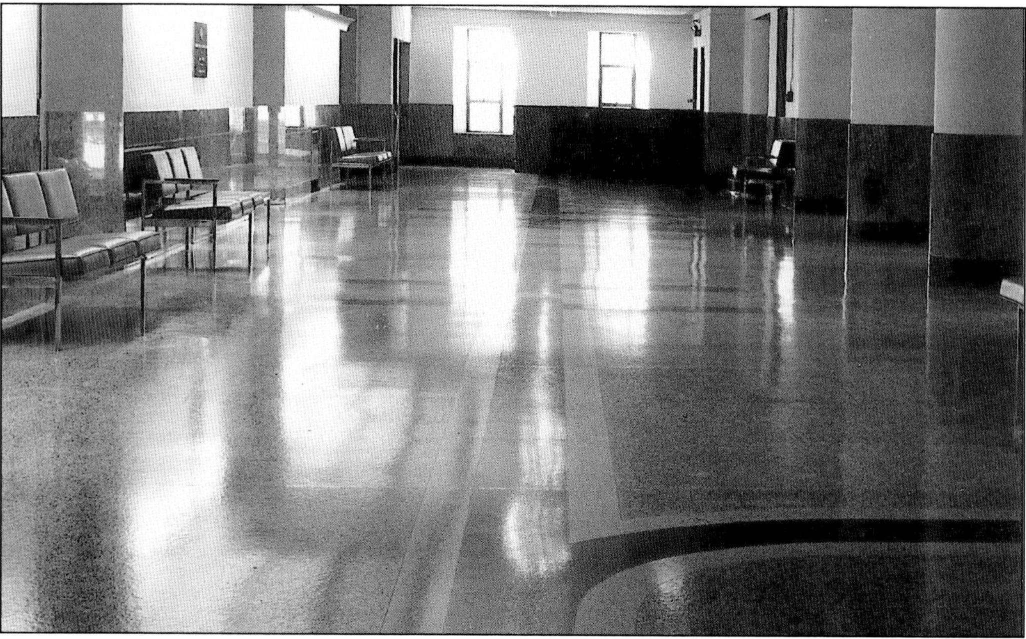

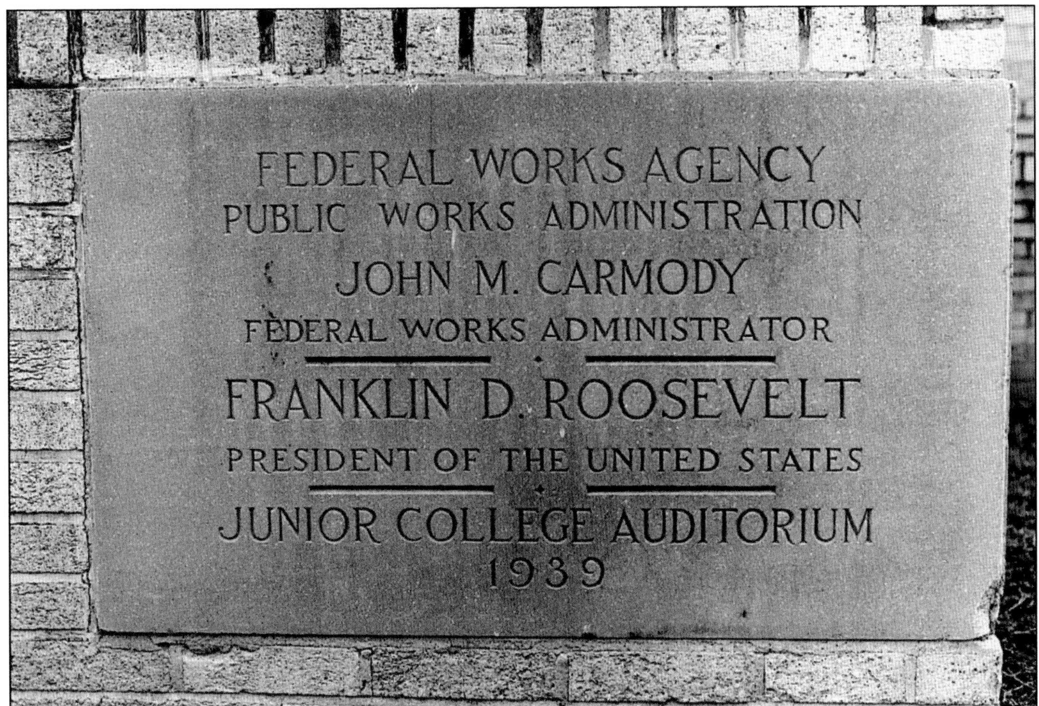

AUDITORIUM CORNERSTONE. The cornerstones of the three original buildings illustrate the contributions made by the Federal Works Agency and the Public Works Administration under the New Deal encouraged by President Franklin D. Roosevelt.

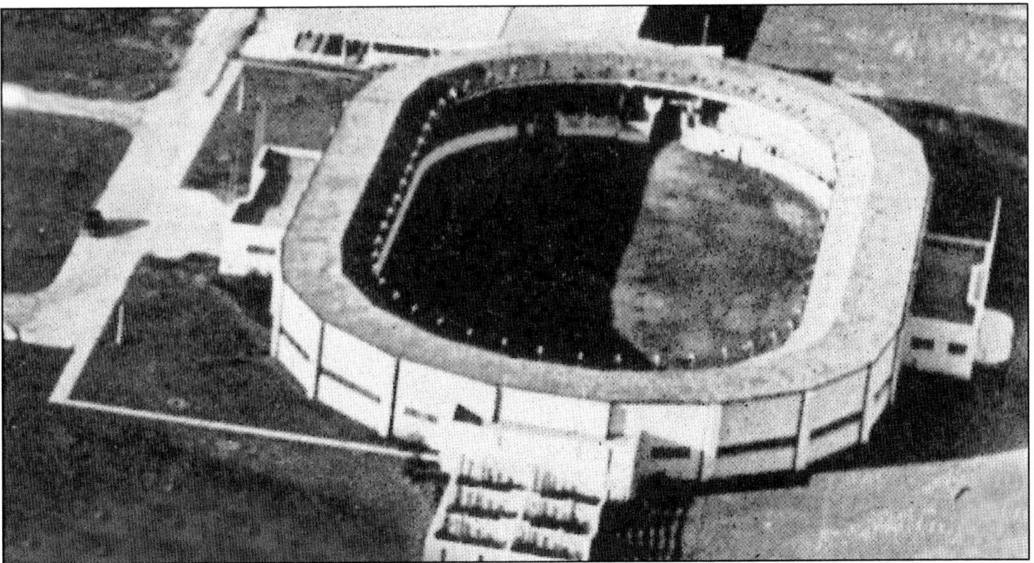

ARENA. When first constructed in 1939, the arena was open as seen in this photograph. Originally designed for livestock shows and rodeos, it was not until about 1950 that a roof was added. The arena could then be used for other purposes, including basketball games, physical education classes, and tennis matches. An annex housing a basketball court was constructed in 1956 and dedicated by Lt. Gov. Lether E. Frazar on December 10, 1956. The arena was renamed the Ralph O. Ward Memorial Arena in 1990 in honor of the former basketball coach.

17

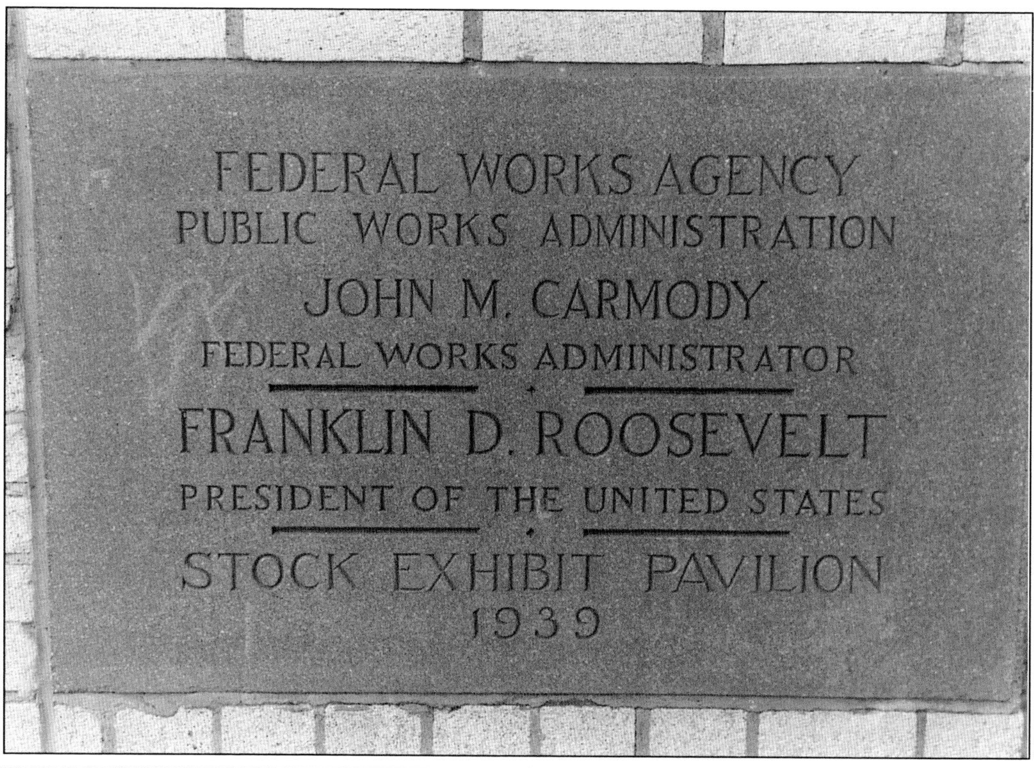

6   LOUISIANA STATE UNIVERSITY

GENERAL INFORMATION

HISTORICAL SKETCH

The Lake Charles Junior College, a branch of the Junior Division of the Louisiana State University, was created by legislative act at the regular session of the state legislature in 1938. The land and the buildings were provided by the Police Jury of the Parish of Calcasieu, the Public Works Administration, and the State of Louisiana.

OBJECTIVES OF THE JUNIOR COLLEGE

It is the purpose of the Board of Supervisors and the Administrative Officers of Louisiana State University to bring, through the Junior College, the facilities of the University closer to the young men and women of Southwest Louisiana and at a greatly reduced cost. The courses offered at the Lake Charles Junior College are therefore the same as those offered in the first two years on the campus of the University at Baton Rouge. High school graduates of Southwest Louisiana who plan to attend the University are urged to spend their freshman and sophomore years in the Lake Charles Junior College.

BUILDINGS AND EQUIPMENT

The campus of the Lake Charles Junior College, which is beautifully landscaped, consists of eighty-seven acres located in the southwest suburbs of the city of Lake Charles. The grounds, buildings, and equipment are valued at approximately $1,000,000.

The administration building is a three-story modern fireproof structure containing classrooms, laboratories, offices, a cafeteria, and the library. Other buildings in the process of construction are an auditorium and a coliseum which is to be used as a gymnasium as well as for other purposes.

THE LIBRARY

The library, ample in size and supervised by a trained librarian, is attractively furnished and generously supplied with books, magazines, and newspapers.

STUDENT EXPENSES

A general fee is charged to all students to defray the cost of the following: matriculation, library, athletics, lockers, and physical examination. The amount of the fee is $20 a semester, payable in advance.

SPECIAL FEES

Special fees are as follows: late entrance fee, $1.00 for the first week, and $1.00 for each additional week or fraction thereof; changes in schedule, unless initiated by the Dean of the College, 25 cents; special examinations, 50 cents.

FEE FOR SPECIAL STUDENTS

All students who take fewer than three courses and who are not candidates for graduation may, in lieu of the regular registration fee, pay $2.25 for each semester hour carried.

ARENA CORNERSTONE. The Louisiana Cattlemen's Association originally wanted the arena to be a stock exhibit pavilion. Burton Coliseum is now used for livestock shows and rodeos, while the arena houses an Olympic-size swimming pool, an indoor track, basketball courts, and more.

FIRST *CATALOGUE*. The first publication of the *Catalogue*, spelled *Catalog* only after 1979, included the general information seen here as well as the costs of books—$12.50 to $25 per year.

Two

CAMPUS SCENES

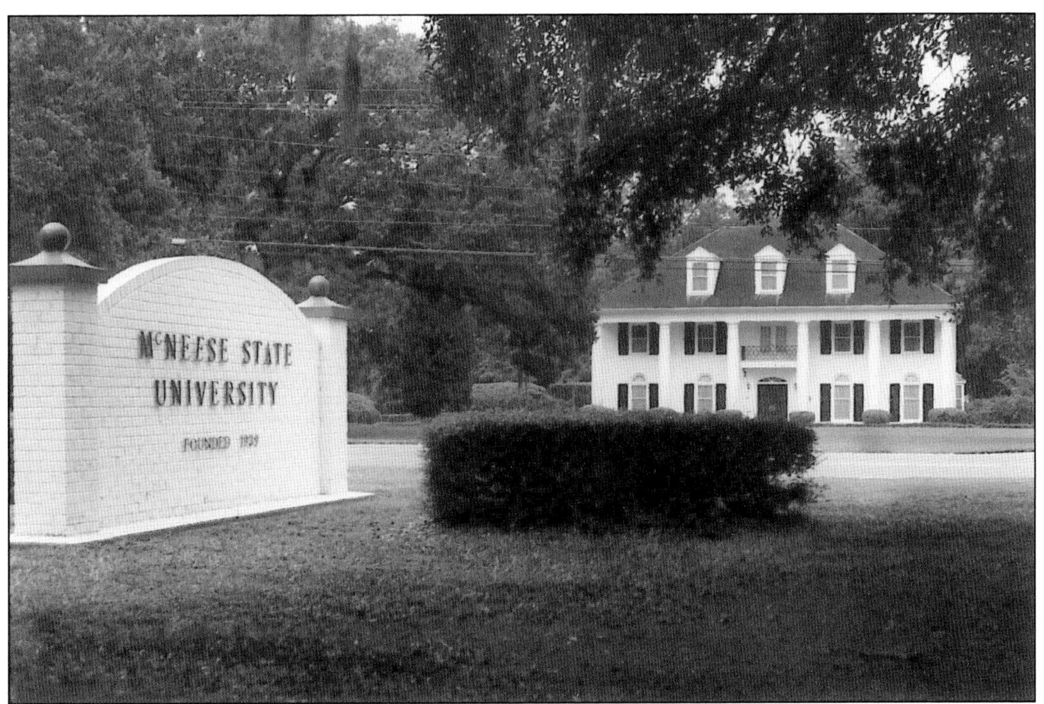

THE PRESIDENT'S HOME AND CAMPUS MARKER. Pres. Wayne Cusic was the first to live in the president's home. He and his family moved into the newly constructed home across the street from Smith Hall at the beginning of the fall semester in 1965. The white brick main campus sign was built in 1974 during the Leary administration. The cost of the sign, $4,069, was paid for from oil lease bonuses. It stands in front of the auditorium and measures 16 feet long, 16 inches wide, and 7 feet tall.

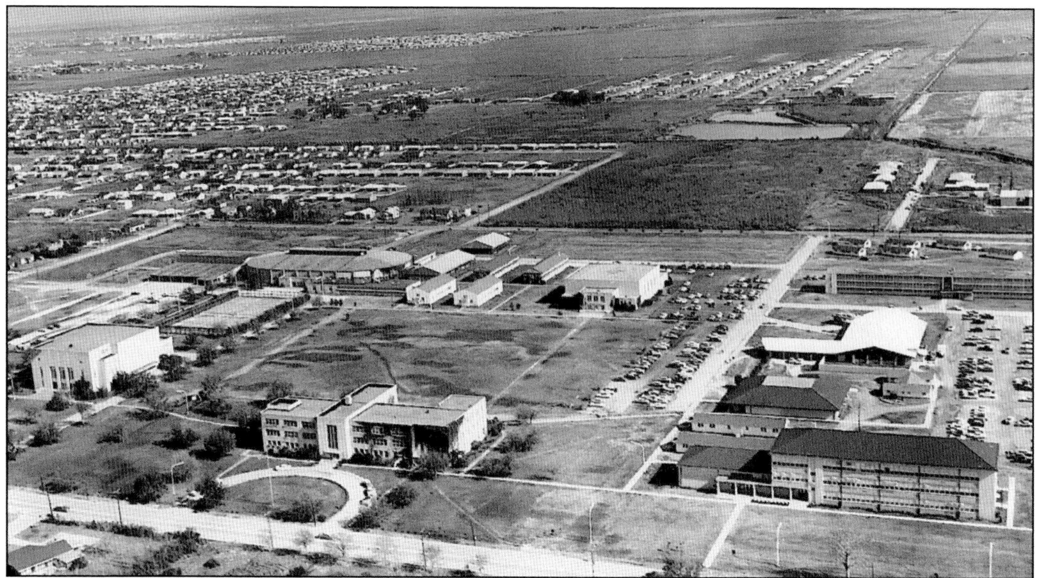

AERIAL VIEW, 1950s. This view of the campus looks east from the main entrance on Ryan Street. Kaufman Hall, with its circle drive, Bulber Auditorium to the left, and the Ward Arena behind it were the first three buildings. To the right of Kaufman Hall is the science building, Frasch Hall, built in 1955. Behind Frasch is the bookstore and student union building, constructed in 1953 and 1956, respectively. The Memorial Gymnasium was built in 1949 and is directly behind Kaufman Hall across the open space or quadrangle.

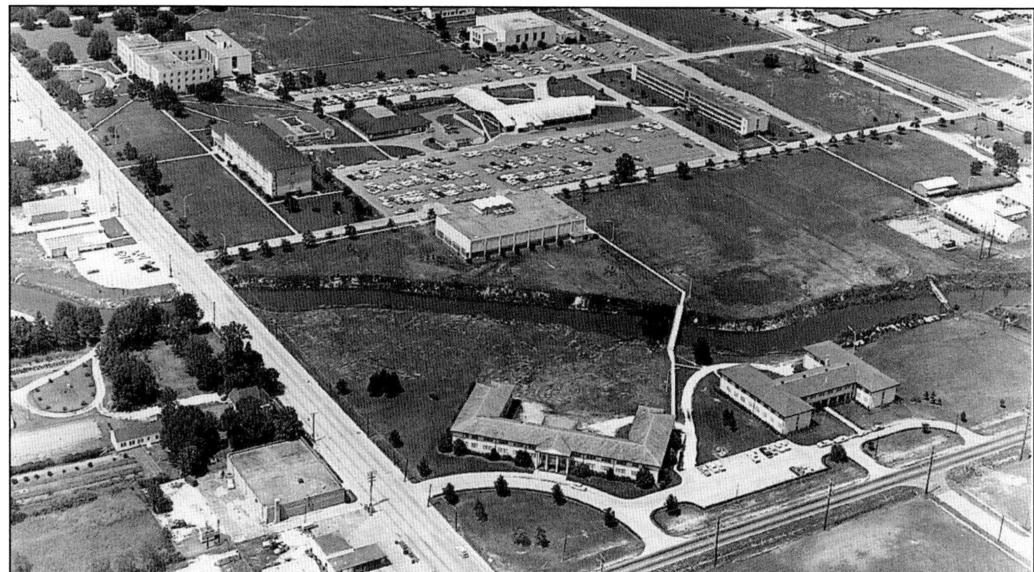

AERIAL VIEW, 1950s. Looking north from McNeese Street, this aerial view shows the two original women's dormitories in the lower right. Sallier Hall, known as Alpha Hall when first constructed in 1956, and Bel Hall, known as Beta Hall when constructed in 1957, were both named for women important to the early history of Southwest Louisiana. The two other women's dormitories, Burton Hall and Collette Hall, were also named for area women. Sallier Hall was named for Catherine LeBleu Sallier, Bel Hall for Della Goos Bel, Collette Hall for Ida King Collette, and Burton Hall for Alice Evelyn Smith Burton.

20

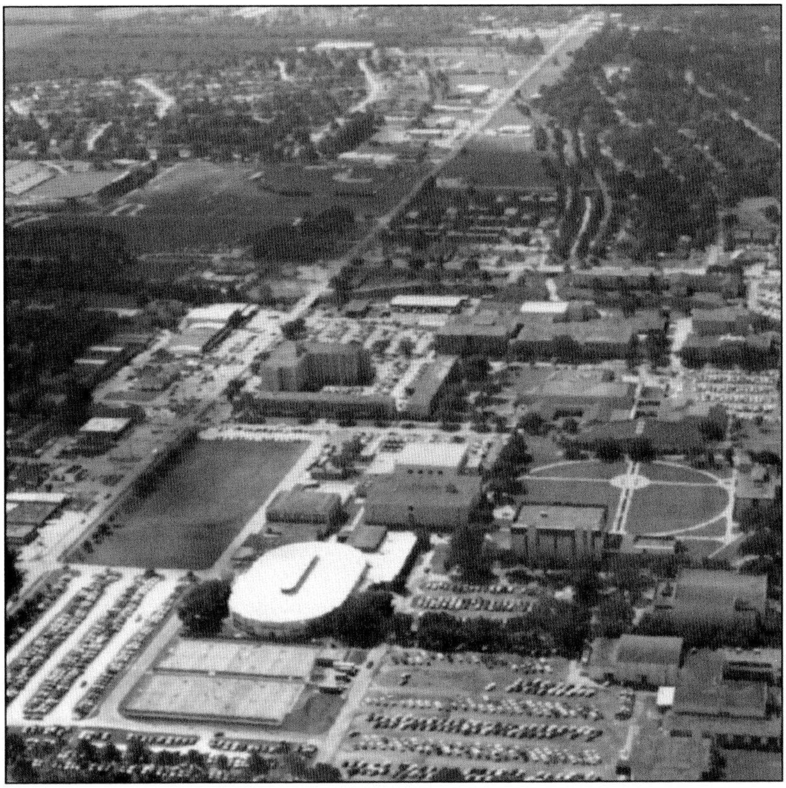

AERIAL VIEW, 1989. At the time of the university's 50th anniversary, the campus had grown to 488 acres owned and 355 leased, with 67 major buildings. This view from the north shows the Burton Business Center on the north side of the quadrangle. At the top left is the football stadium, track, and baseball stadium.

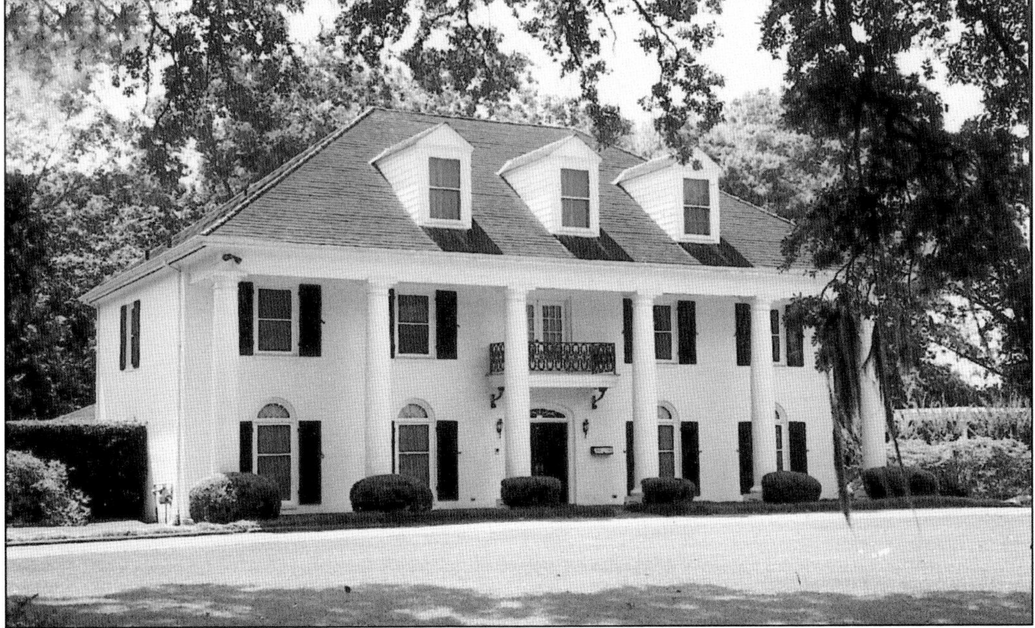

PRESIDENT'S HOME. When the college was first opened there were pear and pecan orchards on this site. Townspeople could drive out to buy fruit and nuts from the owner. Later, Louisiana State University purchased a house close by for use by President Frazar. The current president's home stands on the same site.

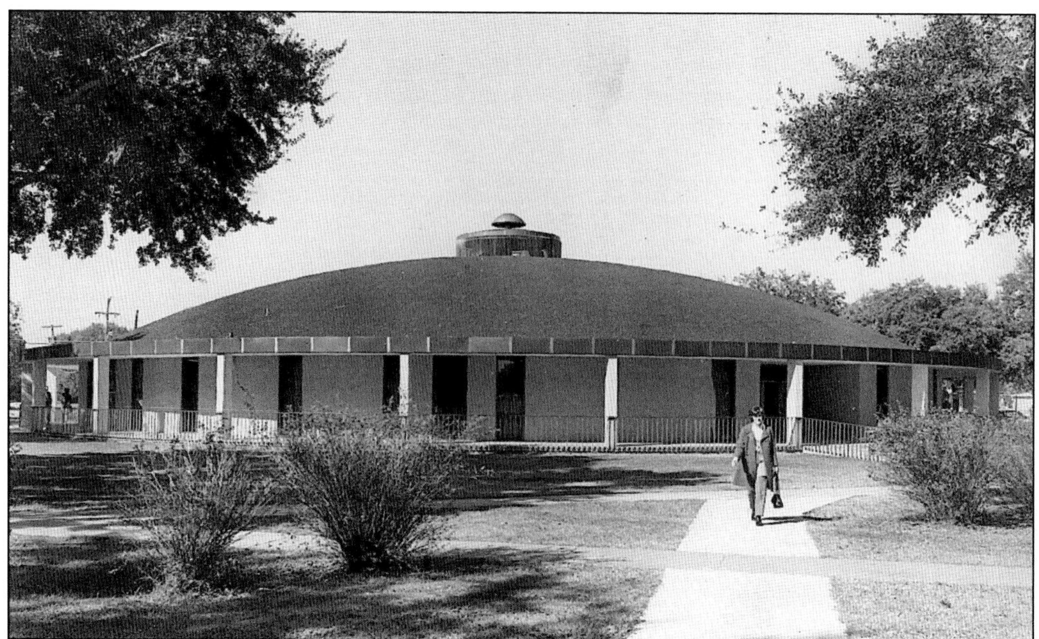

SMITH HALL. The two-story circular administrative building was constructed in 1968. The president's office was housed originally in Kaufman Hall, but with the construction of the new Round Building, the president's office moved. In 1970, it was named for A.D. Smith, former president of the State Board of Education. It is currently used for administrative offices.

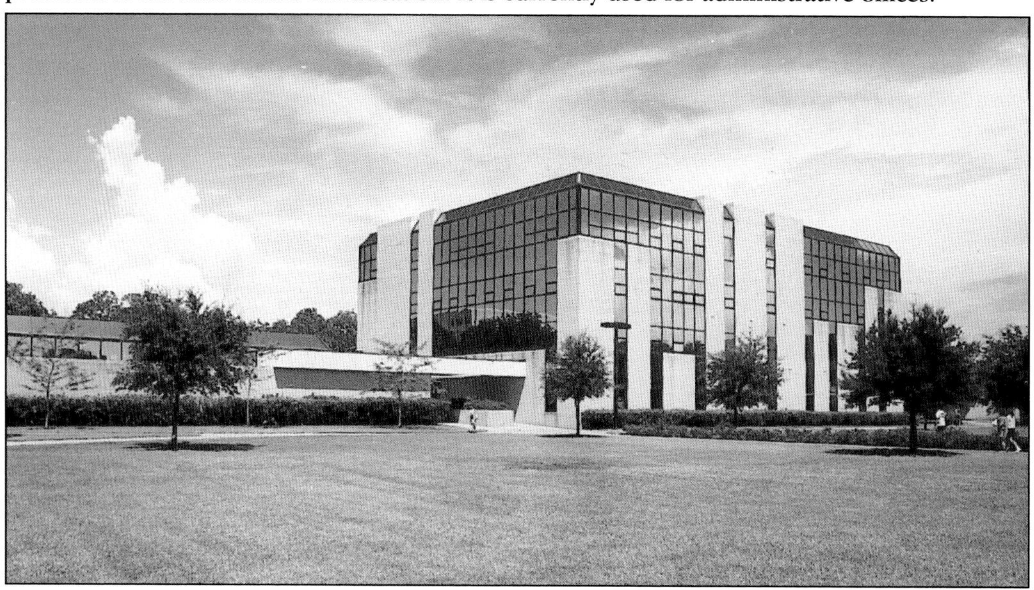

BURTON BUSINESS CENTER. Built in 1984 as the Business and Economic Center for Southwest Louisiana, this beautiful four-story building was renamed in 1998 for William T. and Ethel L. Burton. William T. Burton was chairman of the Calcasieu-Marine National Bank, president of William T. Burton Industries of Sulphur, and a major benefactor of McNeese State University. The Burton Business Center, the BBC as it is commonly called, houses College of Business classrooms, administrative offices, and the Burton Conference Center. The president's office, as well as the offices of the four vice-presidents and other officials, is located on the fourth floor.

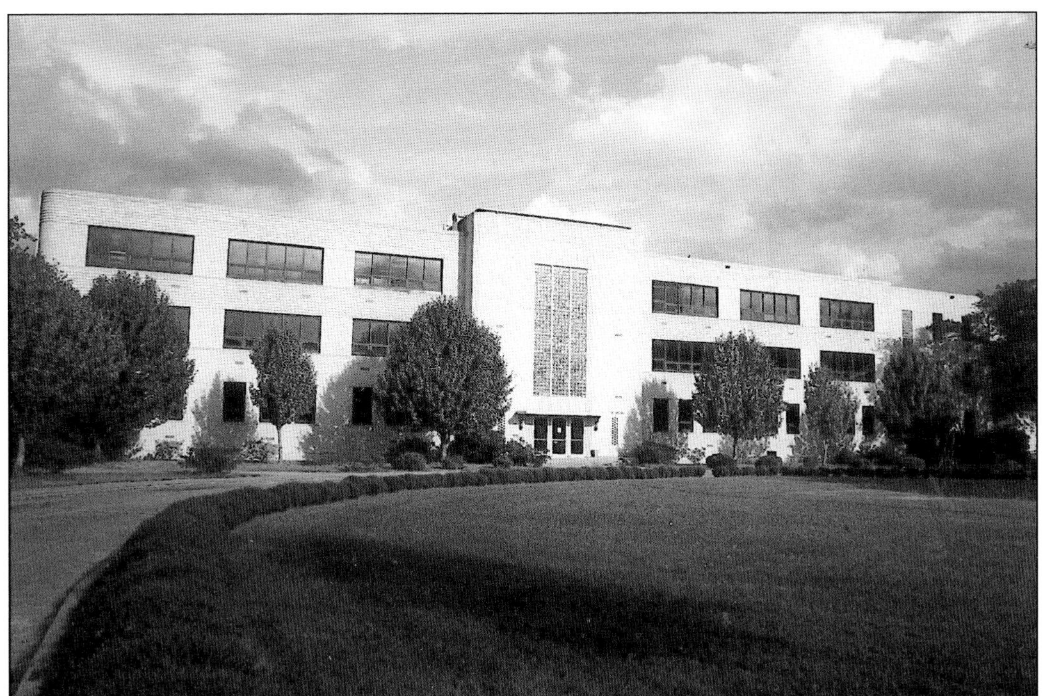

Kaufman Hall. When Kaufman Hall was first built it housed many offices that have been moved to other buildings. In Kaufman were the first library, the first cafeteria, the first bookstore, the first classrooms, and the first faculty and administrative offices.

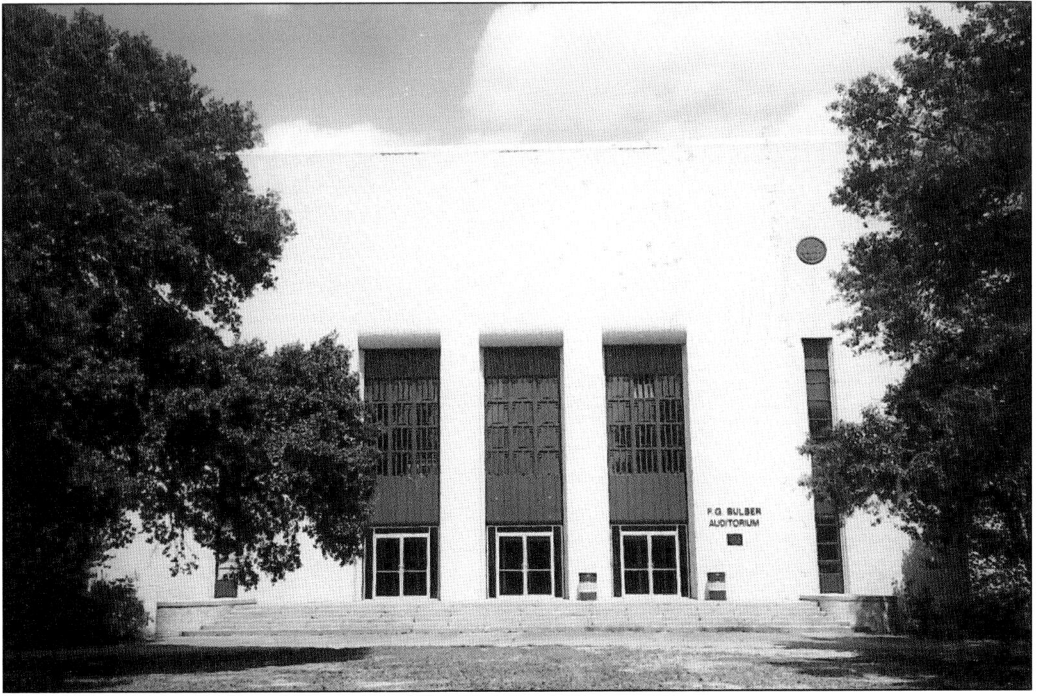

Bulber Auditorium. The Bulber Auditorium is seen above as it looks today, surrounded by oak trees.

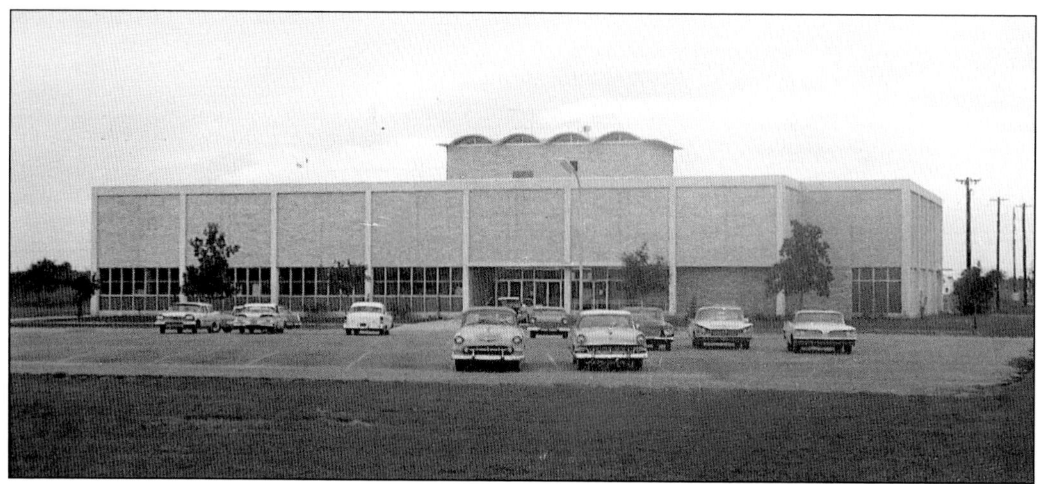

FRAZAR MEMORIAL LIBRARY. The first library on campus was one large room on the south side of Kaufman Hall. Although it was quickly filled to overflowing, a new library did not replace the one room until 1961. Dedication ceremonies, naming the building in memory of Dr. Lether E. Frazar, the former dean and first president of McNeese who had died in 1960, took place in November of that year.

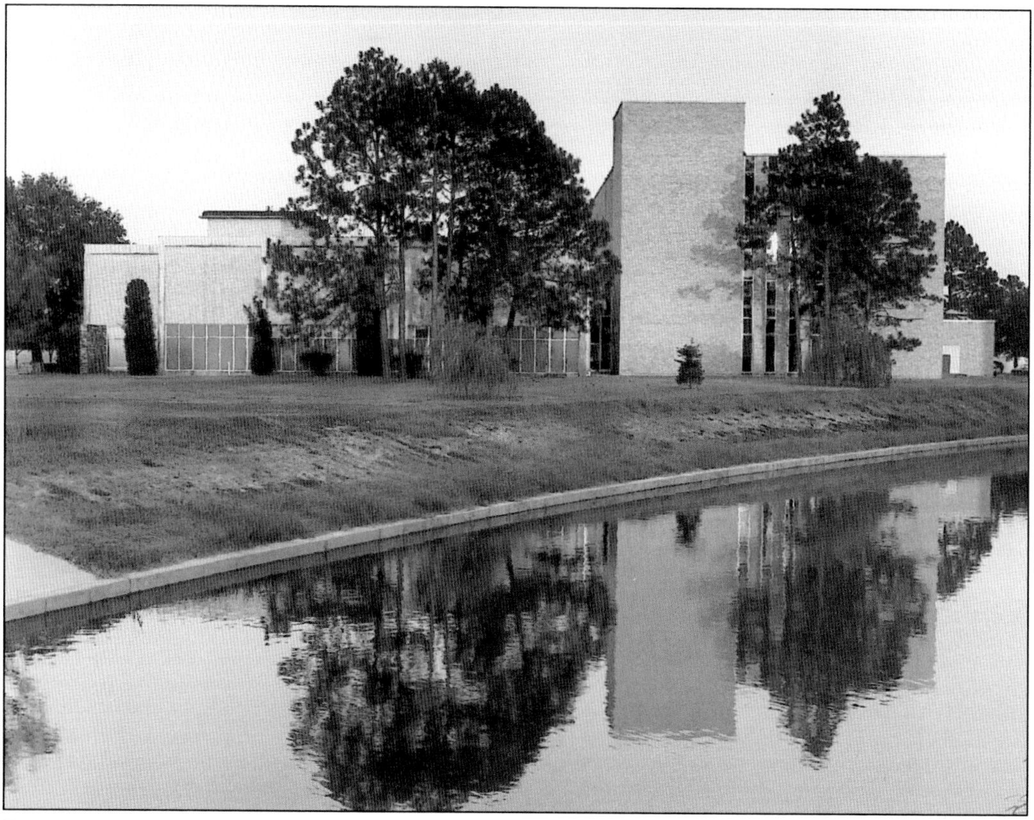

FRAZAR MEMORIAL LIBRARY. The waters of the Contraband Bayou reflect the Frazar Memorial Library, showing the original two-story building and the four-story addition that was constructed in 1974.

24

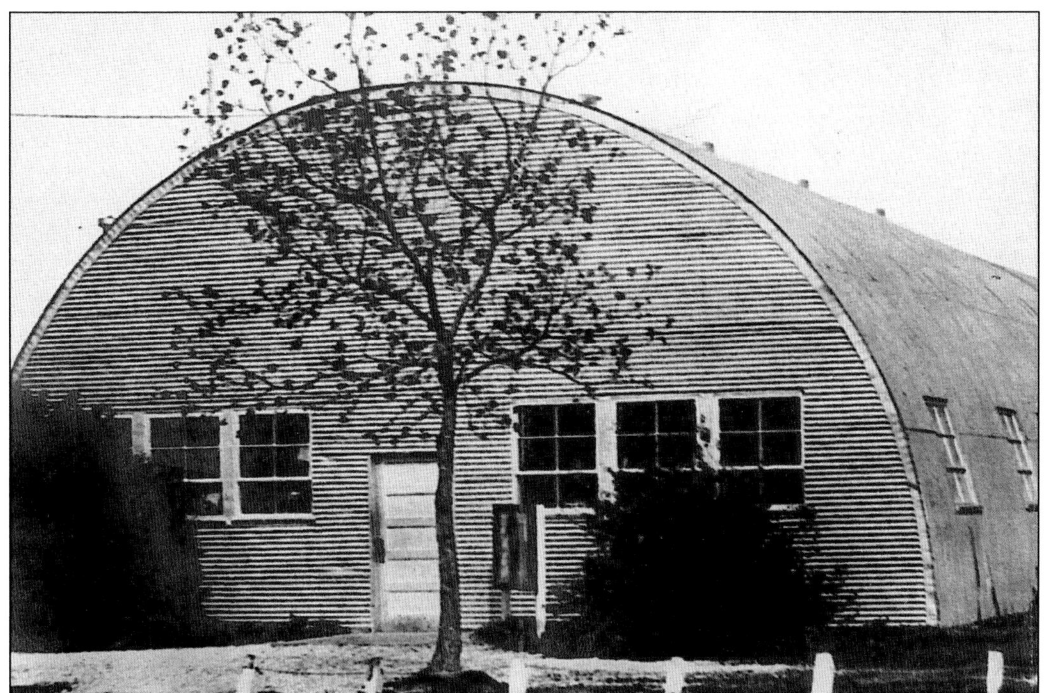

QUONSET HUT—ONE OF MANY. The campus saw many of these small temporary buildings throughout the 1940s and 1950s. This particular one was known as the social room, a forerunner of the student union. Others, obtained from the federal government in many instances, were used for commuter lounges, student organization offices, faculty offices, and classrooms.

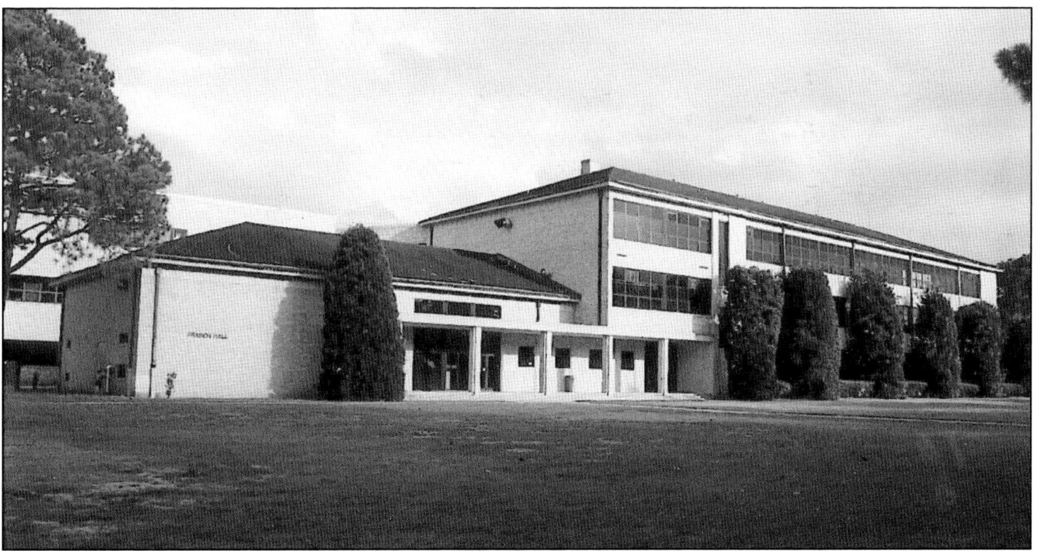

FRASCH HALL. The science building was constructed in 1956; a three-story annex was added in 1993. The building was renamed Frasch Hall in 1965 in honor of Dr. Herman Frasch, a German chemist who developed the modern process for mining sulfur. He first performed this process in west Calcasieu Parish on Christmas Eve 1894. Frasch Hall is currently used for faculty offices and classrooms for the College of Science, particularly the Department of Biological and Environmental Sciences.

25

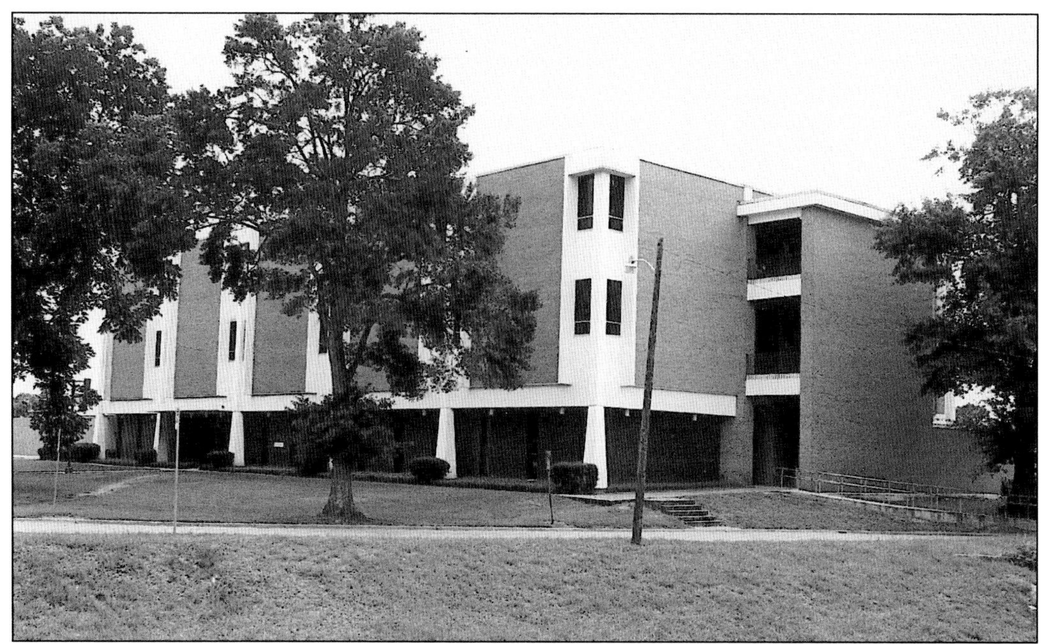

GAYLE HALL. The three-story agricultural building was constructed in 1969 and renamed in honor of Arthur Gayle Sr., a Lake Charles businessman. Gayle, who was instrumental in the founding of the university, was the president of the Association of Commerce in the late 1930s. Gayle Hall is currently used for administrative and faculty offices and for classrooms for the Departments of Agriculture and Family and Consumer Sciences.

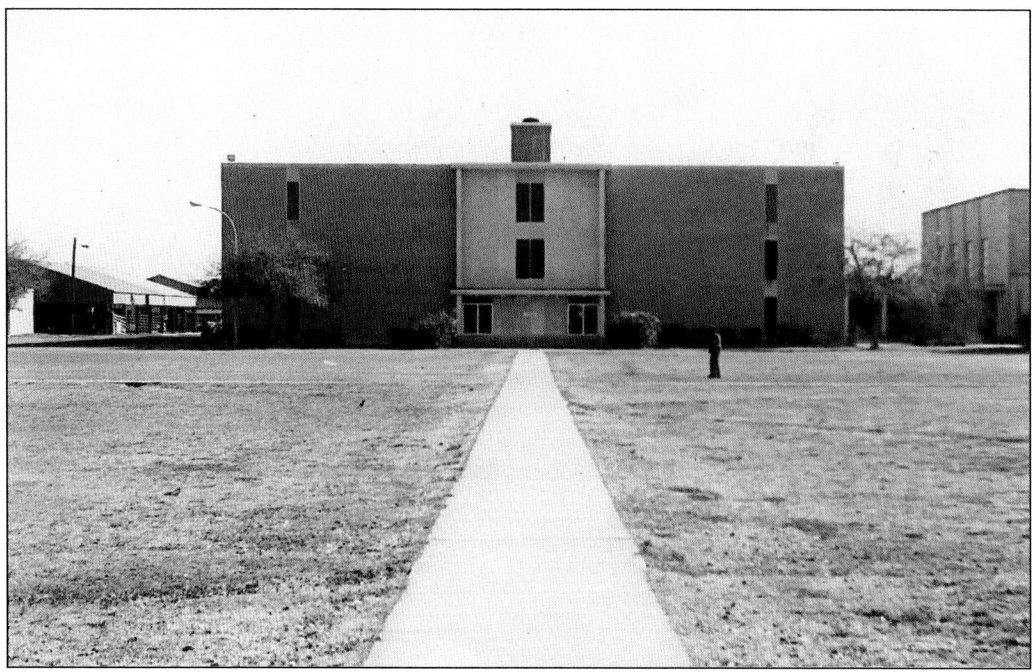

FARRAR HALL. The education building was constructed in 1968 and named for Dr. Joseph T. Farrar, first dean of John McNeese Junior College. It is currently used for administrative and faculty offices and for classrooms for the education and psychology curricula.

26

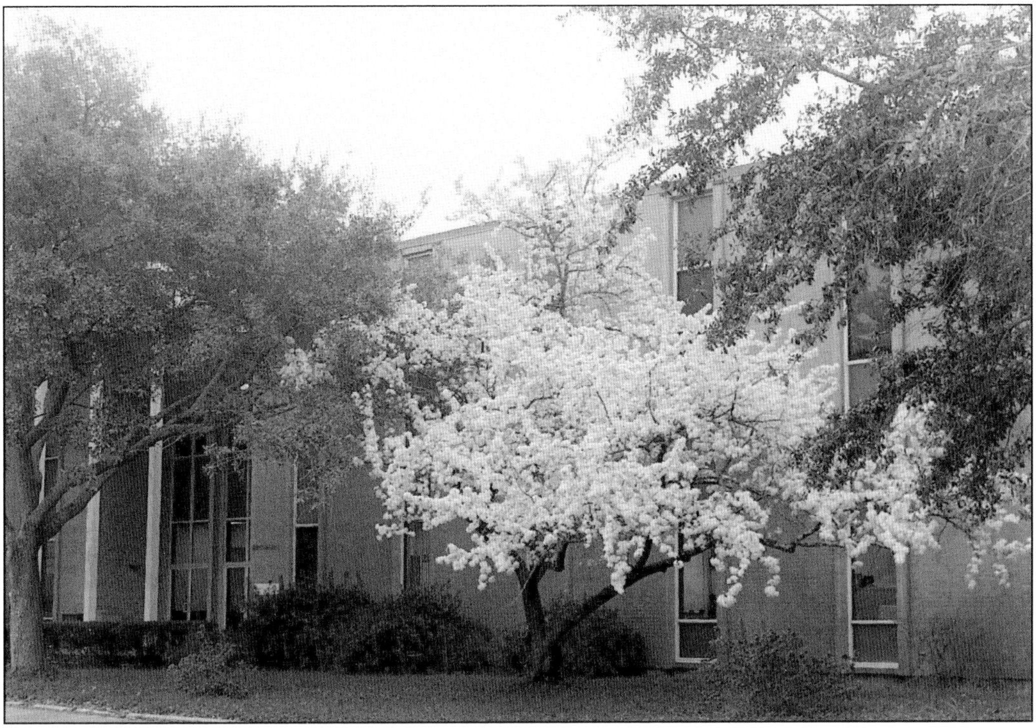

KIRKMAN HALL. Kirkman Hall was named for the pioneer Calcasieu Parish physician, state senator, and first president of the Lake Charles Board of Health, Dr. William Kirkman. It was built in 1969 to house the Departments of Chemistry, Physics, and Mathematics when Frasch Hall became too crowded.

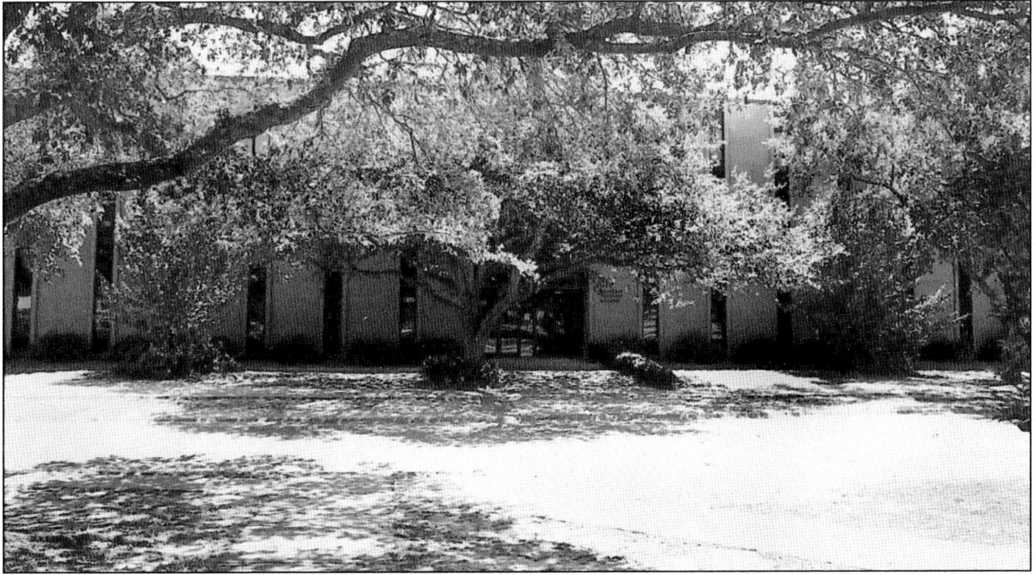

DREW HALL. Harrison C. Drew, a Louisiana senator and philanthropist, was significant in establishing Lake Charles as a center for the lumber, rice, and cattle industry in Southwest Louisiana. This three-story building constructed in 1983 as the Engineering, Technology, and Nursing Building was renamed in 1988 in his memory.

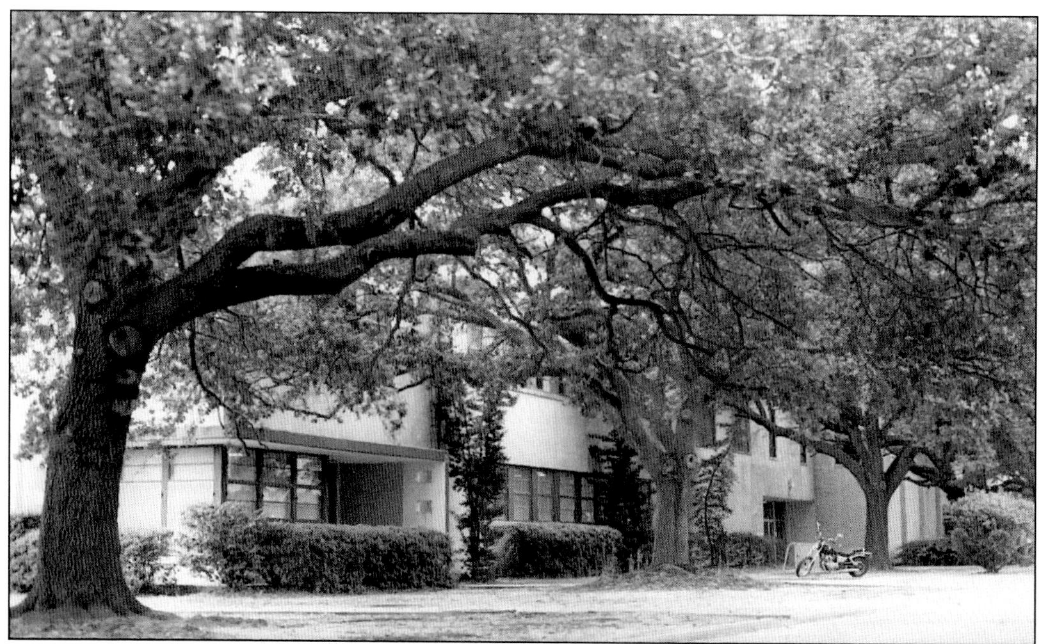

SHEARMAN FINE ARTS BUILDING. Originally constructed around 1950 as the music building, the Shearman Fine Arts Building was renamed in 1991 in honor of Flora I. and Thomas B. Shearman Sr. The Shearman family own and publish the local newspaper, the *Lake Charles American Press.*

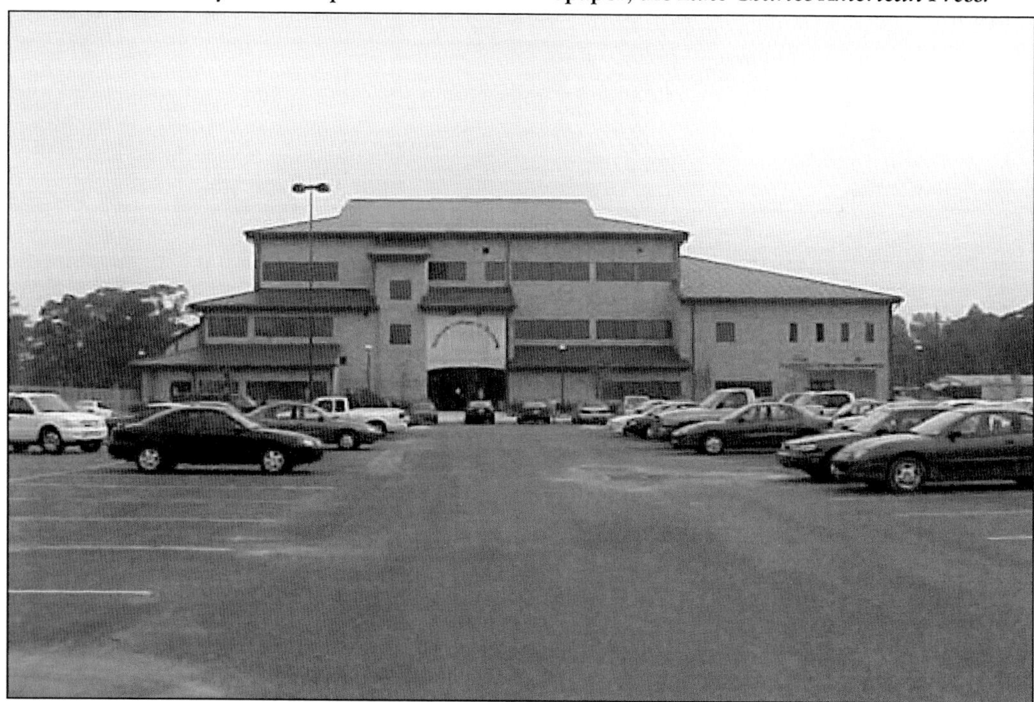

HARDTNER HALL. Completed in the fall semester of 2000 to house the College of Nursing and the Department of Mass Communications, this building was named in memory of Juliet Hardtner. Hardtner Hall also houses the Calcasieu Community Clinic, a free clinic for the uninsured and underserved in the area.

28

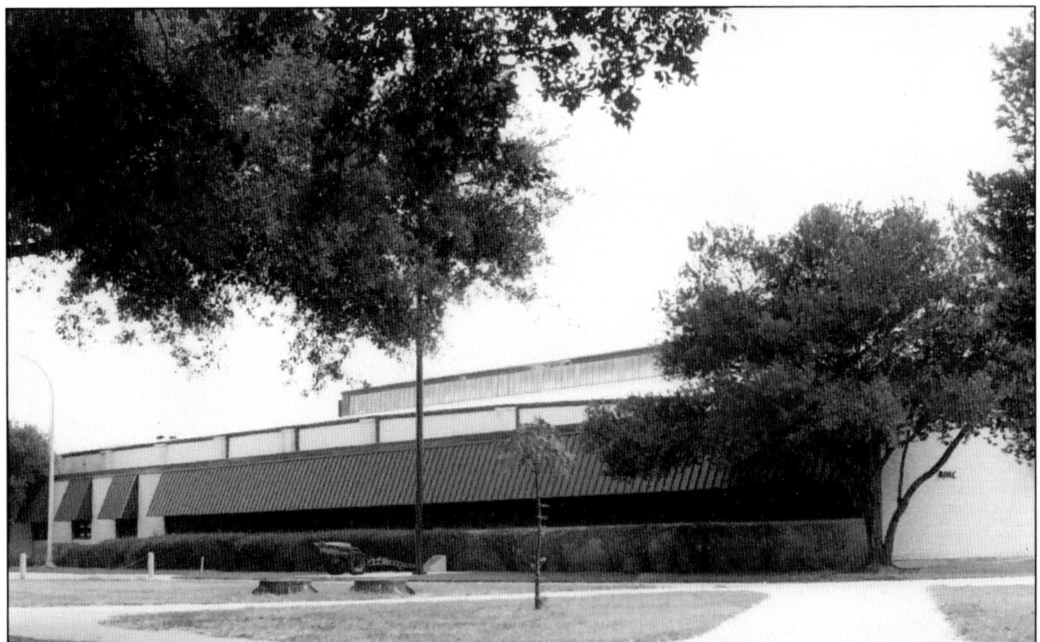

ROTC. The Reserve Officers Training Corps (ROTC) grew out of a voluntary drill team that was formed in 1942. A two-year basic course was compulsory for physically fit, non-veteran males until 1969. The ROTC program ended its 55-year history at McNeese in 1997. The building now houses the Financial Aid Office.

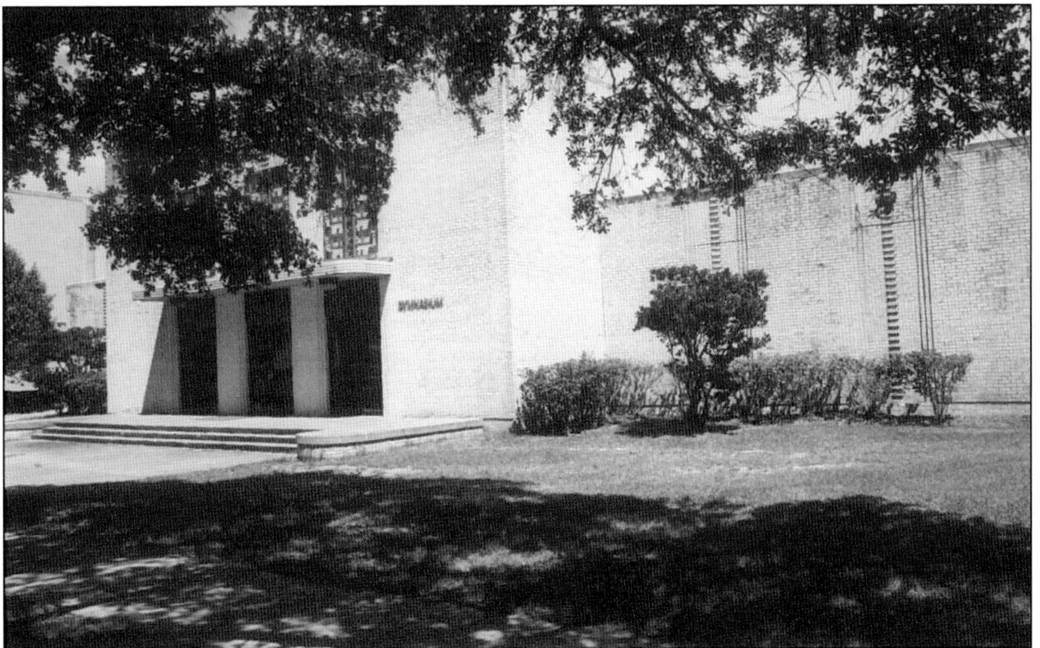

Memorial Gym. The McNeese gymnasium was constructed in 1949. It was renamed the McNeese Memorial Gymnasium in 1965 to honor the memory of students and faculty killed in action during World War II, the Korean War, and the Vietnam War. Students, cheerleaders, and athletes participated in pep rallies held in this gym.

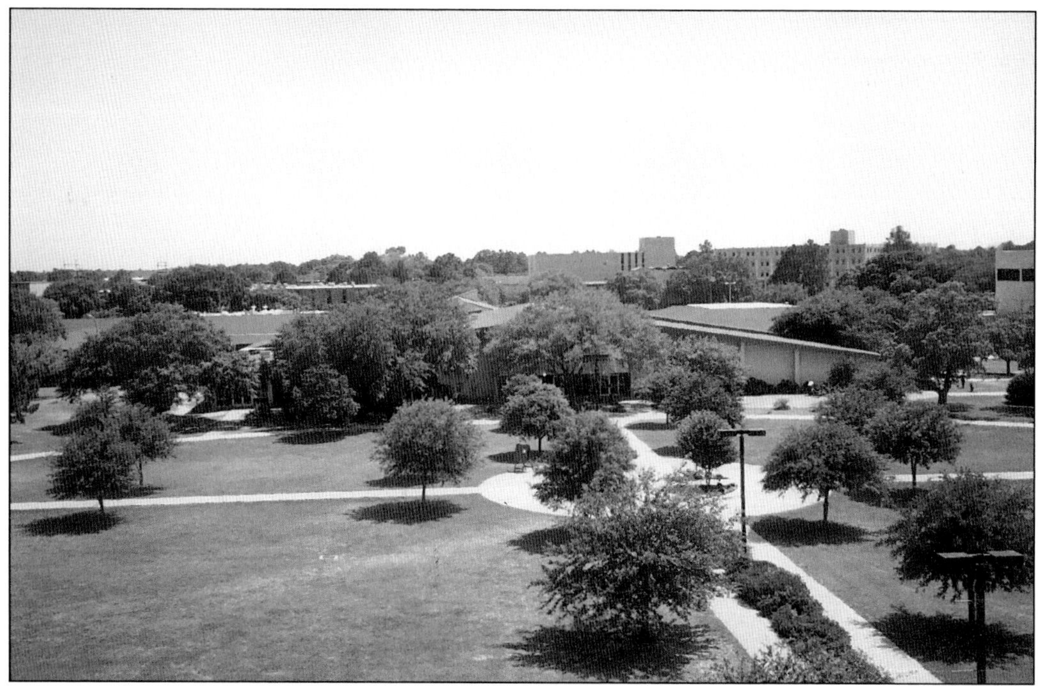

OLD RANCH. The Holbrook Ranch Student Union was originally constructed in 1956. As the university and student needs grew, annexes were added in 1966, 1976, and 1986. The Ranch, as it is called, opens out on the north side into the grassy area referred to as the quadrangle, or the quad. W.A. Holbrook, for whom the union was named, was the president of the Calcasieu Parish Police Jury when McNeese was established as a junior college.

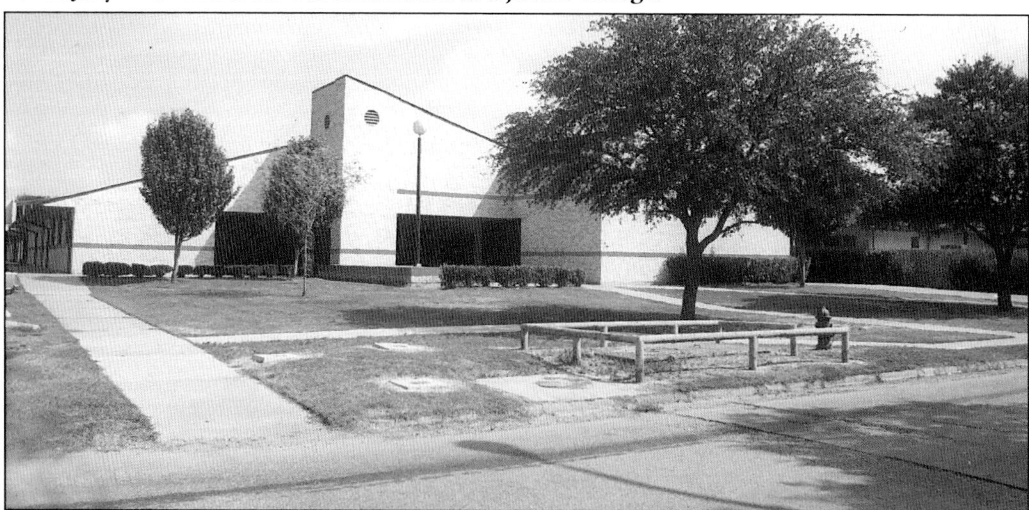

NEW RANCH. The section of the student union more commonly referred to as the New Ranch houses the post office, student services, the print shop, the photography studio, and the president's dining room. The older part of the union houses the cafeteria, the *Log* office, Media Services (formerly News Bureau), a computer lab, the bookstore, the ballroom, meeting rooms, and other university organization offices. Parra Ballroom was named for Leland Parra, a McNeese graduate and past president of the Alumni Association, who worked for the growth of the university.

30

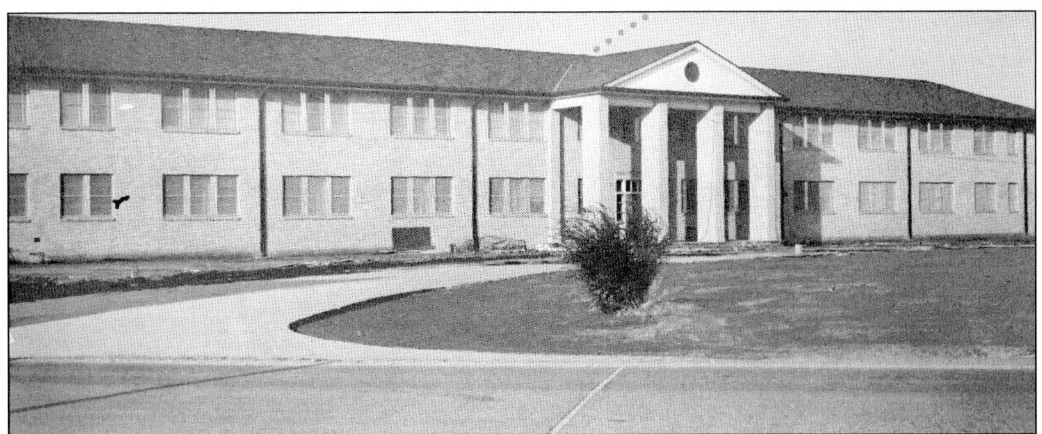

SALLIER HALL. Built in 1956 and originally called Alpha Dorm, Sallier Hall was the first women's dormitory. It was renamed for Catherine LeBleu Sallier, the wife of Charles Sallier, one of the earliest area settlers and the man for whom the city and lake are named. Sallier Hall is still used as a dormitory today, although it is now co-ed.

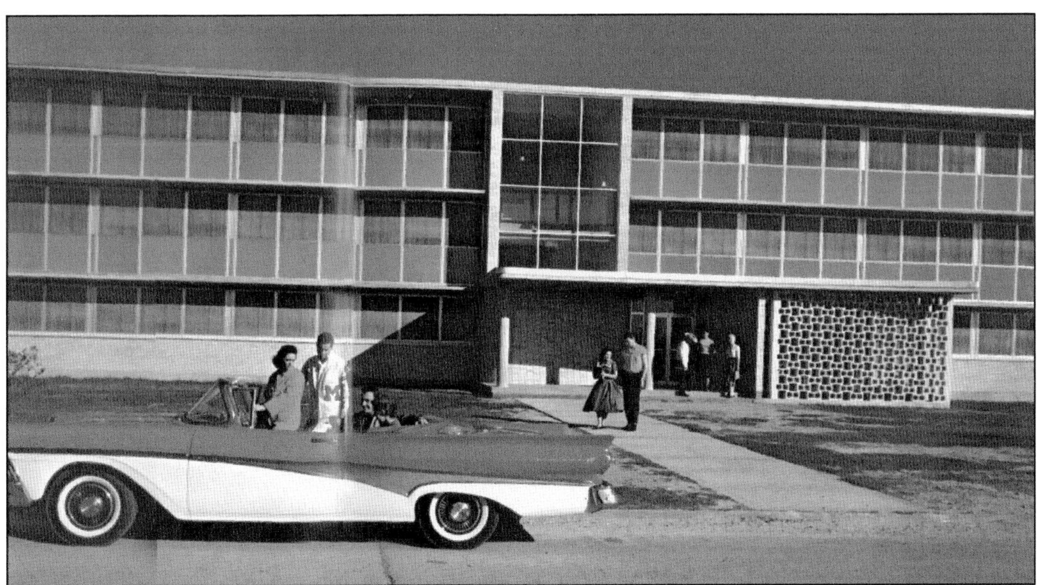

WATKINS HALL. The first men's dormitory was christened the Blue Dorm when it was built in 1957 because the bottom panes in all the windows were blue. Zigler Hall, built in 1964, was known as the Red Dorm for the same reason. These dorms were also called Wrangler Hall and Bronco Hall, respectively, in keeping with the cowboy theme. Watkins Hall was named in honor of Jabez B. Watkins, who was responsible for bringing many settlers from the Midwest to this area in the late 1800s. Zigler Hall was named for Fred Zigler, a Jefferson Davis Parish businessman and philanthropist, who created a foundation to give financial aid to college students.

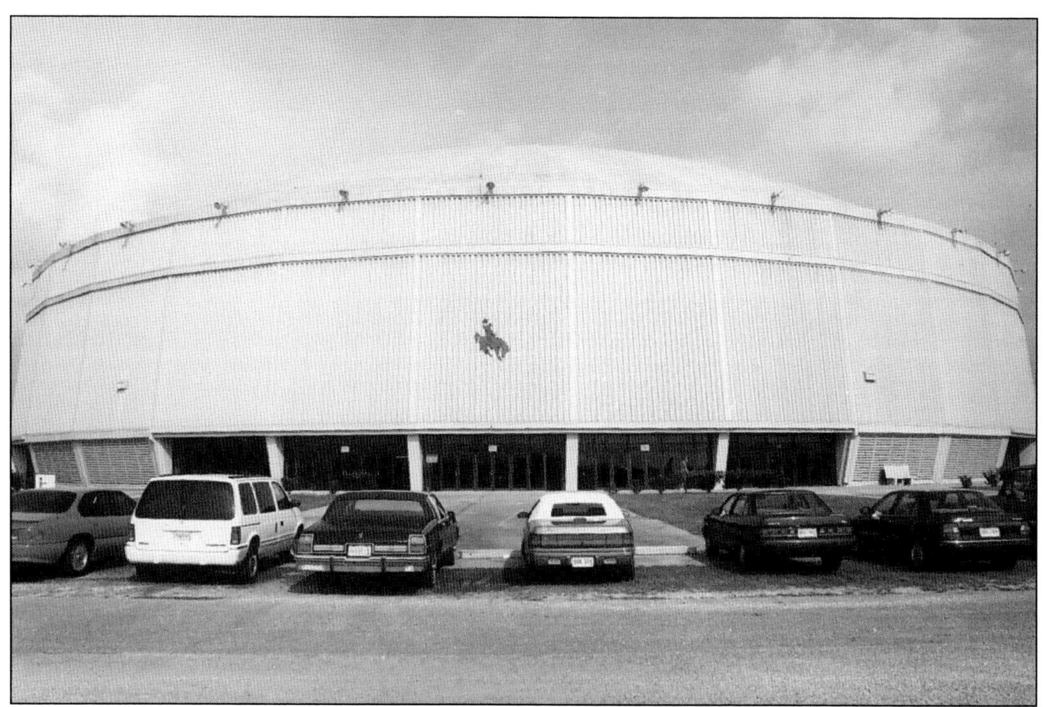

BURTON COLISEUM. Burton Memorial Coliseum is located south of the main campus and is used for commencement ceremonies, basketball games, rodeos, and other university and area events. It was built on land donated by William T. Burton and named for him. The coliseum was acquired during Jack Doland's presidency. It is described as a 40-acre, $13.5 million omni-dome.

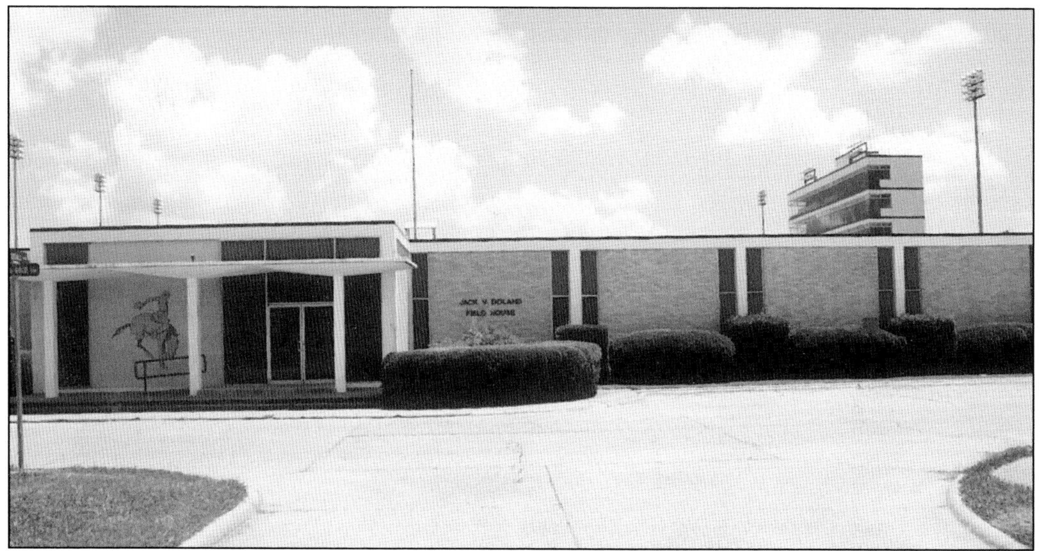

FIELD HOUSE. The Jack V. Doland Athletic Complex includes all the athletic buildings and fields on the McNeese campus. The field house and ticket office were built with the stadium in 1964. The complex was named in 1992 for Dr. Jack V. Doland, former McNeese head football coach (1970–1979) and president (1980–1987).

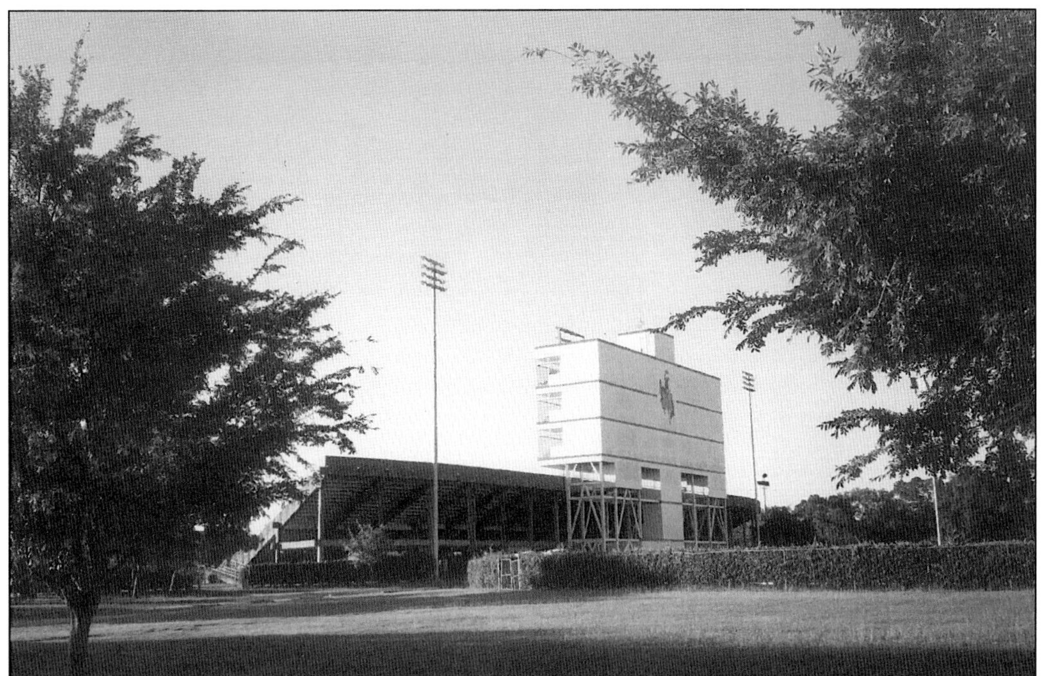

FOOTBALL STADIUM. Cowboy Stadium, home to the McNeese Cowboy football team, was constructed in 1964 and first used in 1965. Sen. Guy Sockrider, a longtime supporter of the university, made the formal dedication along with other dignitaries from the State Board of Education, the Louisiana Legislature, the Calcasieu Parish Police Jury, and the Association of Commerce.

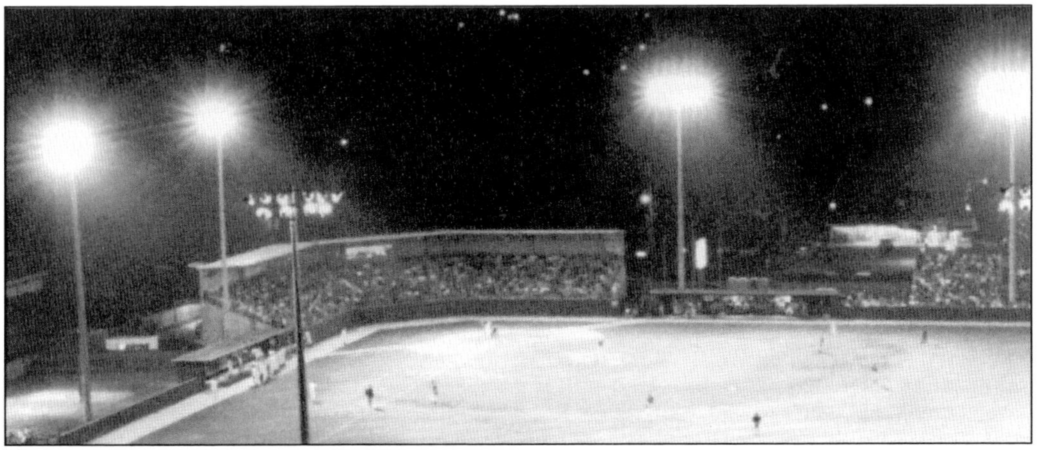

BASEBALL STADIUM. Cowboy Diamond was originally constructed in 1965 and renovated in 1986 to seat 1,500. The complex is named for the son of Frank Landry Sr., who was a guiding force in lighting the field and in the construction of the complex. The Frank E. Landry Jr. Baseball Complex houses dressing rooms, offices, meeting rooms, indoor hitting and batting facilities, and training rooms.

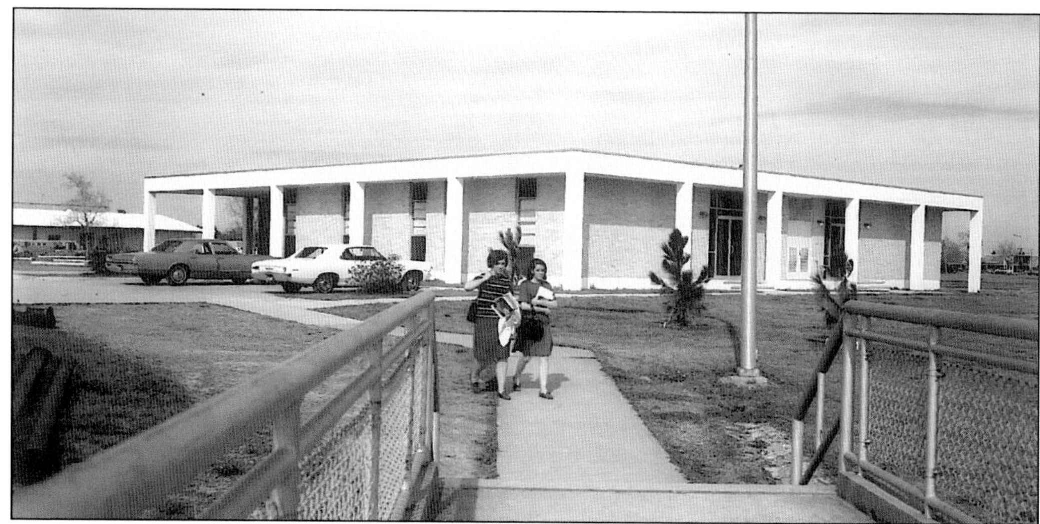

WATKINS INFIRMARY. The Watkins Infirmary opened in 1966—although medical treatment was available to students much earlier—and was named for Dr. Thomas Henry Watkins, an early 20th-century Lake Charles surgeon. Located on the north bank of the Contraband Bayou beside the Frazar Memorial Library, the infirmary staffs full-time nurses who treat illnesses and emergencies, teach preventative medicine, and inform students on health issues.

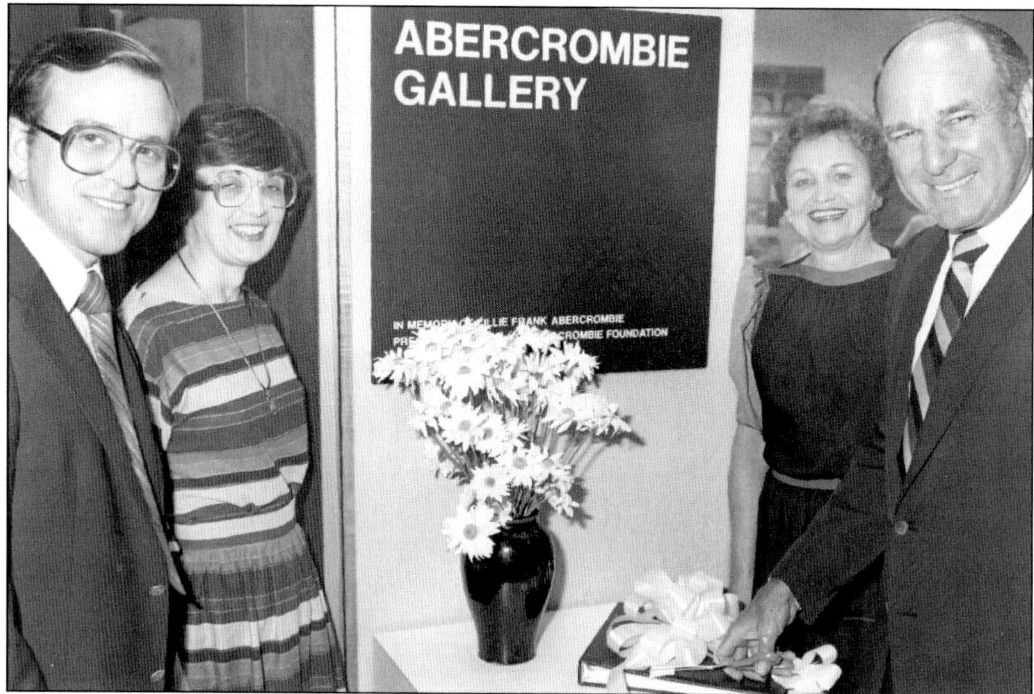

ABERCROMBIE GALLERY. Abercrombie Gallery in the Shearman Fine Arts Building was named for Lillie Frank Abercrombie by the J.S. Abercrombie Foundation in 1983. The gallery is used to exhibit student and faculty art as well as special shows including the National Works of Art on Paper, a competition established at McNeese in 1988. In this photograph, Vice President for Academic Affairs and Mrs. Robert D. Hebert and President and Mrs. Jack V. Doland attend the opening of the gallery.

34

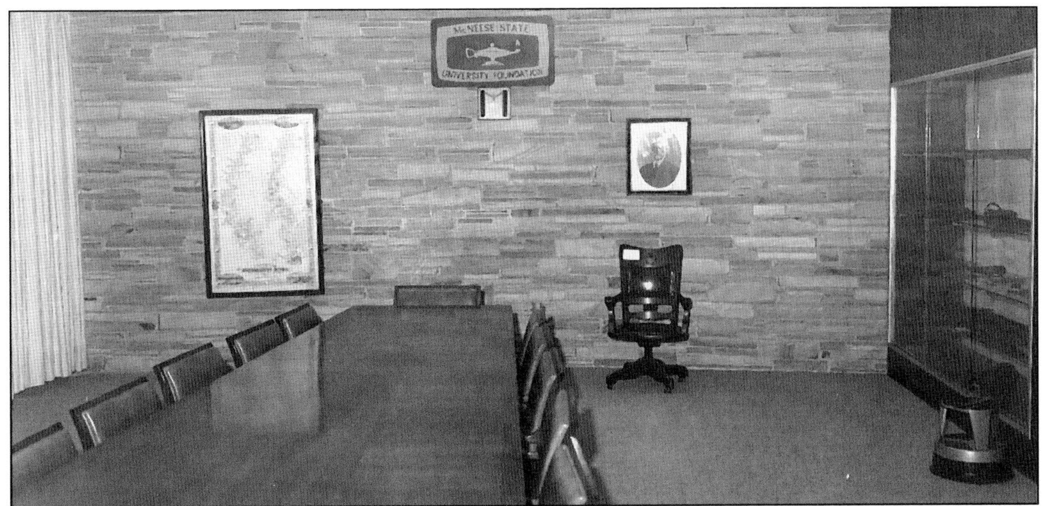

McNeese Room. The university community is welcome to use the McNeese Room in the library whenever a large boardroom is needed. The solid wood table measures over 25 feet long and almost 6 feet wide. The McNeese Room is named in memory of John McNeese. A painting of him, his office chair, and several pieces of furniture from his home are on display there. For many years, the McNeese Room served as the best location on campus to welcome dignitaries, bestow awards, and sign important documents.

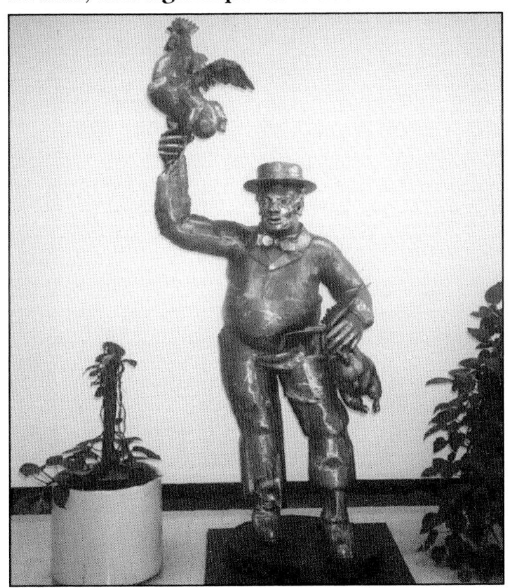

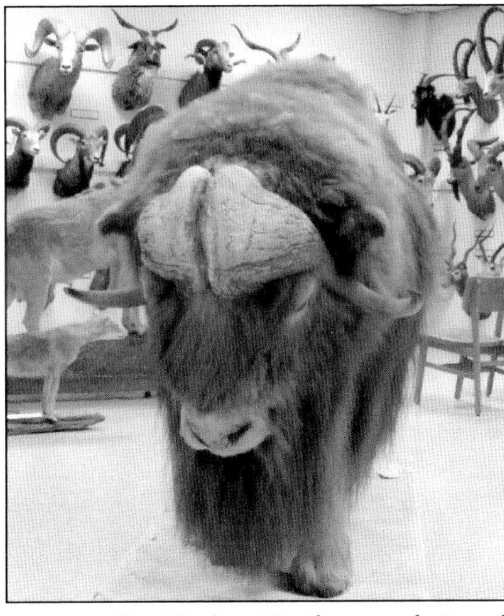

(Left) **Chicken Vendor.** Crafted in steel by artist Al Lavergne, the Chicken Vendor was designed to commemorate Louisiana's French markets. Lavergne stated that in years past it was not uncommon to see vendors selling their live goods on the street corners and at the junctions along the roads. The statue was part of an exhibit of Lavergne's steel sculptures in the library in 1986 and has graced the front entrance of the Frazar Memorial Library since then.

(Right) **Seale Museum.** The Seale Museum in Frasch Hall, a taxidermy museum of large animals, was named for Dr. William Arnold Kent Seale, a sulphur surgeon. He and Francis Mire, a Lake Charles attorney, were enthusiastic wild game hunters who collected the specimens from around the world before donating them to the university.

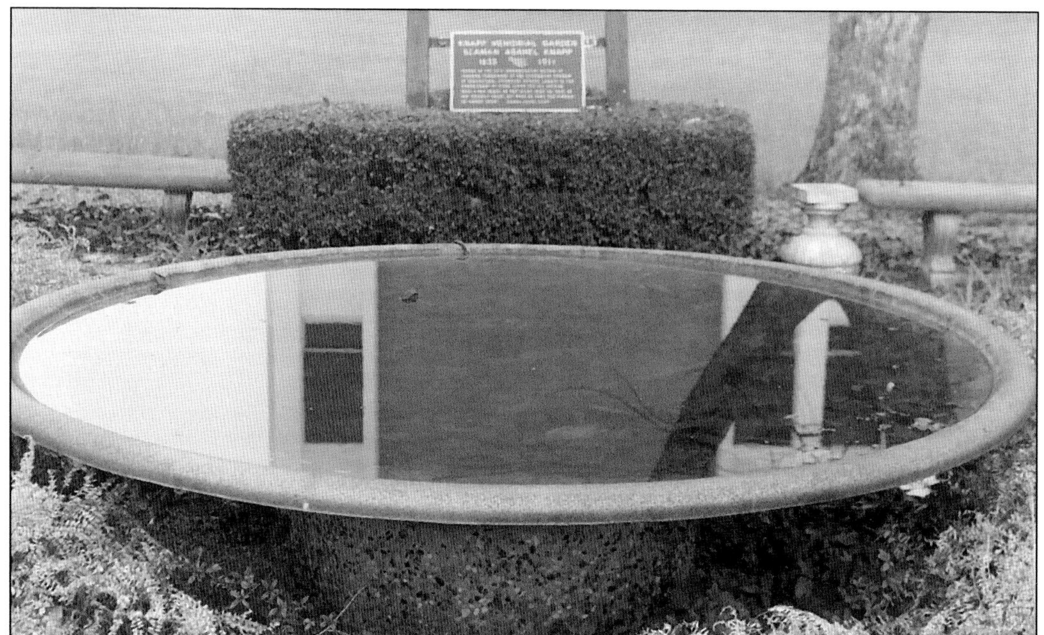

KNAPP FOUNTAIN. The Knapp Memorial Garden, Fountain, and Plaque were placed in front of Gayle Hall in 1975 in order to commemorate the deeds of Seaman Asahel Knapp. Jabez B. Watkins and the North American Land and Timber Company brought Knapp to Southwest Louisiana in 1885 from Ames, Iowa, where he was president of Iowa State College. It is primarily through Dr. Knapp's efforts that rice production has become a major industry in the Southwest Louisiana area.

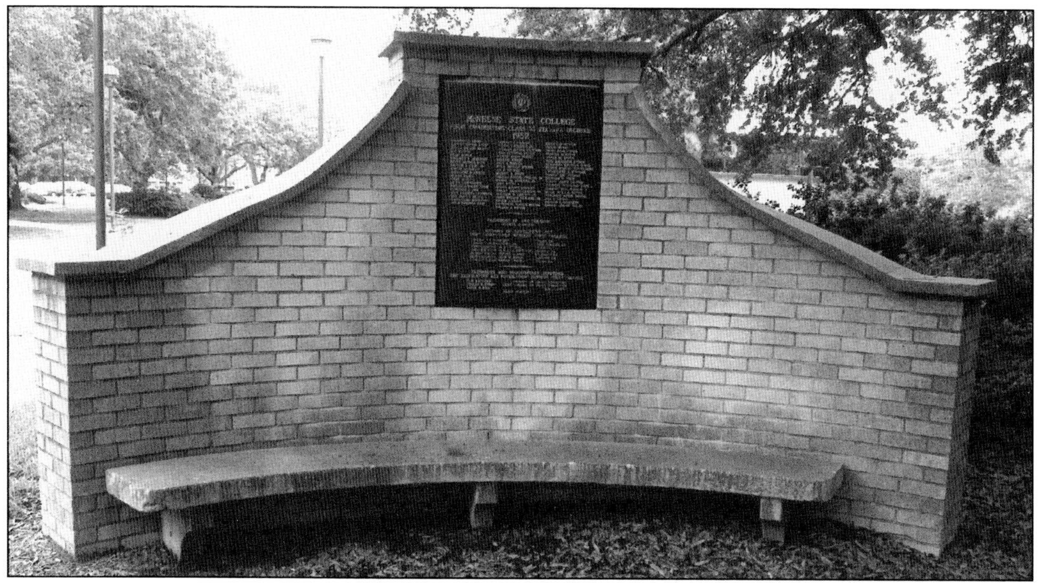

MEMORIAL BENCH. This brick and concrete bench sits behind Smith Hall in an area surrounded by azaleas and live oaks. The plaque lists the names of the first graduating class to receive degrees in 1952 after McNeese had become a four-year institution. It honors not only those who graduated but also those who were responsible for writing and defending the legislative act that provided for four-year status.

Three

STUDENTS AND CAMPUS LIFE

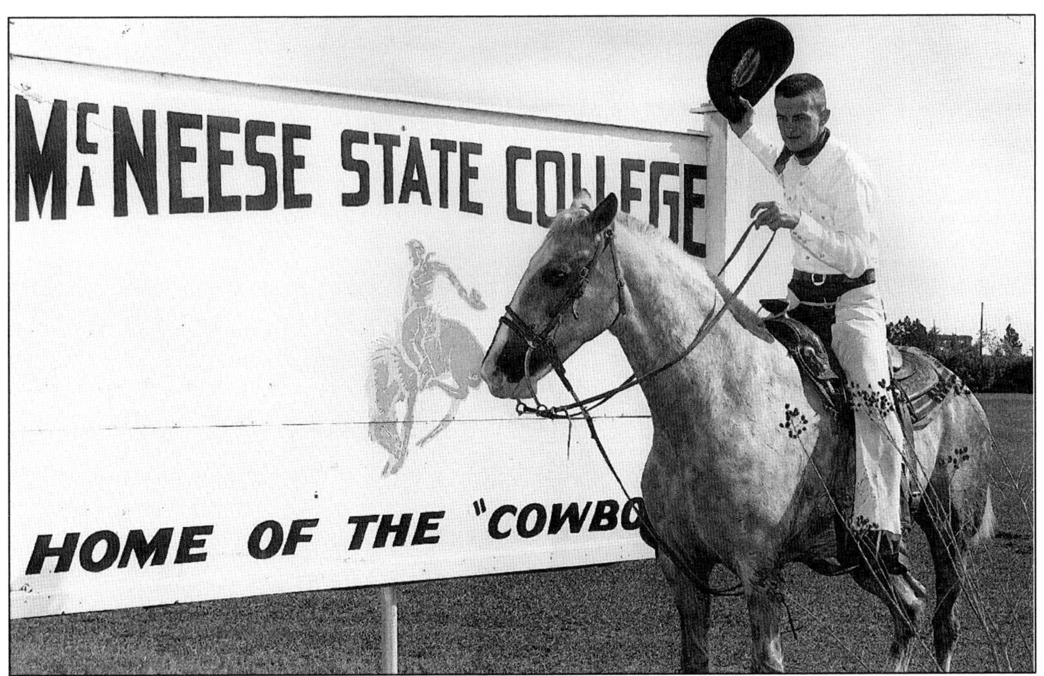

COWBOYS AND COWGIRLS. In the early days of the college, some students would ride their horses to campus and tie them up while attending class. Rodeo was one of the most popular activities of the early students. It's not surprising that the names "cowboys" and "cowgirls" were chosen to designate McNeese's athletic teams. In this photograph, Robert Peshoff shows how he and his horse would have posed for the school logo.

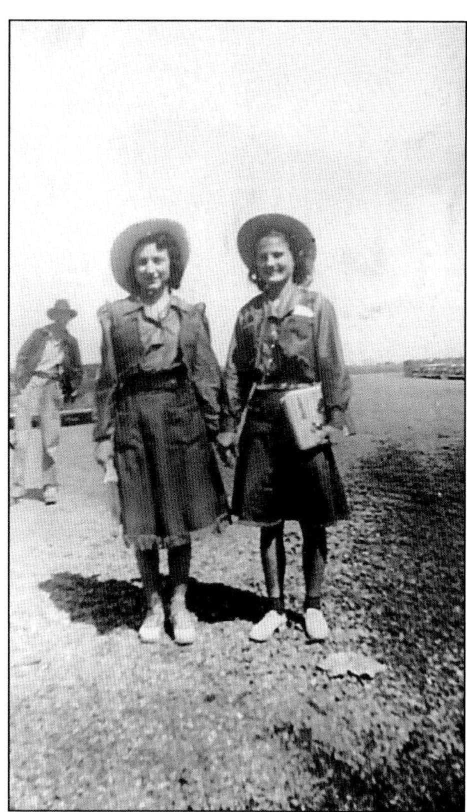

COWGIRLS. In these early photographs, the cowboy-cowgirl theme can be seen developing. Teresa Viglia and Hazeldine Lane dress the part as they attend classes during the first semester of Lake Charles Junior College.

BROWN BAGGIN'. "A bunch of us had a great time at the Sugar Bowl across from McNeese. It was a little sandwich shop right across the street and it was called 'Shug's.'" Johnny Daugherty, class of 1939–1941, remembers one of the class's favorite hangouts. Teresa Viglia and Dahlia Cook pause to have their picture taken on the way back from purchasing their lunch. Teresa Viglia Mistretta recalled that Shug's was a fun place to visit and that the class enjoyed the hot dogs and hamburgers. She also remembered the cows that were kept nearby. According to classmate Richard See, owner Shug Collins kept a jukebox stacked with the students' favorite records.

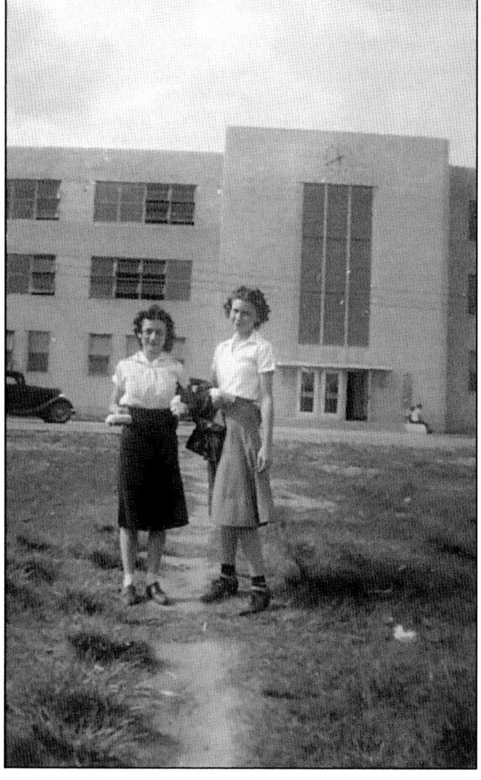

38

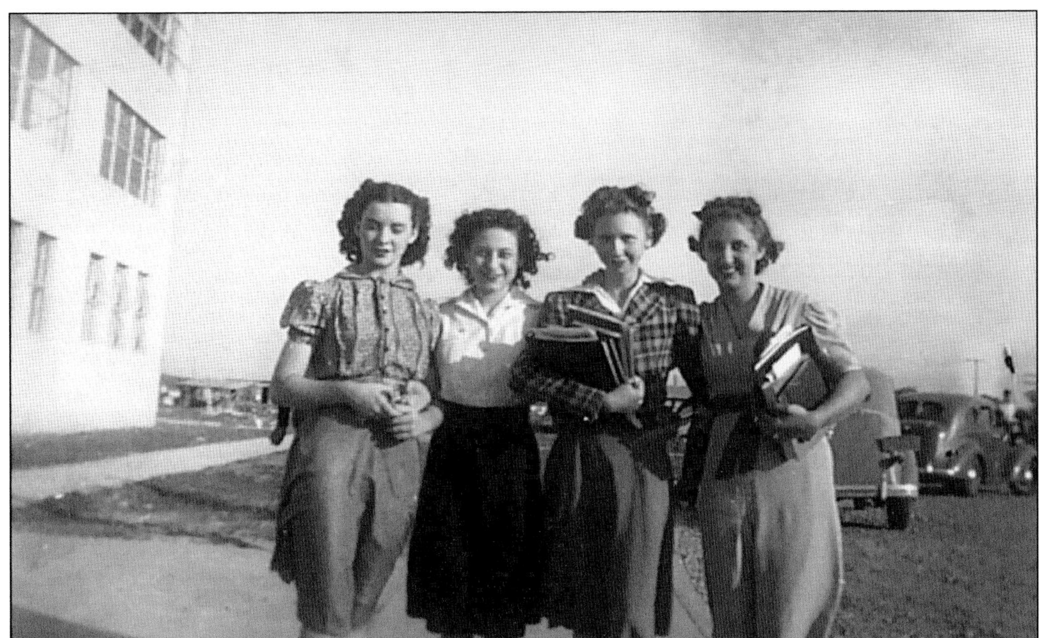

FOUR FRIENDS. Speaking of the first class, Margaret Andrus Roberts said, "It was a small group, and we knew each other. Everyone was friendly. It was just a good feeling to be here." Teresa Viglia Mistretta said, "We were all like a big family out here." These four girls, Kathleen Bordelon, Teresa Viglia, Dahlia Cook, and Evelyn Schauer, were part of the close-knit group of students in the first class.

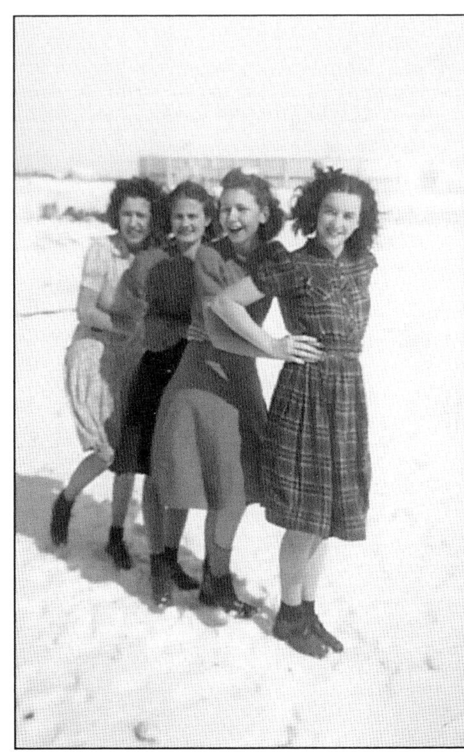

A RARE SNOWFALL. These four classmates enjoy a rare snowfall in the winter of 1940, sans coats. They are Martha Caldwell, Hazeldine Lane, Dahlia Cook, and Kathleen Bordelon. The newly constructed arena can be seen in the background.

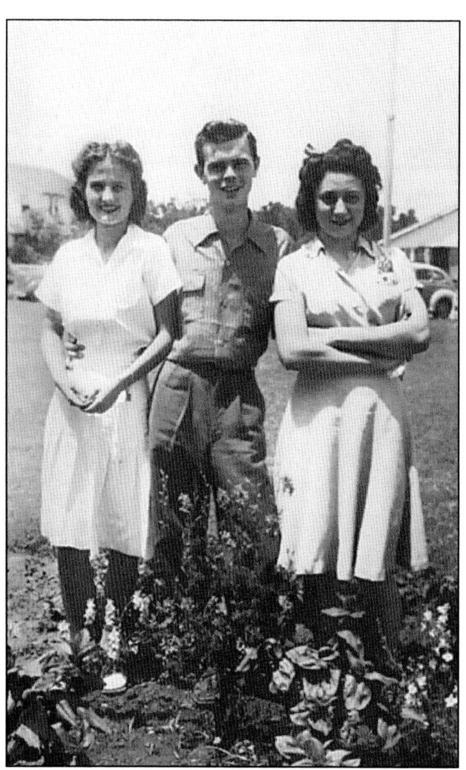

College Chums. Hazeldine Lane, Roy French, and Teresa Viglia were part of the first class at Lake Charles Junior College. According to another classmate, Colleen Doane O'Neal, some students did not attend college when they first graduated from high school but waited several years for the junior college to open. "They just waited until McNeese came," she said. Classmate Ernest Levingston declared, "To me it was a godsend. I was always dreaming of going to college, I didn't know if I ever would or not, but it just so happened everything fell together. The year I moved to Lake Charles is the year they opened up so there was no way I wasn't going."

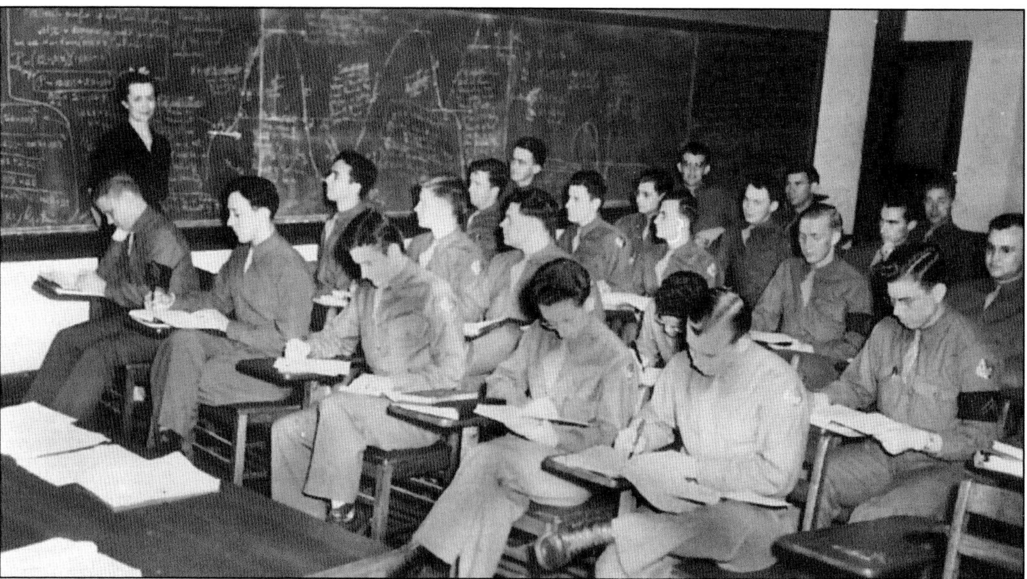

Soldiers in the Classroom. The Louisiana Maneuvers took over the campus in 1941 with Lt. Gen. Walter Krueger making the auditorium his headquarters. Planes took off and landed on an airstrip marked off on the grass. Dwight D. Eisenhower bivouacked on McNeese property. By 1942, the college had organized a Reserve Officers Training Corps on campus, and students as well as faculty participated in various related wartime activities. Two hundred Army Specialized Training Program (ASTP) students arrived on campus in August 1942 to take part in the special program of classes organized by the Army at colleges across the country.

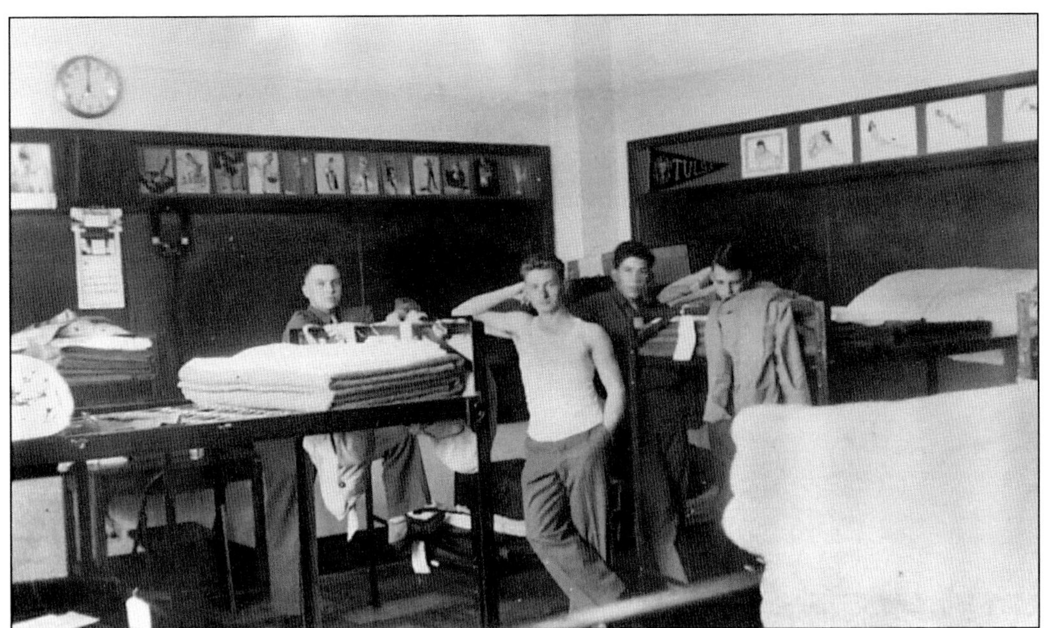

BUNKS IN THE CLASSROOM. Kaufman Hall was remodeled to provide sleeping quarters for the ASTP soldiers in former classrooms on the second and third floors. The civilian students had finished their summer term early to make room for the influx of soldiers, but the two groups combined when the fall classes began in September. Most of these soldiers went on to infantry divisions in European battlefields.

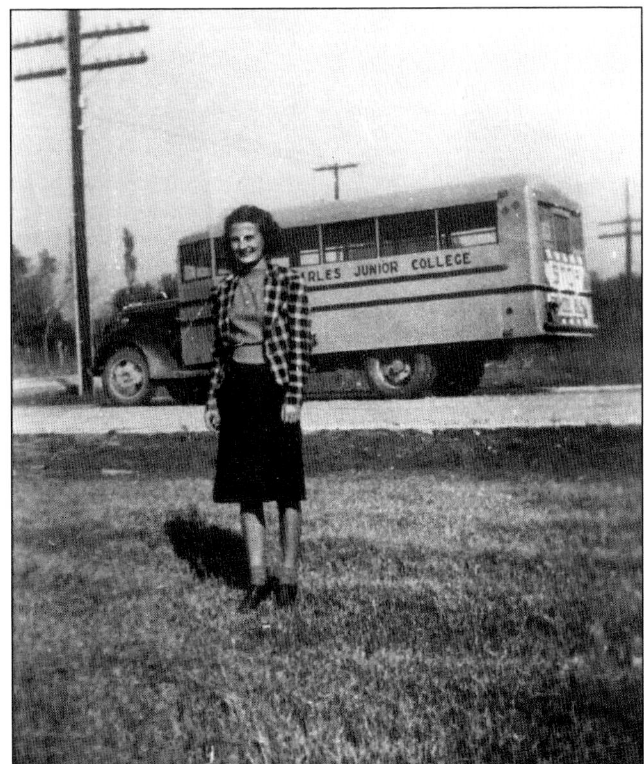

COLLEGE SCHOOL BUS. "George Ashy drove an old beat-up school bus from Oakdale to Lake Charles every day and back. He brought about 25 students from the Oakdale area." According to Johnny Daugherty, students rode horseback, carpooled in Model A Fords, rode the Lake Charles Junior College school bus, or found other ways to get to campus. Hazeldine Lane stands in front of the bus.

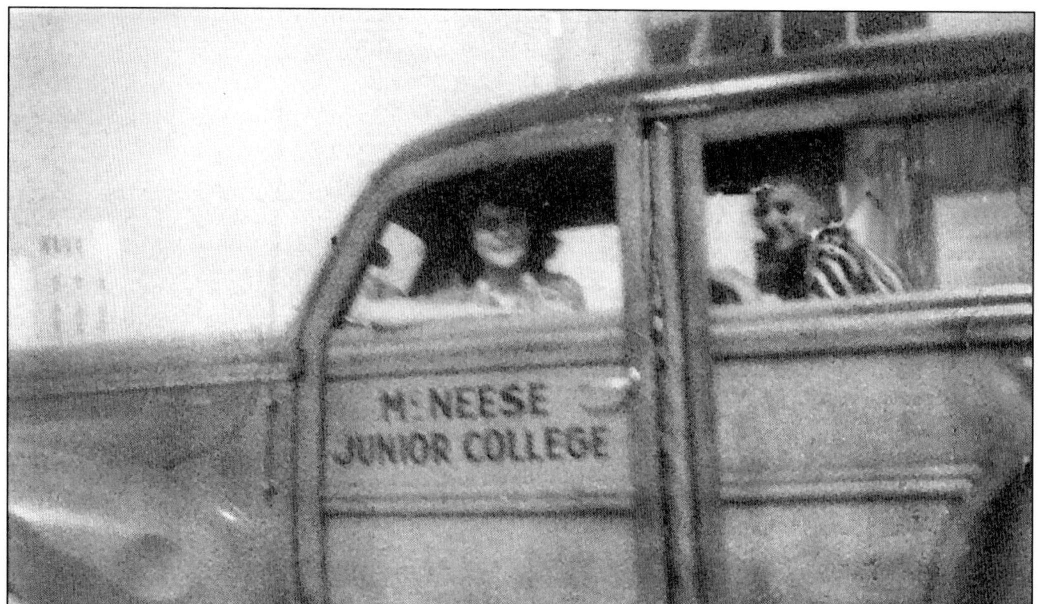

COLLEGE STATION WAGON. Two unidentified students sit in a station wagon used during the early 1940s to bring students to campus. Gasoline was rationed during the war so students as far away as Jennings took advantage of any opportunity to get to class. During the 1950s buses from Oakdale, DeRidder, and Vinton brought students to the Calcasieu Parish Courthouse where they could get a bus to the campus. Buses made seven round trips daily from the courthouse to the campus.

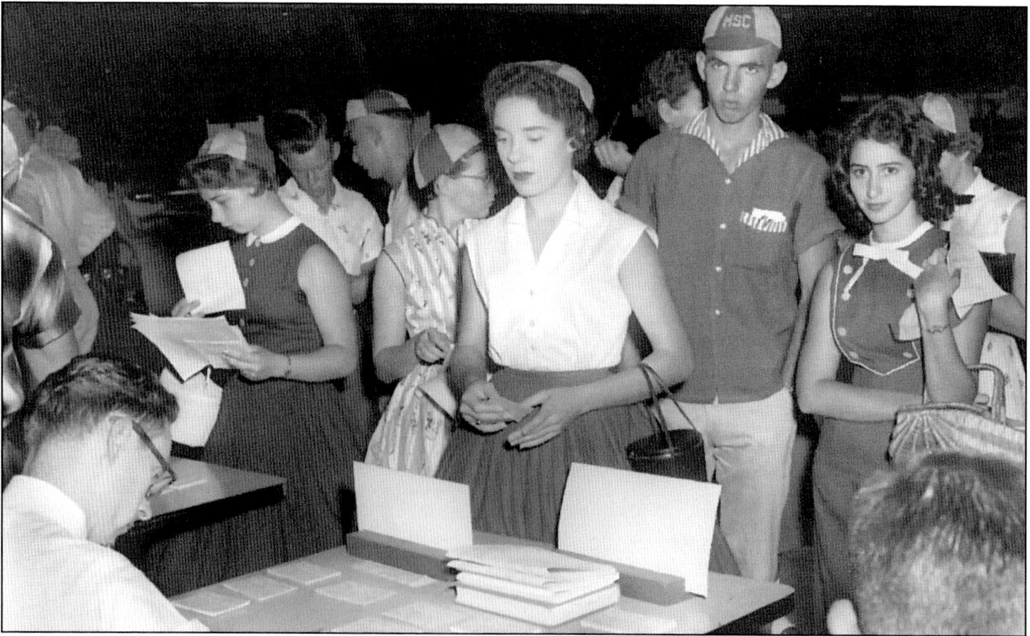

REGISTRATION IN THE 1950s. Students seen in these photographs from the 1950s patiently stand in line waiting to register for classes. During the 1950s students picked up cards, filled out schedules, and kept their fingers crossed that they would get the preferred classes, teachers, and time slots. Saturday classes were held until 1970.

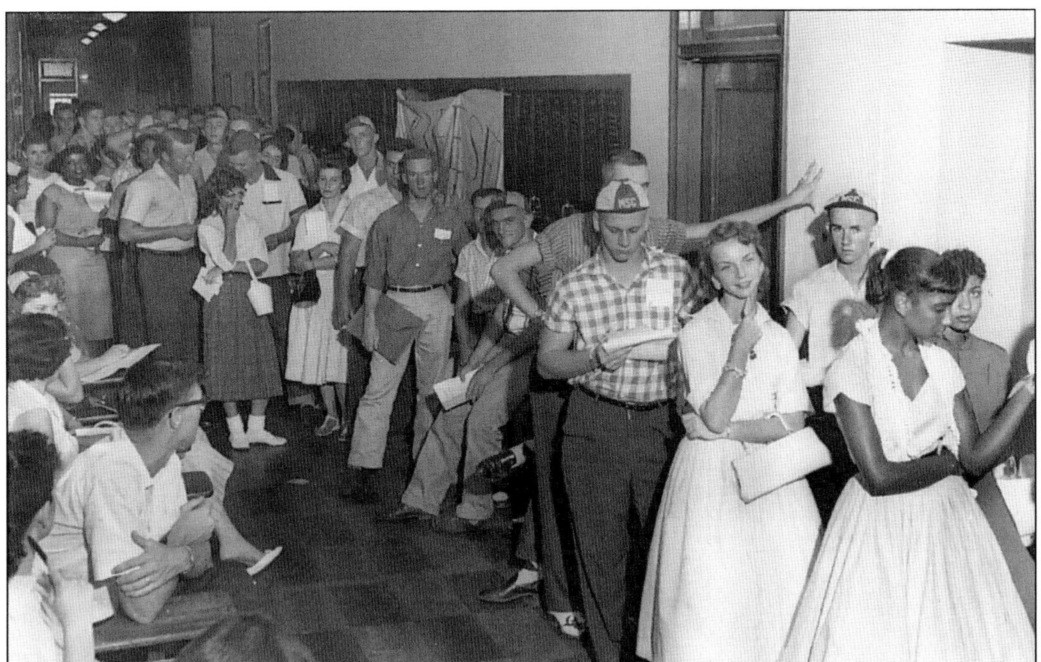

REGISTRATION BLUES. The registration process usually involved picking up class cards for each course listed on registration schedules, standing in long lines, and walking from one location to another to hand in cards and pay fees.

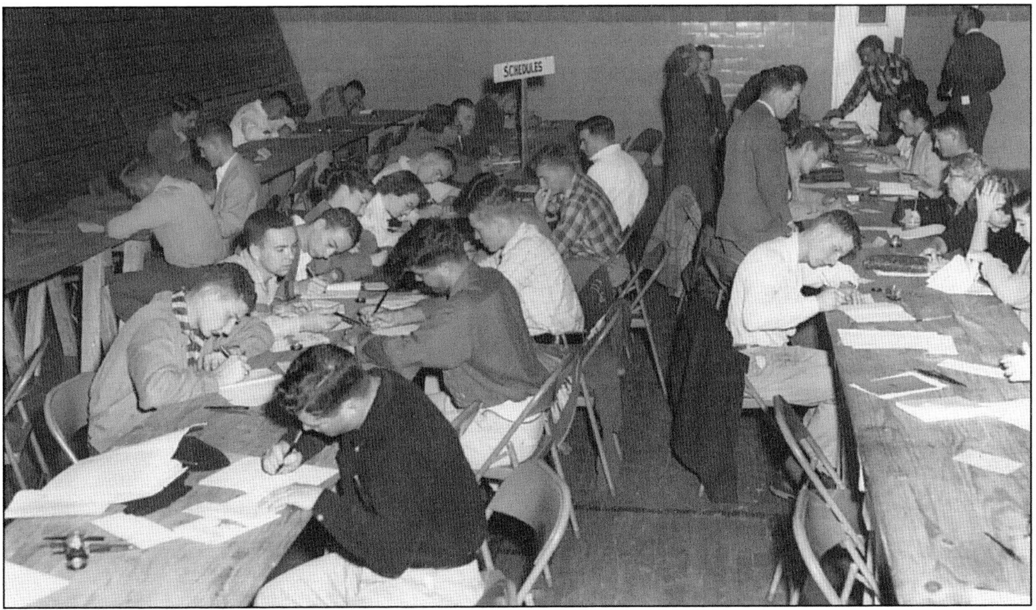

REGISTRATION HOPES. Until recently, registration has been handled by the Registrar's Office. Mrs. Inez S. Moses, who received the Alumni President's Cup in 1963 and retired in 1968, was in charge of this office for many years. Her successors were Billy Brown and Linda Finley. Currently, the student and the advisor direct the registration process. Advisors in any department can schedule students' classes at their desks using computer technology. Online and telephone registration have also become popular options.

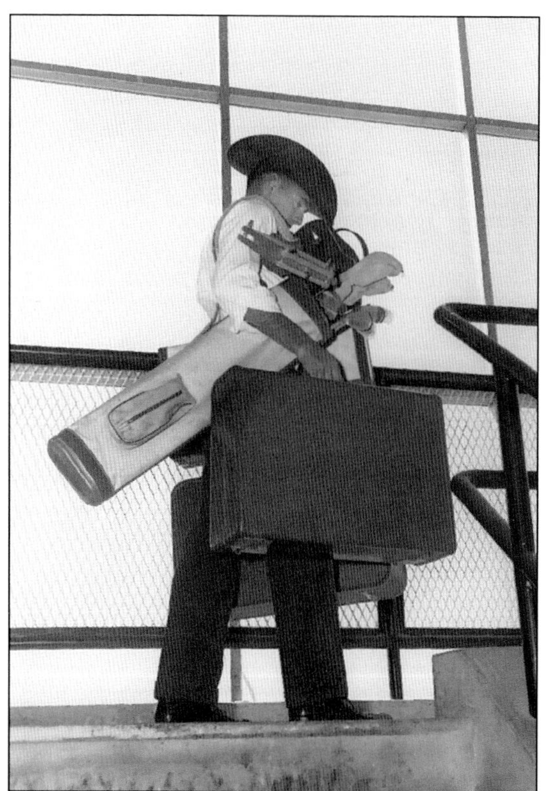

WISHFUL THINKING. A young male student moves into Watkins Hall anticipating having the time to play a few rounds of golf during class breaks. It is likely that the only time time he would have been able to play was during physical education class. Early students carried full loads, had scheduled study times, and curfews.

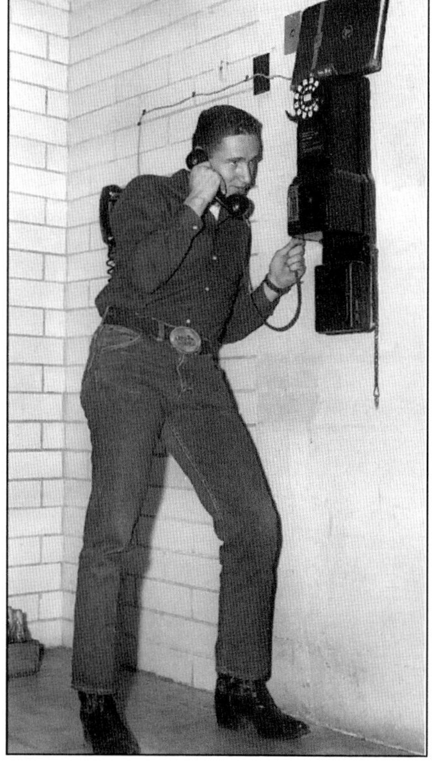

DATE NIGHT. Students living in residence halls were allowed late hours for date night only once a week. Luckily, young couples had many other opportunities to get to know each other with all the social activities planned on campus. In addition to organized club activity, students could attend parties, picnics, games, rodeos, pep rallies, dances, receptions, teas, fashion shows, and parades. There was even a Social Committee that worked to keep everyone involved and happy.

DRESSING UP. There were many opportunities for young ladies to don their gowns as McNeese sponsored several formal events. The ROTC Military Ball, the Homecoming Dance, the Spring Dance, and beauty pageants such as LaBelle and the Homecoming Court were very popular. During the early years, photographs of the girls chosen to represent each club or organization were sent to a famous person for judging. It must have been quite an honor to be picked by actor Gregory Peck as the most beautiful girl on campus, as happened to Theresa Vidrine in 1948.

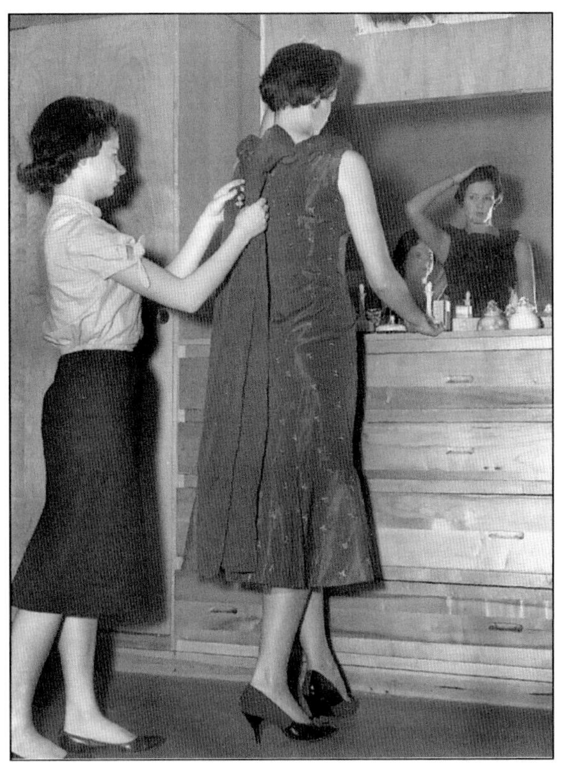

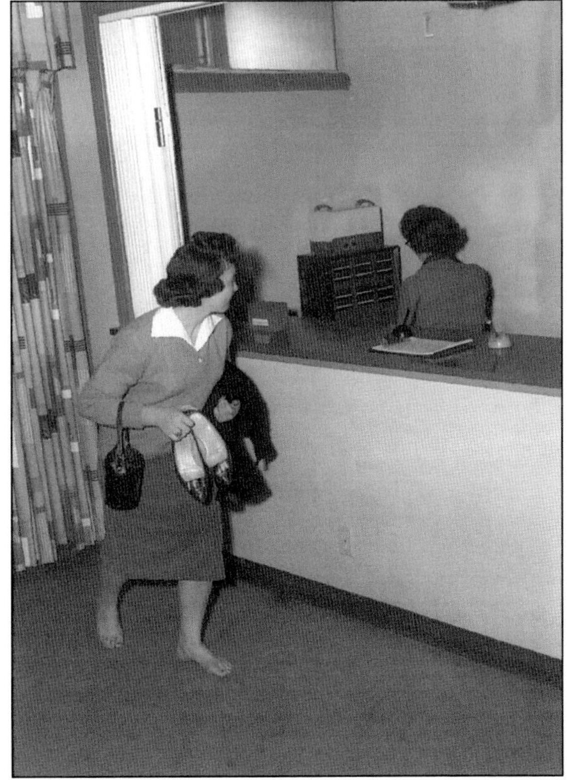

SNEAKING OUT PAST CURFEW. The *Cowboy Corral*, the official handbook of student life, listed rules and regulations governing men and women students in residence. These emphasized the highest standards of social conduct and enforced such standards with daily sign-in times, inspections, enforced study periods, nightly checkups, and dress codes. Dress codes existing in the 1950s stated that shorts, slacks, and blue jeans could not be worn by women students outside the dormitory except for sports, picnics, and special assignments such as backstage work.

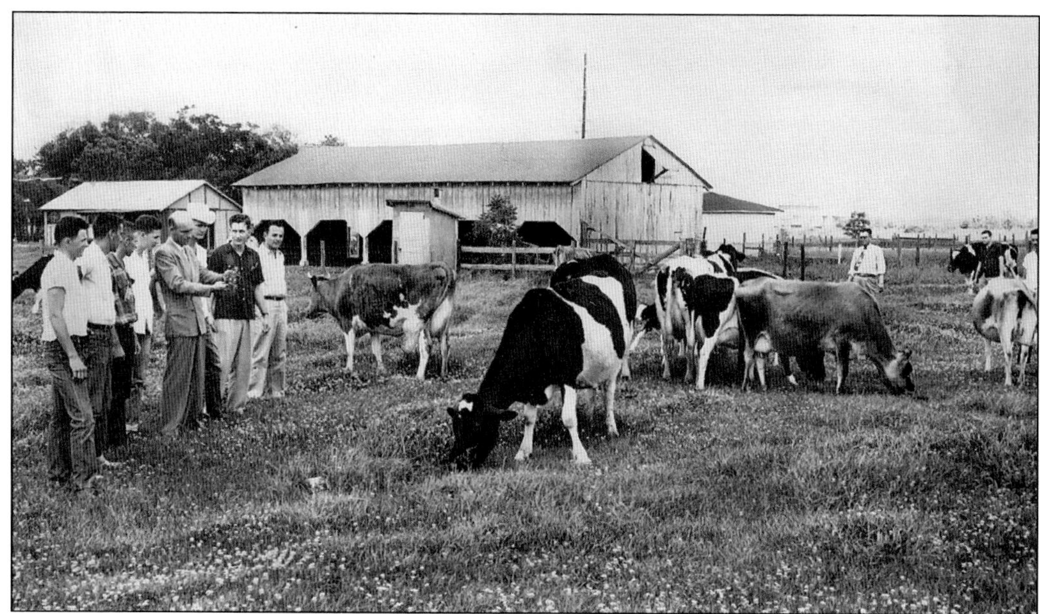

FARM. Dr. Onis D. Hyatt, head of the Department of Agriculture for a number of years, lectures students at the McNeese Farm. The 280-acre farm was purchased in 1955 from the Arthur L. Gayle family. It is located east of Louisiana Highway 14 and is still used today. The homestead and surrounding acreage were converted into an experimental station for the agriculture curriculum. Dr. Hyatt received the Alumni President's Cup in 1966.

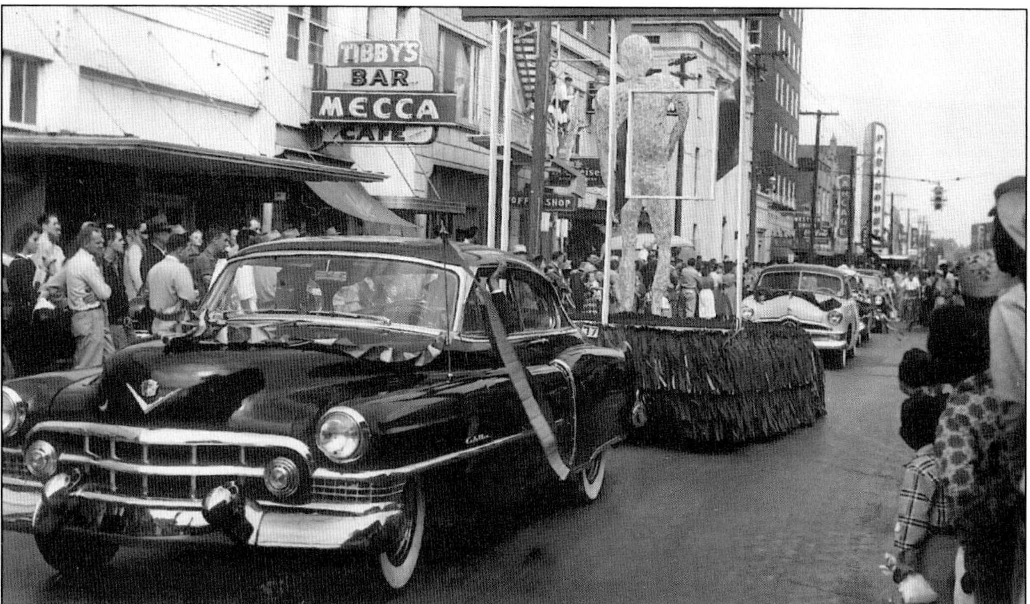

HOMECOMING PARADE. The first Homecoming Parade was held in November 1945, although it was called McNeese College Day. Sponsored by the Lake Charles Lions Club, the parade consisted of horses, floats, bands and other marching groups, and decorated cars. The winner of the prize for the best decorated car was the McNeese family car in which two daughters of John McNeese rode. The football game was played at Lake Charles High School football stadium. Gov. Jimmie Davis crowned the first Homecoming Queen, Adrienne Managan.

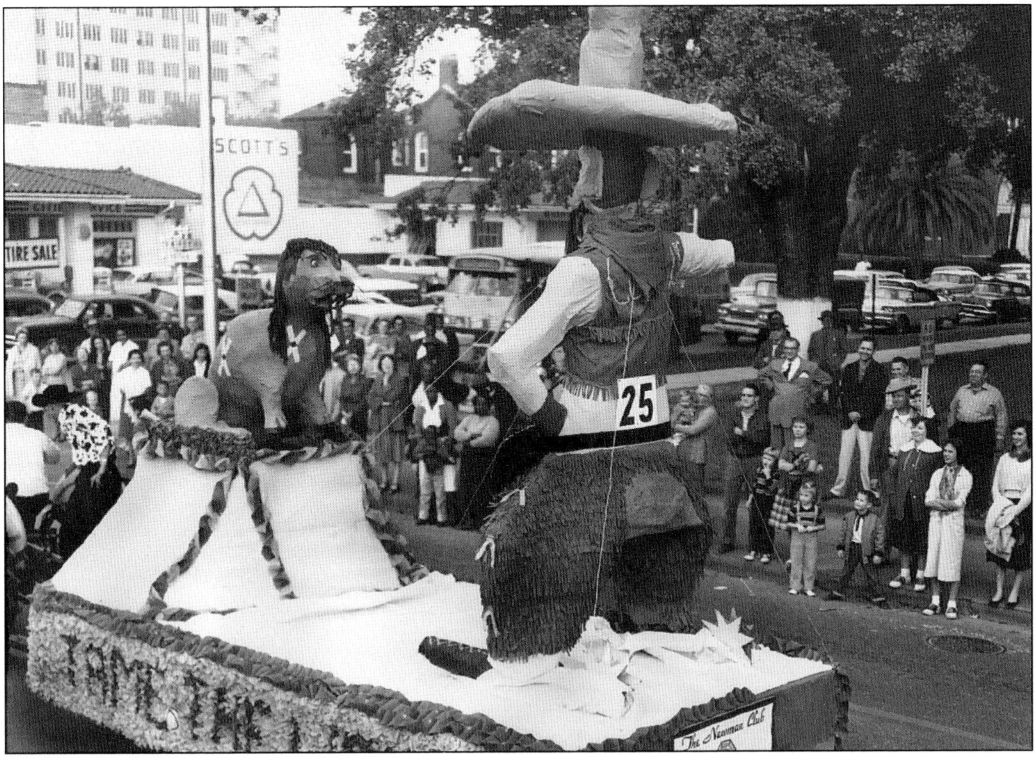

A GREAT TRADITION. McNeese students
have observed Homecoming since the
first one took place in 1945. The parades
with their elaborate floats and marching
bands were always the highlight of the
festivities leading up to the football game,
the presentation of the Homecoming
Court, and the Homecoming Dance.
In this photograph, spectators line the
street to enjoy floats such as this one
called "Tame the Lions," made by the
Newman Club.

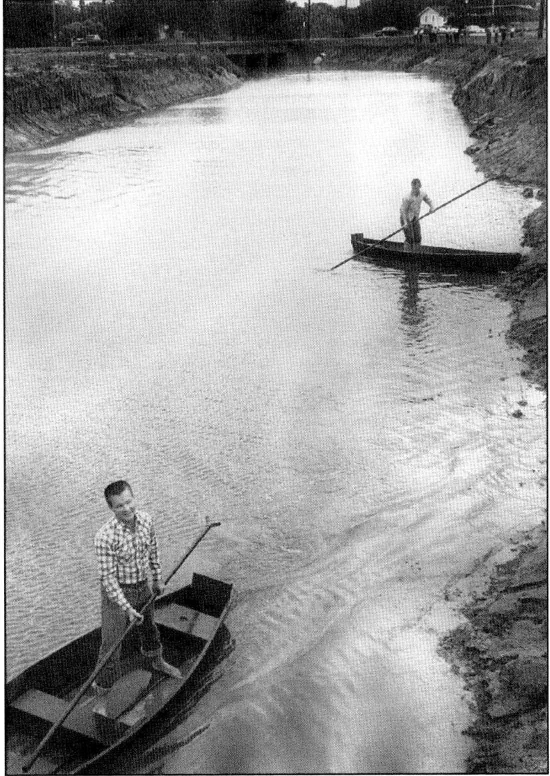

CANOE RACES. Pirogue (canoe) races down
Contraband Bayou were favorite activities
during Greek Week and, in earlier
years, Aggie Day. Greek Week features
fraternities and sororities in competition
against each other in activities ranging
from chariot races and egg tosses to
swimming and tug-of-war. Aggie Day was
sponsored each year by the Agriculture
Department. Students dressed like
cowboys and cowgirls, participated in
tractor driving contests, duels, talent
shows, square dances, and other events.

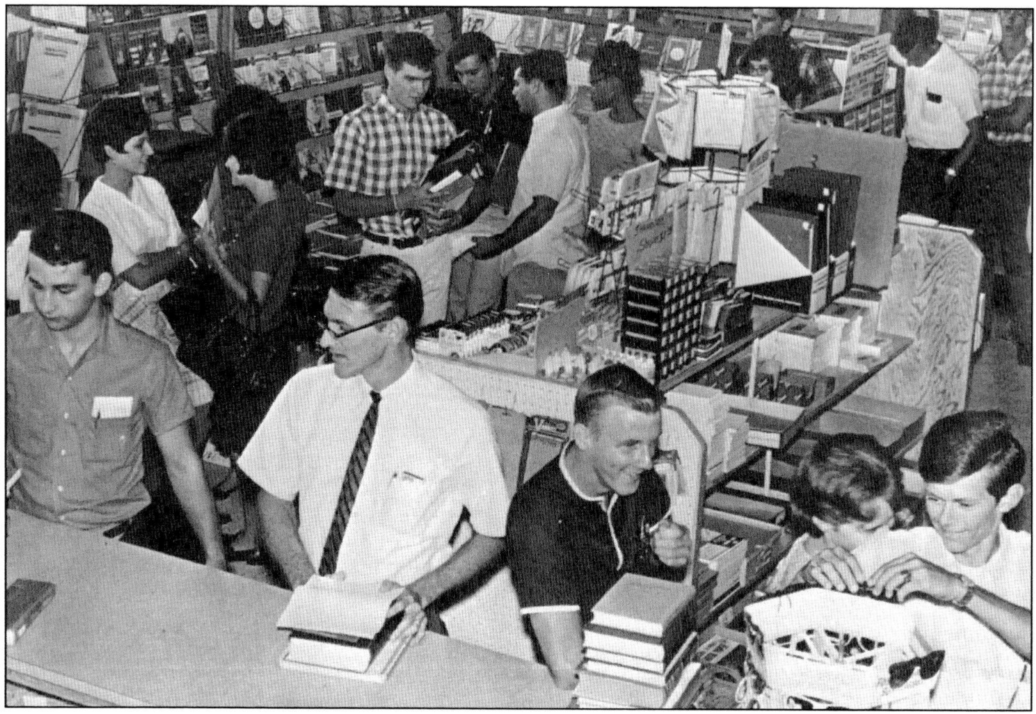

McNeese Bookstore. The McNeese Bookstore was first located in Kaufman Hall but moved to the Ranch shortly after its construction. Brownie Boozer ran the bookstore for many years, followed by Eugene Rainbolt, Myrtle Underwood, Fern Foster, and Denise Sims. Mrs. Boozer received the Alumni President's Cup in 1972. The bookstore has always tried to provide students with school supplies as well as daily necessities, especially in the early days when local stores were not as easily accessible to the students on campus.

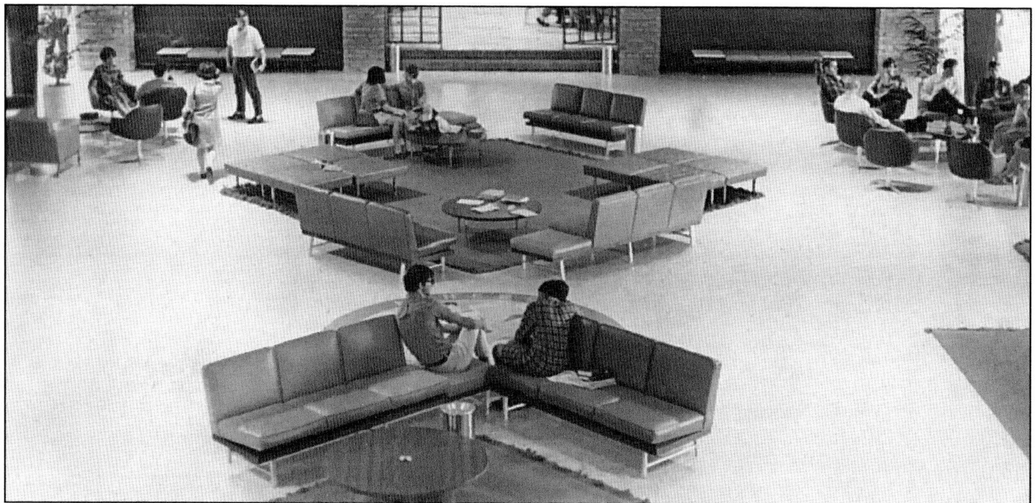

Student Union. "You can't miss the Ranch, for everyone moves in that direction," stated the *Corral* in 1959. The main lounge of the Holbrook Ranch Student Union has been a meeting place for students for many years. It must have proven one of the most popular hangouts on campus; for many years the student handbook warned students to "enjoy the Ranch, but don't major in it."

Fallout Shelter. A survival test was held in 1961 in a fallout shelter located near the president's home. In this photograph, Easton Thibodeaux, left, with the Calcasieu Sheriff's Office, and Everett B. Waddle, McNeese freshman, prepare to move into the radiation shelter. Other students participating in this test under the leadership of Dr. Robert H. Pittman were Kelly B. McWright and Dan R. Sistrunk. The shelter was constructed using funds provided by the Office of Civil and Defense Mobilization.

Pine Haven Apartments. Pine Haven Apartments were built south of campus in the early 1960s and included 96 apartments for married students and their families. Along with Sun Village, these two complexes provided much-needed married student housing.

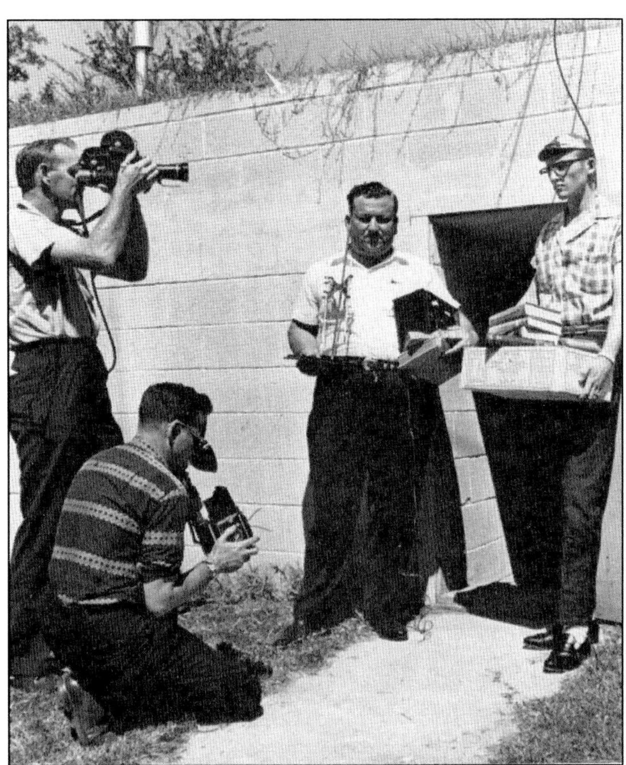

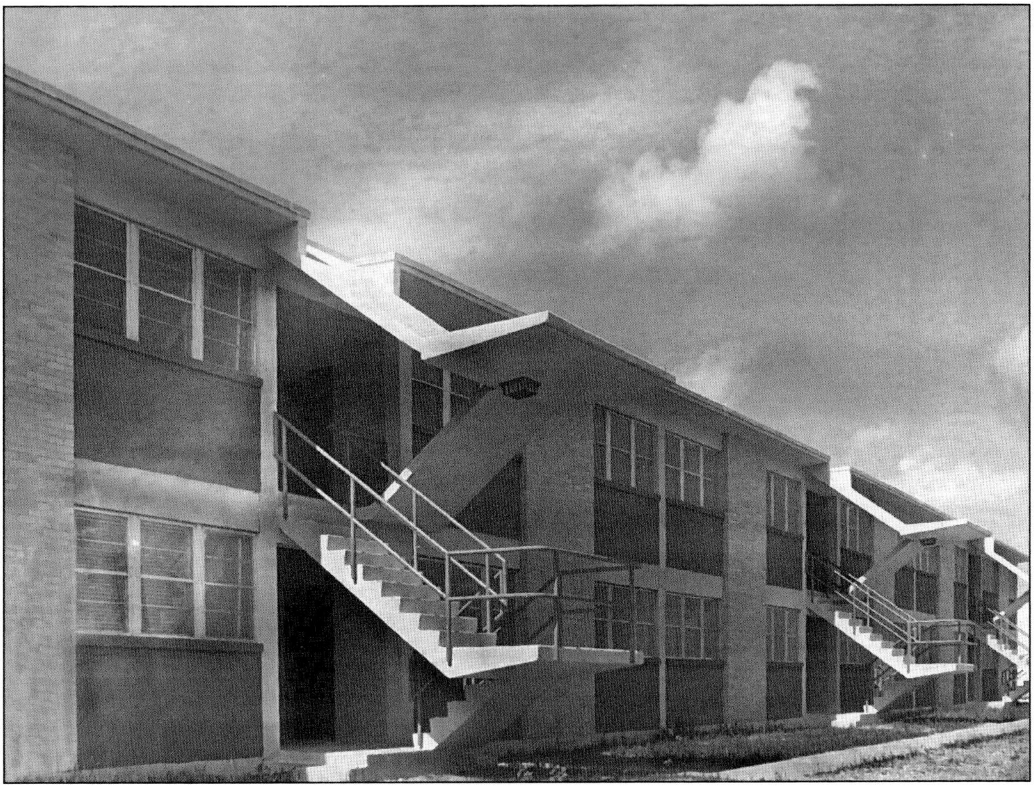

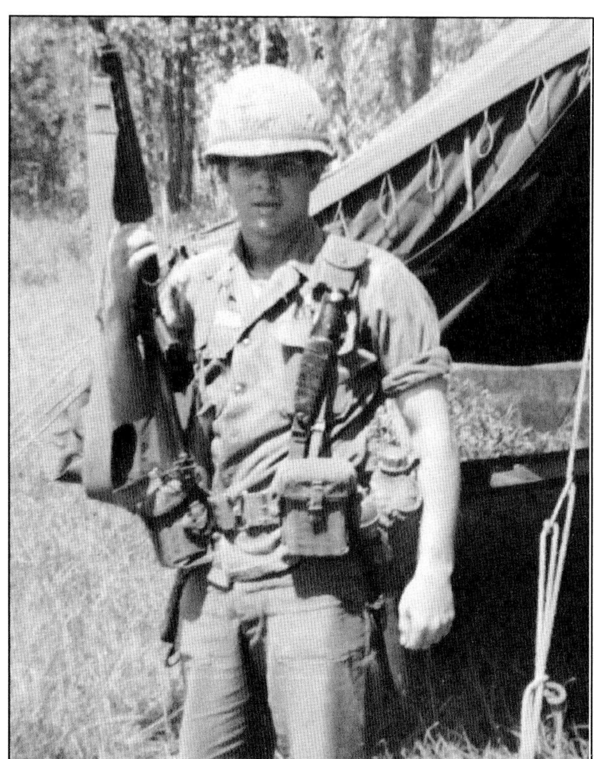

DONALD CHARLES CORNETT. Cadet commander in the McNeese ROTC and president of the student body, 1962–1963, Donald Charles Cornett was active in the college's social life and an honor student. He graduated from McNeese in 1964 and went into the Army. He was killed in action in the Ia Drang Valley in South Vietnam in 1965. The 1966 *Log* was dedicated to his memory.

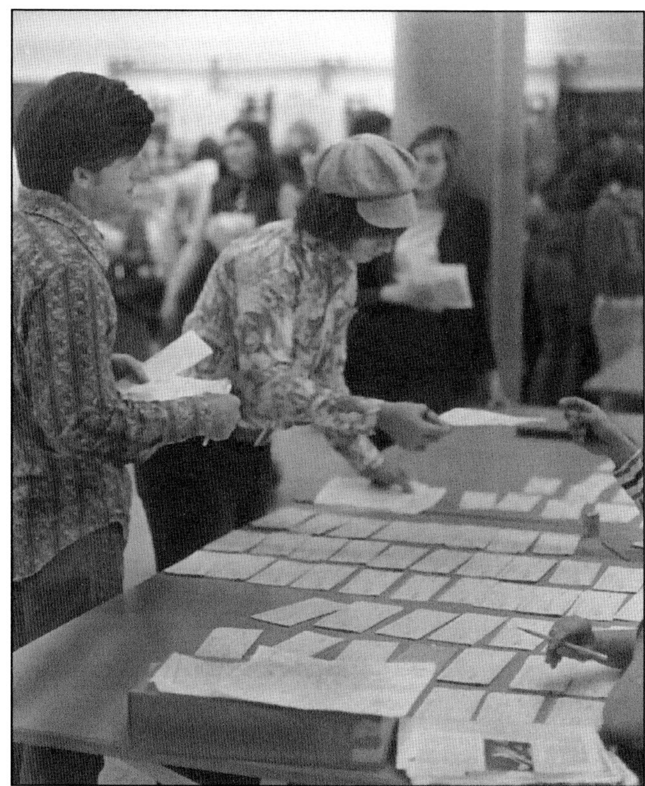

REGISTRATION IN THE 1970s. In the 1960s and 1970s students picked up IBM cards for the classes they wished to schedule. Students today are able to register from home using web-based technology.

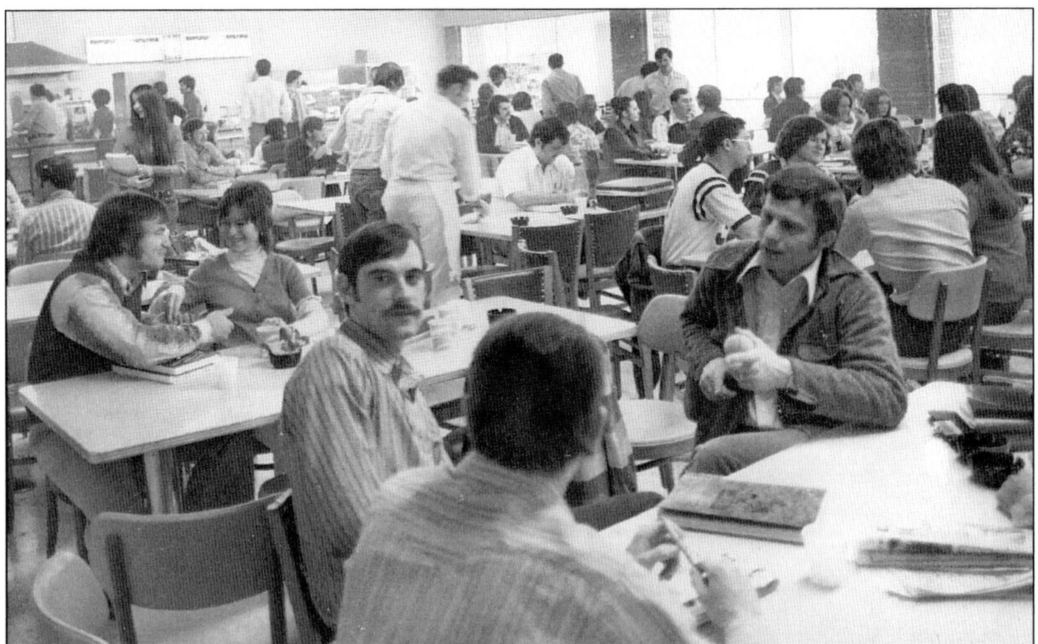

CAFETERIA. Throughout the years the cafeteria has changed along with the university, from providing three regular meals a day to fast food, from bag lunches to catered affairs, from coffee shops to midnight breakfasts. The cafeteria has historically provided a place for students to meet.

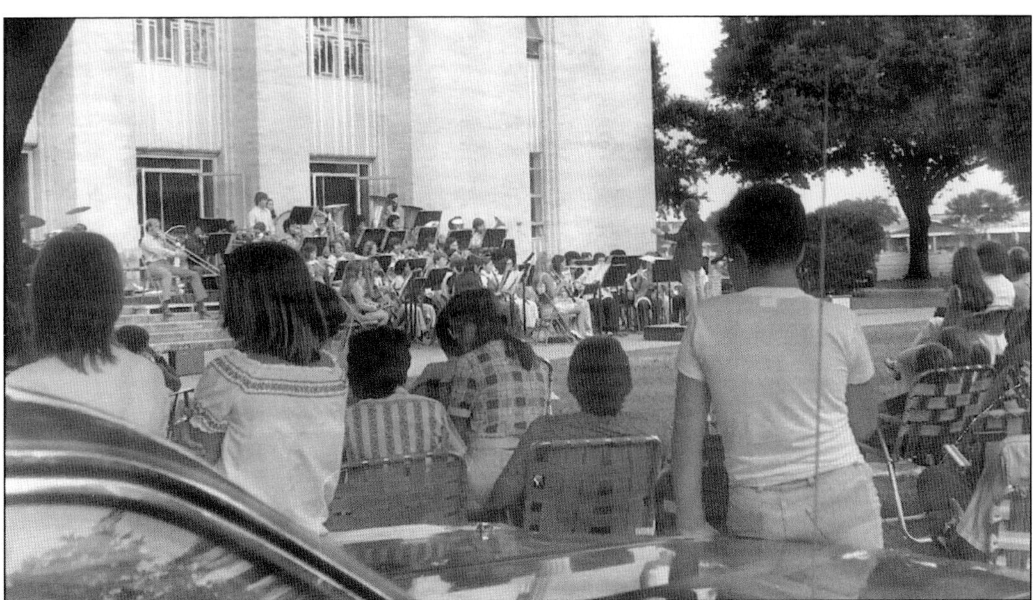

ORCHESTRA. The McNeese Music Department and the Lake Charles Lions Club began an alliance in 1943 designed to bring musical theatre and light opera to Lake Charles. For more than 30 years, these spring operas funded scholarships in music and theatre arts. The music department offers a wide range of courses, in addition to opportunities to participate in the Cowboy Marching Band, the University Chorus, the A Cappella Choir, or the McNeese Orchestra. In this photograph, the orchestra presents a summer concert on the front steps of the auditorium.

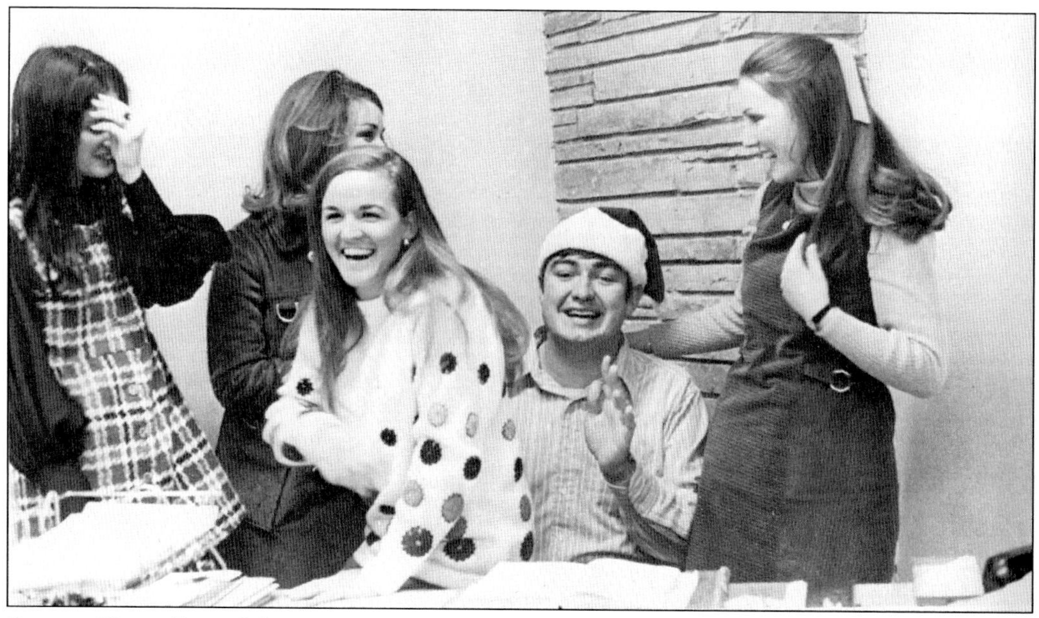

Ben and Willie. Two of the most active students on campus in the early 1970s were Willie Landry and Ben Mount. Willie, seated on Ben's lap in this 1971 *Log* photograph, later became Mrs. Mount as well as Lake Charles's first female mayor and is currently serving as state senator. Ben was Student Government Association (SGA) president and later became a successful local attorney and historic preservation advocate.

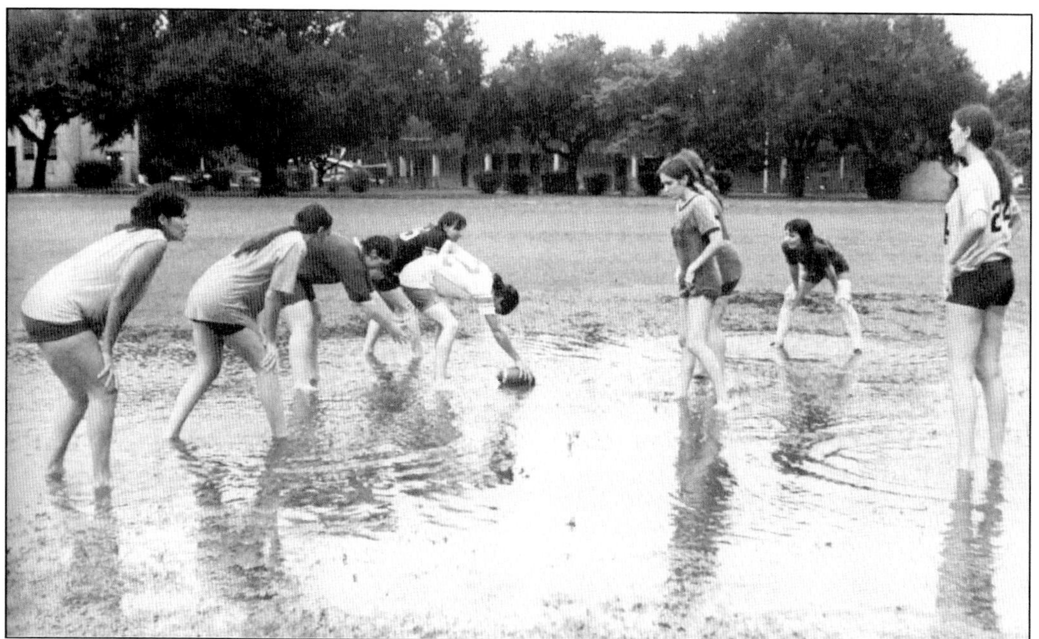

Intramural Sports. Intramural sports emphasize participation and recreation. Competition is designed for those students not formally competing in any athletic program. Participation does not require intense training or a high level of skill—just a desire to relax through recreation, enthusiasm, and interest. In this photograph taken in 1974, a muddy game of touch football is in progress.

52

SPRING FLING. An afternoon free of classes and filled with fun! Spring Fling is an annual tradition at McNeese, and students love it. The main attraction, as seen in this 1986 photograph of Angie Bertrand, is the gigantic, all-you-can-eat, crawfish boil. In addition, there is music, games, and merrymaking. Then it's back to class the next day to get ready for final exams.

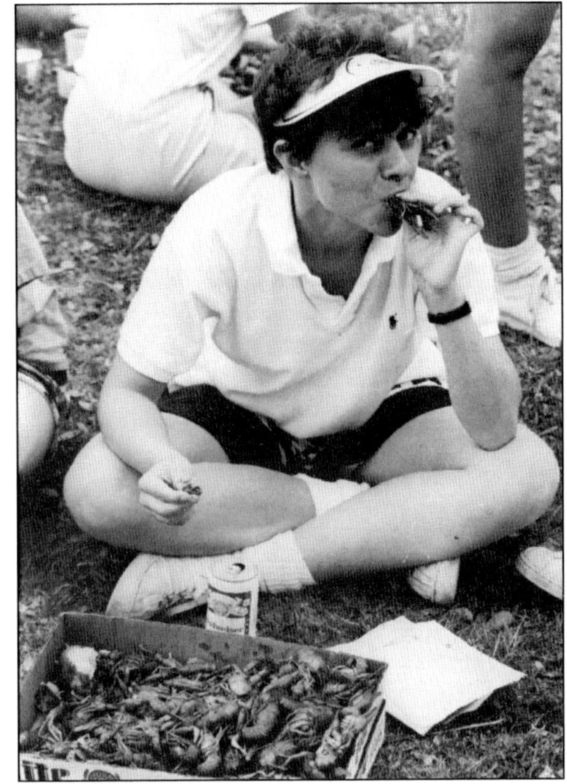

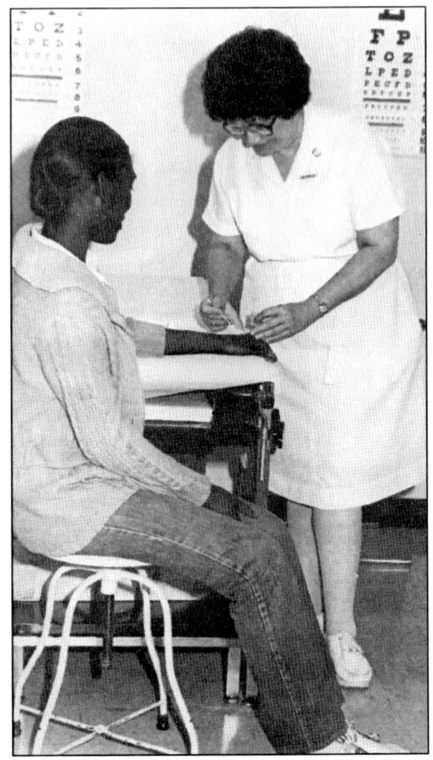

TREATMENT AT THE INFIRMARY. Nurse Josie DiGiglia treats an injured student, Virginia Miller, in the infirmary in 1983.

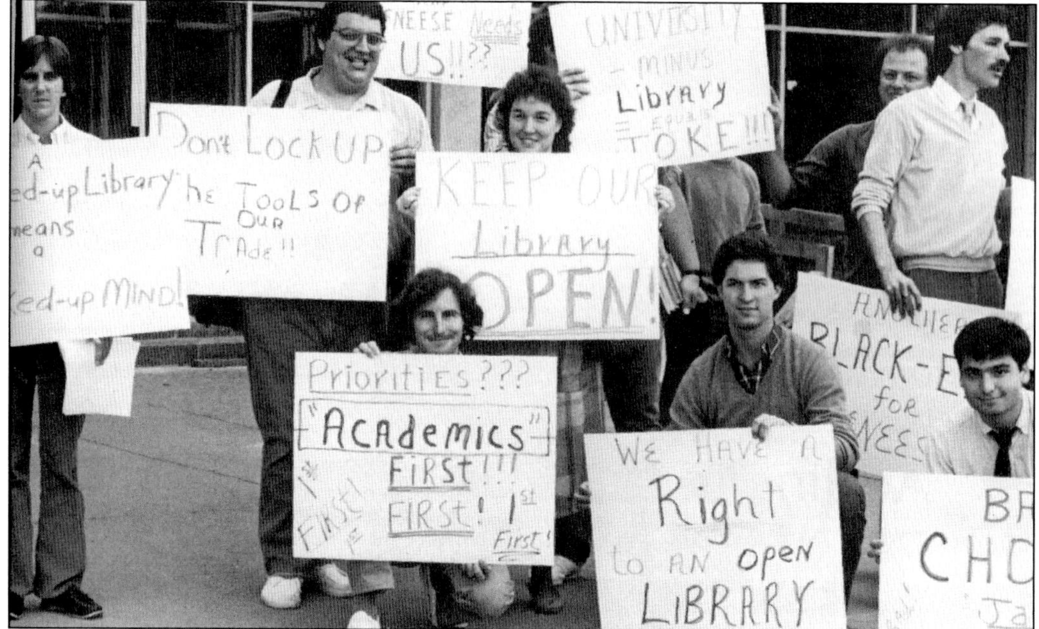

LIBRARY PROTEST. Student protests, letters, and petitions followed the administration's decision to shorten library hours by closing on weekends. In this 1986 photograph a group of picketing students demonstrate student involvement that led to a reversal of the decision and the reinstatement of weekend hours. The library continues to offer many services to the community.

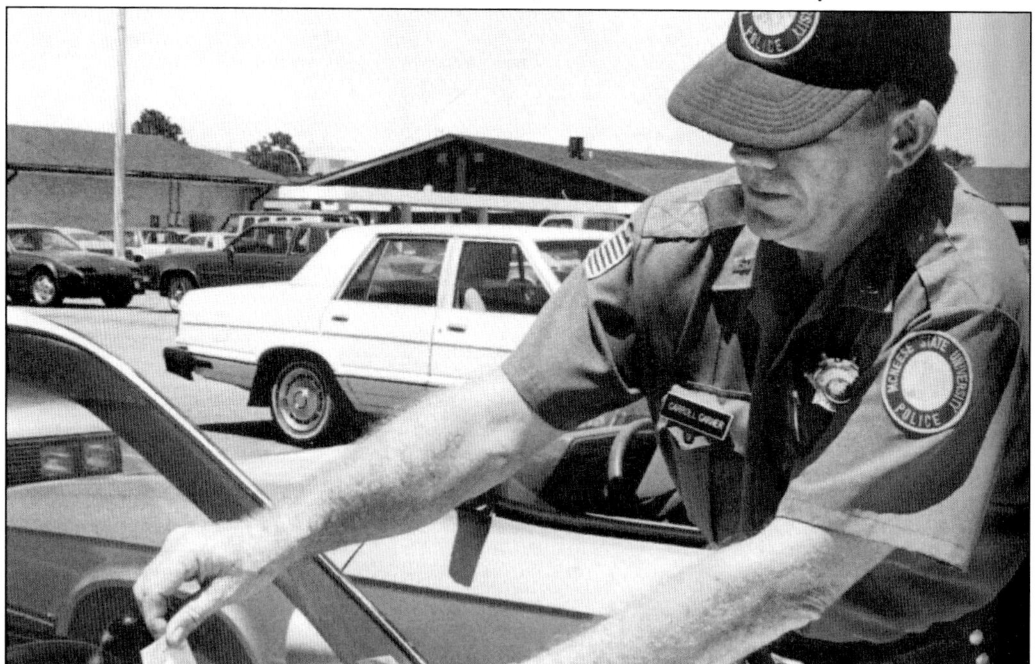

UNIVERSITY POLICE. Officer Carroll Garner tickets an illegally parked car in this 1986 image. The goal of the University Police Office is to protect students, faculty, and their property. Formerly directed by Byron Petry and Charles Goen, the office is now run by David Benada. Before the organization of this office, night watchmen such as H.L. Kickendahl patrolled the campus.

54

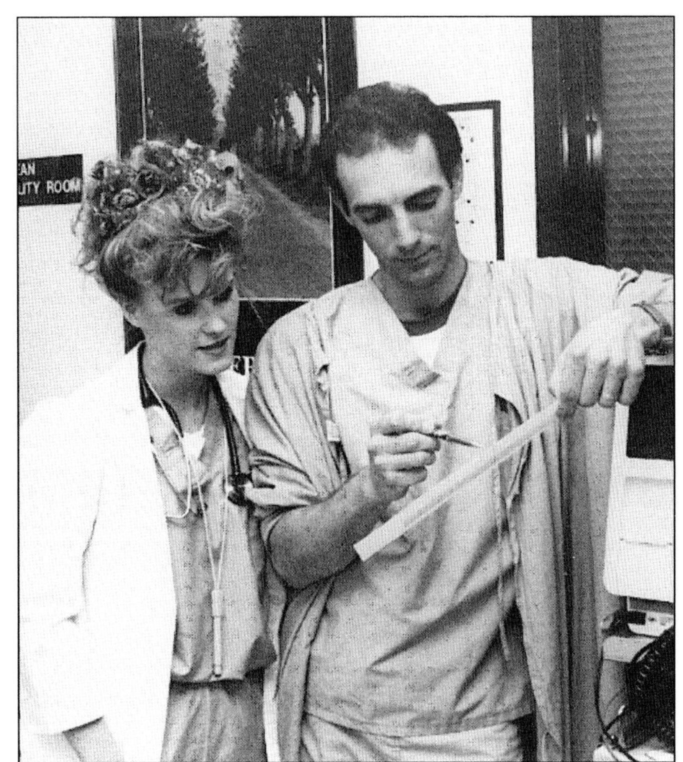

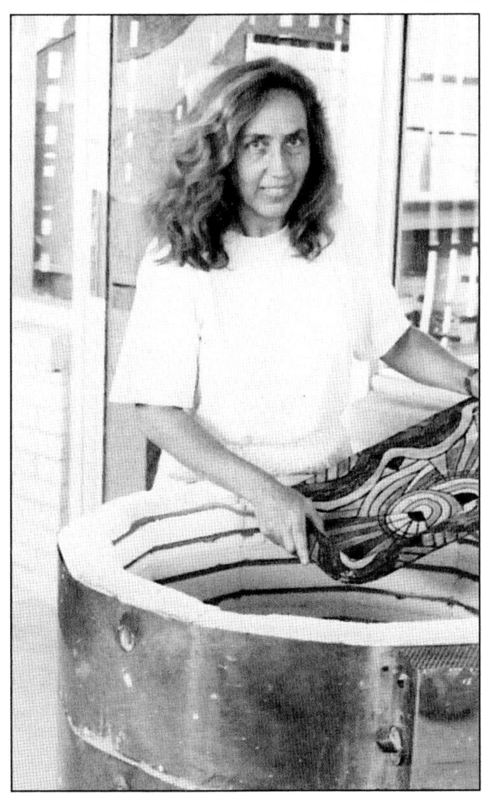

ART CLASSES. Students in the visual arts
curriculum may choose classes in advertising
design, drawing, painting, printmaking,
photography, or ceramics. Students exhibit their
work several times a year, and those persons
lucky enough to get to the student art sales early
can go home owning a piece of original artwork.
In this photograph, Charlene Kaough holds a
ceramic tray.

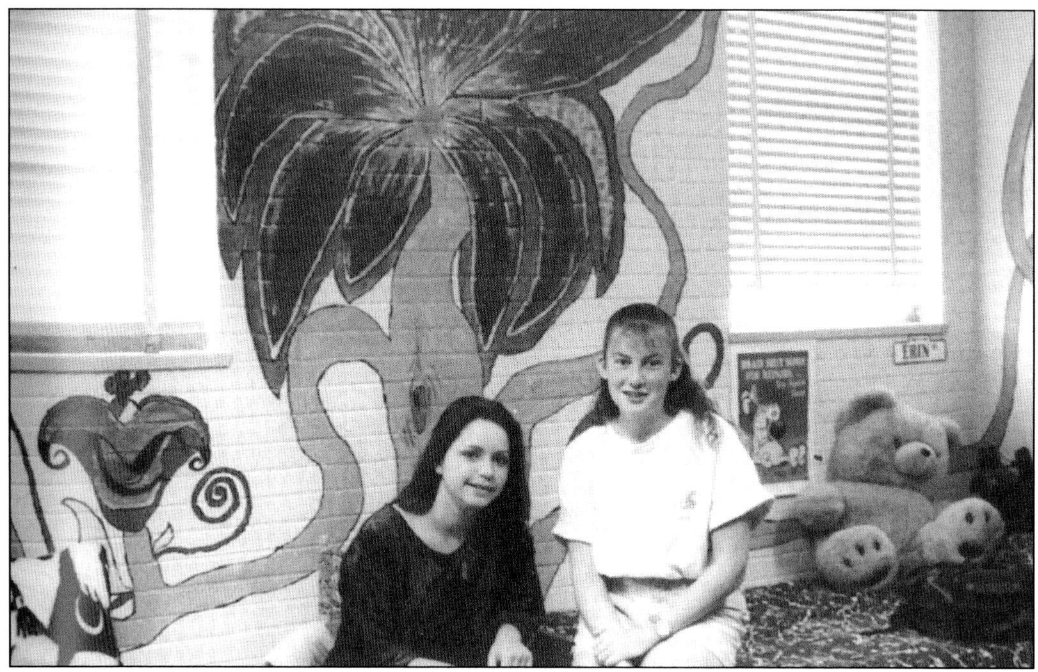

Dorm Art. This 1995 photograph shows the result of a dormitory room-painting contest. Amy Marie Sternadel, left, and Erin Cheevers won first place for the colorful flowers and trees that adorned the walls of their Burton Hall dorm room.

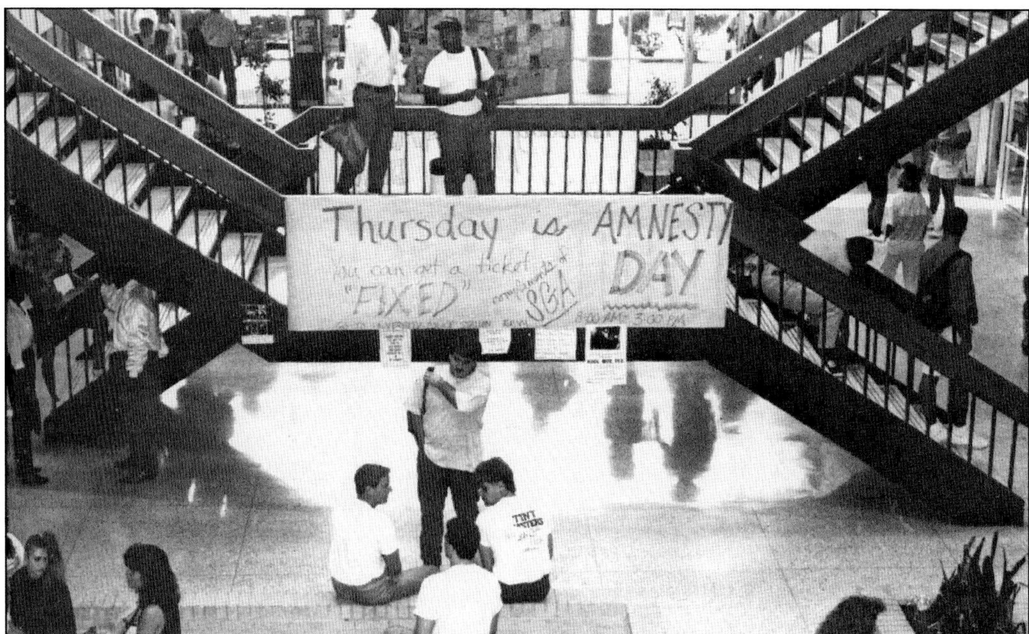

Amnesty Day. Students are happy to observe Amnesty Day when parking fines may be pardoned. This is one of the many benefits of an active SGA. Throughout the years, from the first Student Senate, then Student Council, to the present SGA, this organization has done much to generate school spirit and cooperation by promoting activities for student participation and by supporting and representing students to the faculty, administration, and community.

56

Four

FACULTY

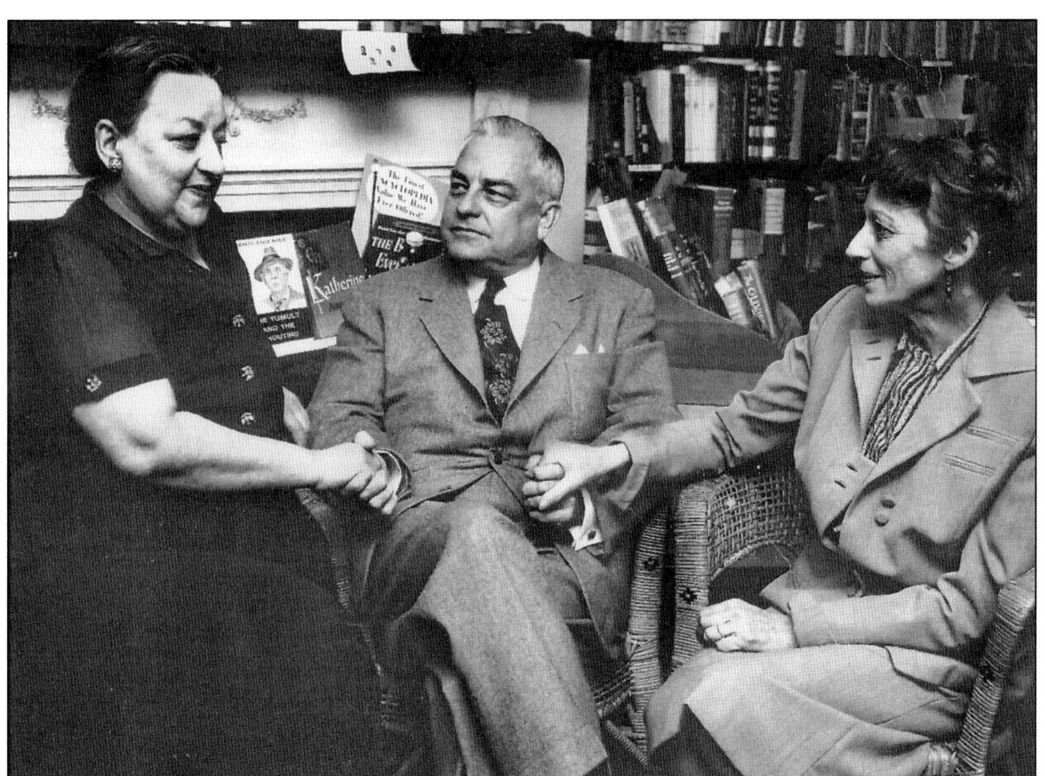

ROSA HART, LETHER E. FRAZAR, AND MARGERY PARSONS WILSON. President Frazar joins hands with Rosa Hart, left, director of the Lake Charles Little Theatre, and Margery Wilson, director of McNeese's Bayou Players. This photograph was taken in 1953, illustrating the cooperation of the two groups of performers who would soon join forces to stage Shakespeare's *King Henry IV, Part I*. Margery Wilson directed the Bayou Players for a quarter of a century through 84 plays. She received the Alumni President's Cup in 1967, and retired in 1969.

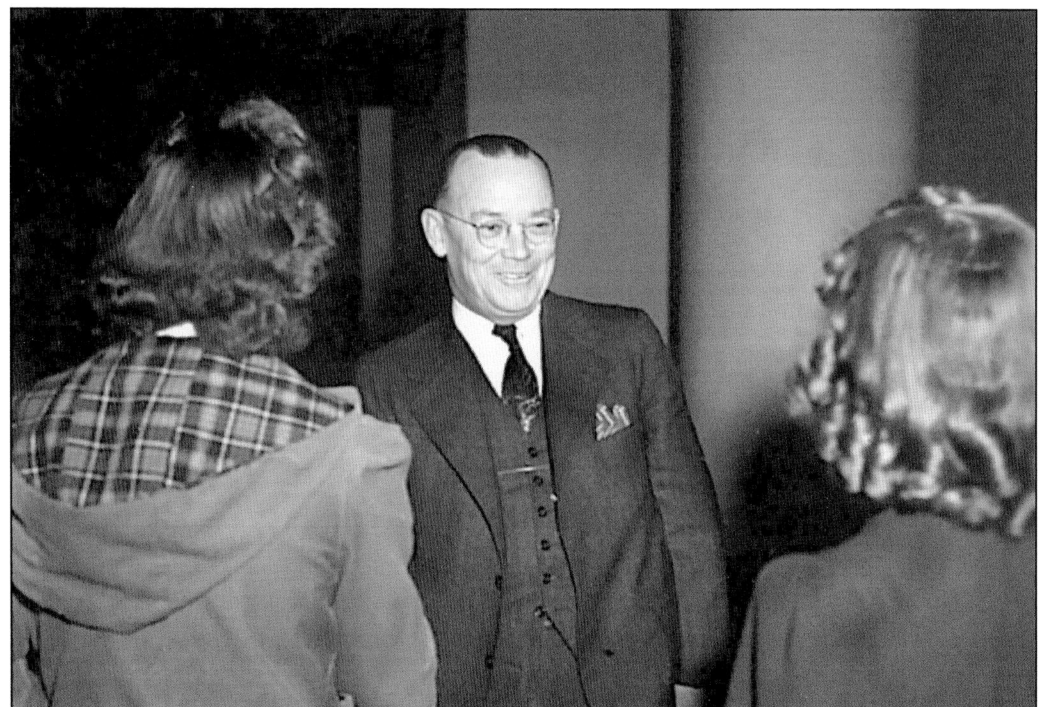

DR. JOSEPH T. FARRAR. The deans of Lake Charles Junior College, later John McNeese Junior College, while the school was still under the administration of Louisiana State University, were Dr. Joseph T. Farrar, Dr. William B. Hatcher, Dr. Rodney Cline, and Dr. Lether E. Frazar. Pictured here is Dr. Farrar, the first dean of the school, who was a well-liked and popular administrator. He went on to become the president of Louisiana State Normal School, now Northwestern State University in Natchitoches.

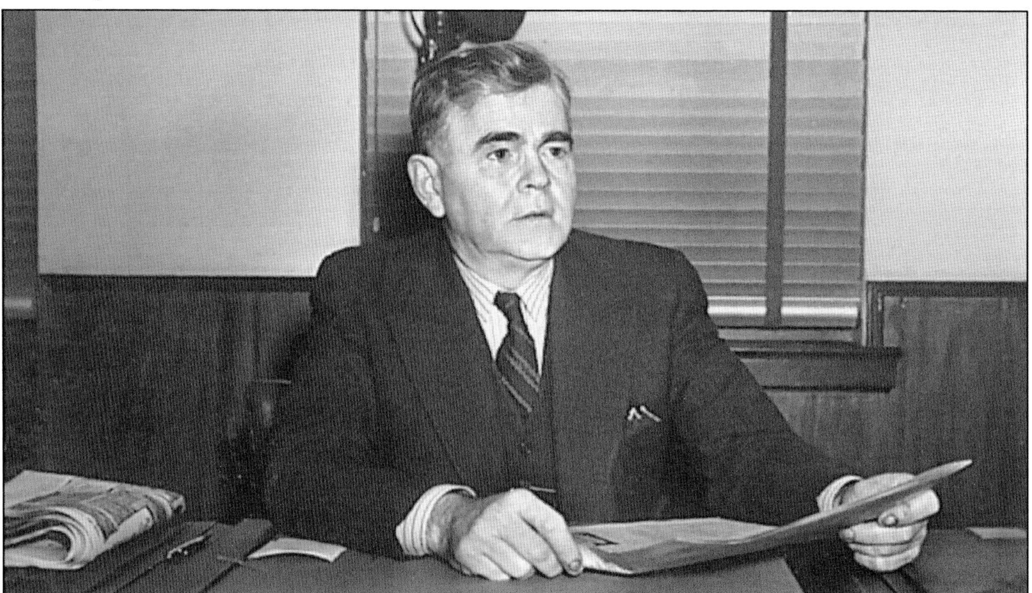

DR. WILLIAM B. HATCHER. Dr. Hatcher served briefly as dean during the 1940–1941 academic year, replacing Dr. Farrar. Hatcher went on to become president of Louisiana State University.

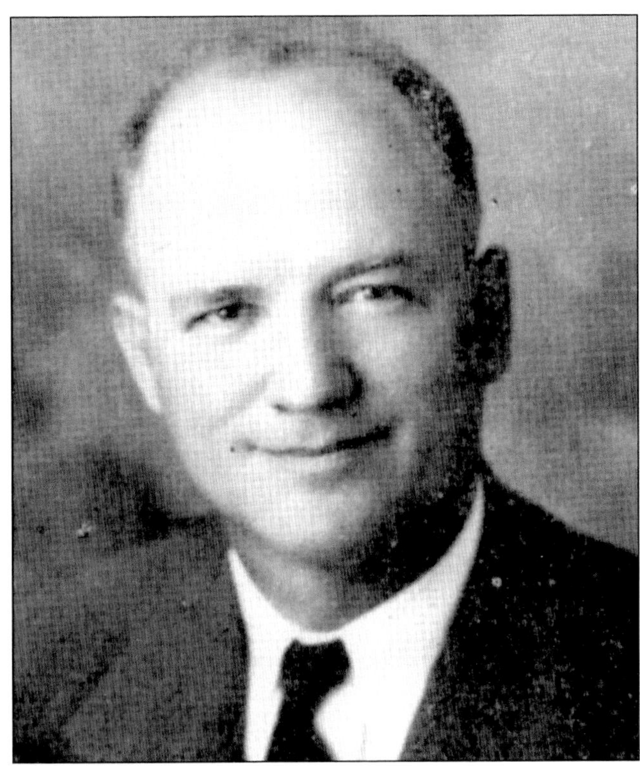

DR. RODNEY CLINE. Cline succeeded Hatcher as dean in 1941. He was from Lake Charles and a graduate of Lake Charles High School. Cline taught at Central School before going to Louisiana State University and Peabody College for his master's and doctorate degrees. He went on to become dean of Northeastern Center, now the University of Louisiana-Monroe. Cline served at McNeese during the height of the Second World War. Not many records remain from his tenure since the school newspaper and yearbook were not published during those years. His farewell address to the faculty and student body does exist, however, and it emphasizes his desire that the college continue to prosper.

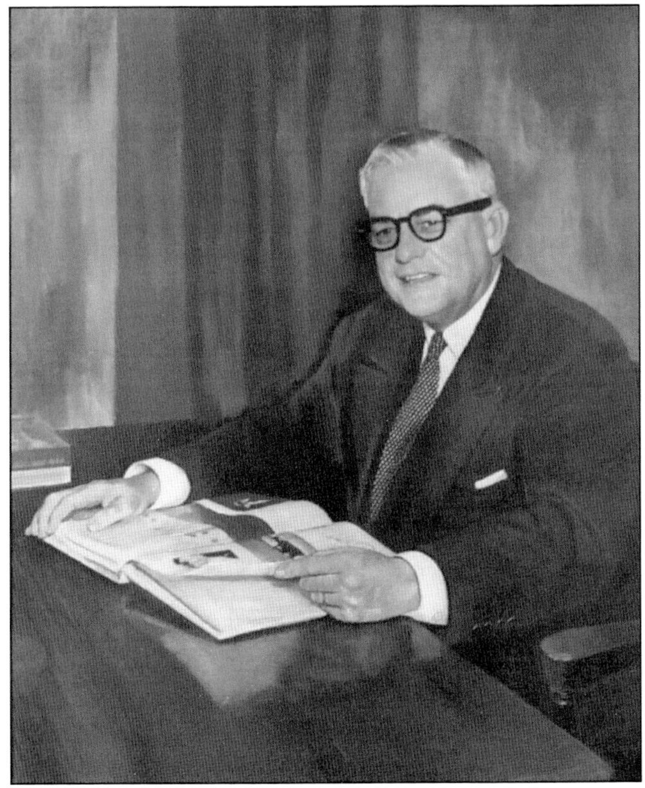

DR. LETHER EDWARD FRAZAR. Dr. Frazar was chosen to succeed Dean Cline in 1944. Described as affable and outgoing, Frazar relished leading cheers at pep rallies and presiding over Honors Day assemblies. He was referred to as a champion of the student body and was a popular and effective administrator. He had served as president of Southwestern Louisiana Institute before coming to McNeese. He worked with local politicians during the early 1950s to make McNeese a degree-granting, four-year institution. Frazar retired from McNeese in 1956 in order to run successfully for lieutenant governor on the Earl Long ticket. Frazar Memorial Library, dedicated in 1961, was named in his honor. Frazar died in 1960, cutting short his promising political career.

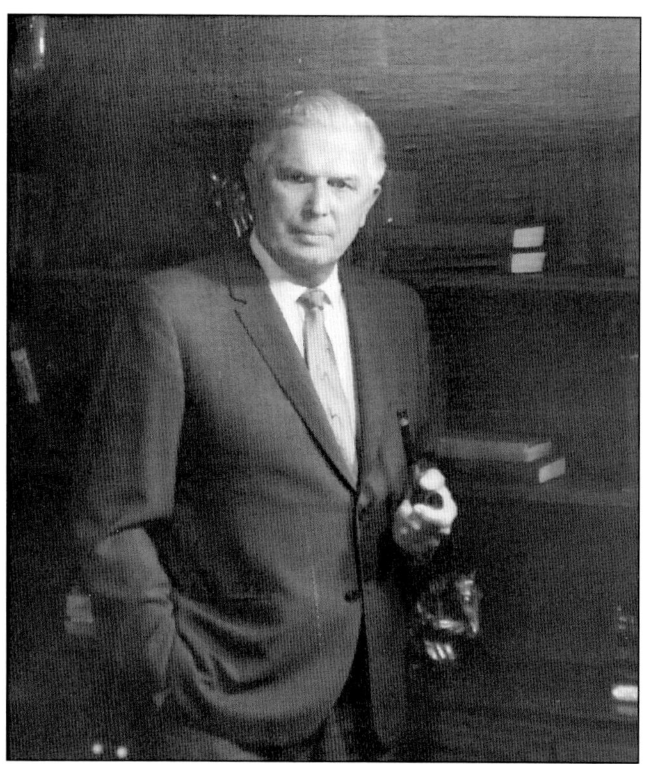

Dr. Wayne N. Cusic. Wayne N. Cusic came to McNeese in the fall of 1940 to teach physical education and to coach basketball. By the early 1950s, he had served as counselor for men, assistant professor and Head of Health and Physical Education, professor and Head of the Department of Education, and Dean of Men. When President Frazar retired in 1955, Cusic was named his successor by the State Board of Education. He remained in this position until his retirement in 1969. Cusic was known as a man of unimpeachable integrity and inflexible will. Dr. Cusic received the Alumni President's Cup in 1960.

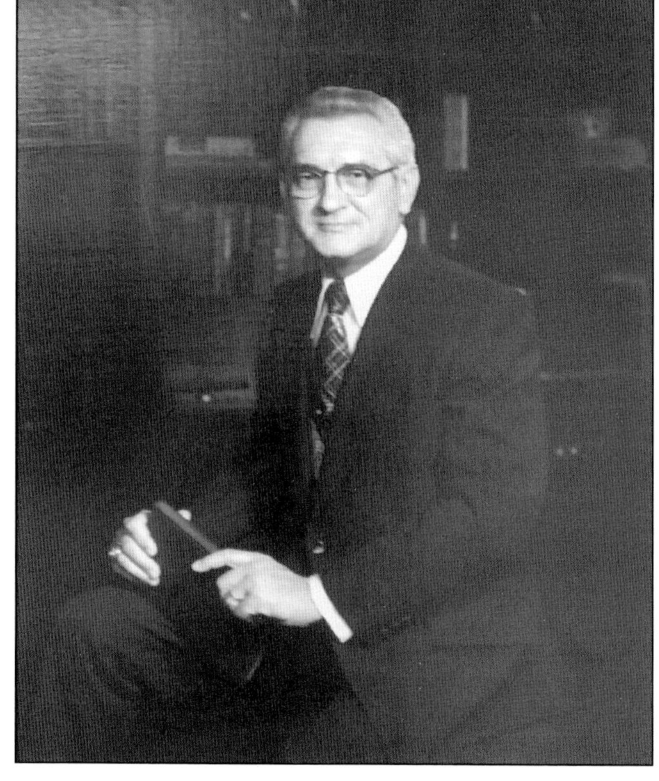

Dr. Thomas S. Leary. Former head of the department of engineering, Dr. Thomas S. Leary became president in 1969. The campus witnessed much dissension and unrest during his 11-year tenure in office. Protests over dress code and hair length regulations were interspersed with more serious race relations issues and declining enrollment figures. Also during Leary's tenure McNeese experienced its last name change, becoming McNeese State University during the 1970 Louisiana Legislative Session. Dr. Leary received the Alumni President's Cup in 1969.

60

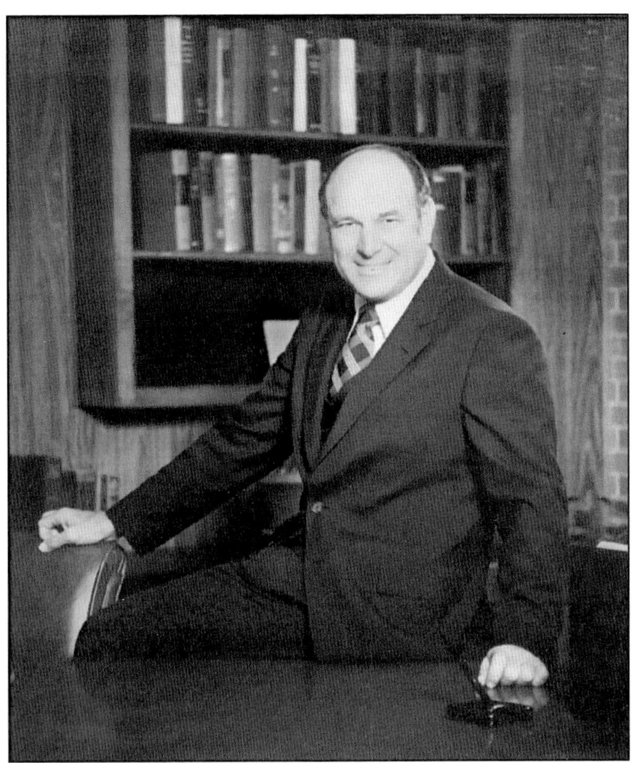

DR. JACK V. DOLAND. Jack Doland played football and basketball for McNeese during its first season of intercollegiate athletics in 1945, and was chosen head coach for the football team in 1969. When Dr. Thomas Leary resigned from the presidency in 1979, Doland, to the surprise and shock of the entire campus, was chosen to succeed him. He became the second coach to be named president of McNeese. He officially took office on July 1, 1980, and soon proved to be an effective administrator. He gained the support of the campus and the community, improved the image of McNeese, and revived student and community pride in the university. Dr. Doland resigned from the presidency in 1986 in order to seek successfully a position in the Louisiana State Senate.

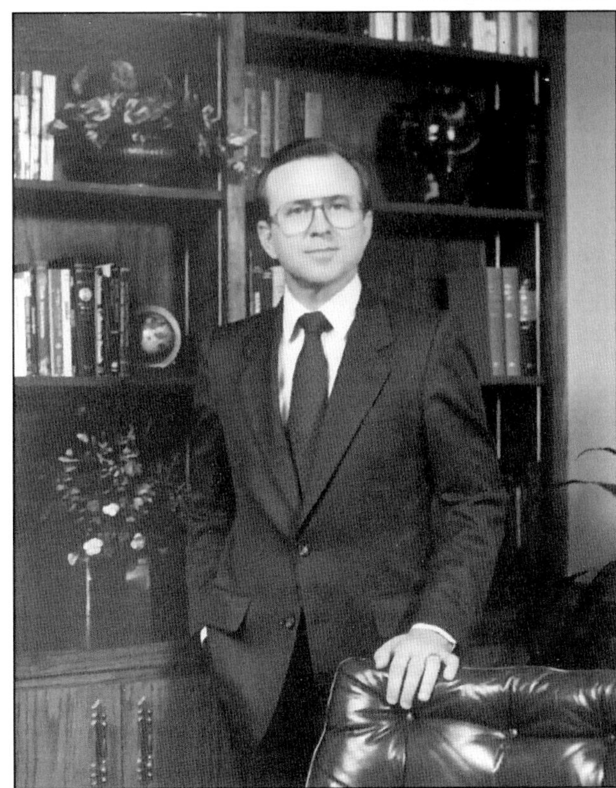

DR. ROBERT D. HEBERT. Dr Robert D. Hebert joined the History Department in the fall of 1969. He served as the first chairman of the new Faculty Council when it was established in 1973, and the first director of the Division of Basic Studies when it was established in 1979. President Doland selected Hebert to serve as academic vice president in 1980, a position he retained until he was chosen to replace Doland as president in 1986.

61

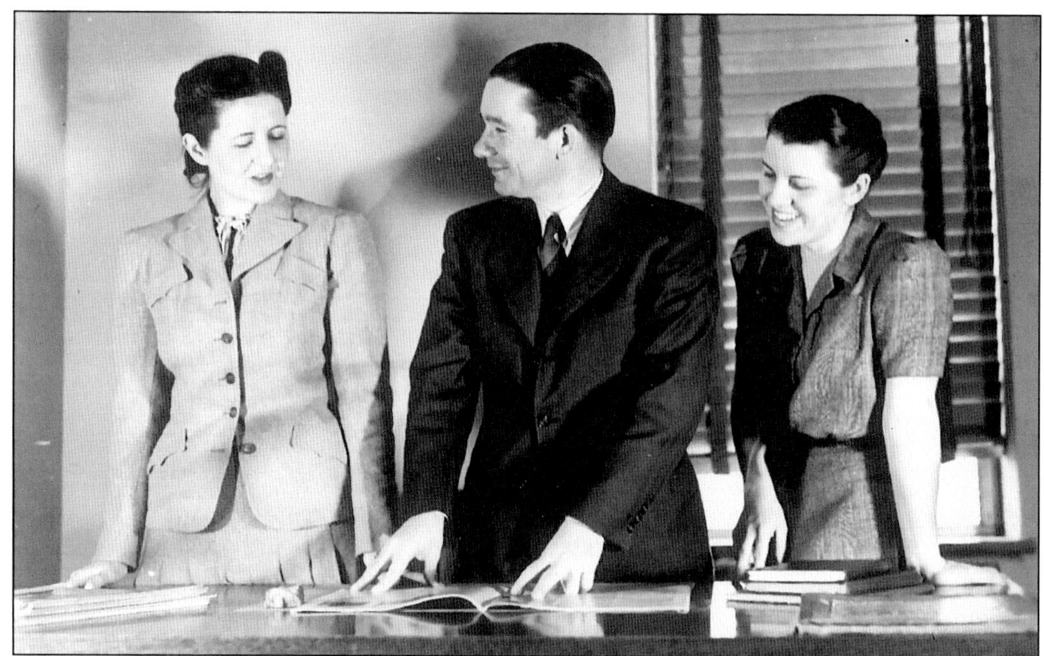

MURIEL CLARE ROGERS, FRANCIS G. BULBER, AND KATHLEEN ALLUMS. Dr. Francis G. Bulber began his career at McNeese in the fall of 1940, retiring in 1974 as dean of the College of Music, after 34 years of service. Bulber received the Alumni President's Cup in 1959. Two other early music faculty members, Muriel Clare Rogers (left) and Kathleen Allums, join Dr. Bulber in this photograph. Allums, one of the original faculty who came to McNeese in 1939, received the Alumni President's Cup in 1968, and remained at McNeese until her retirement in 1979.

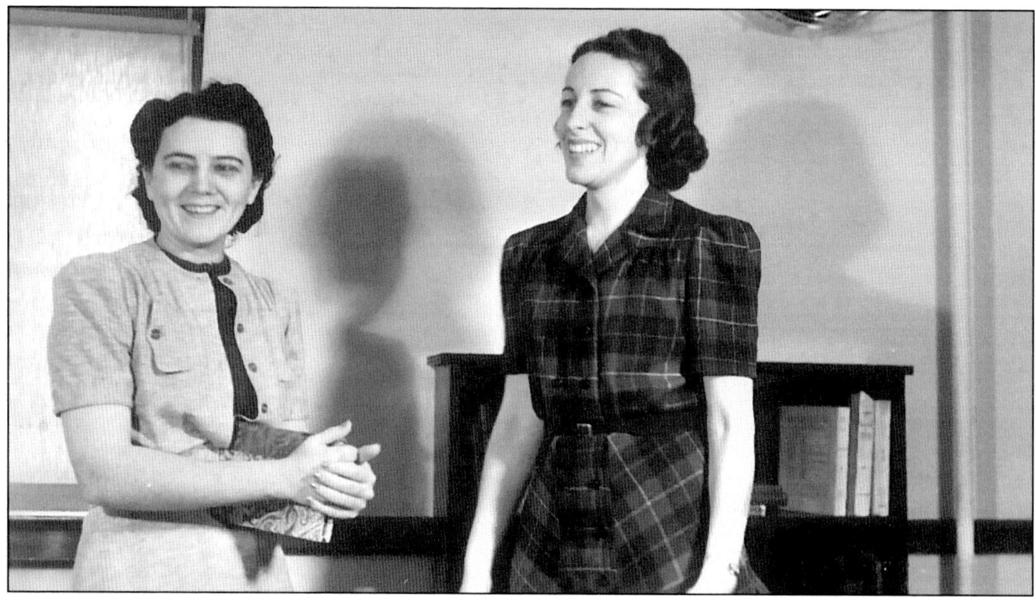

DOLIVE BENOIT AND FREDA SCOGGINS. Dolive Benoit, left, and Freda Scoggins came to McNeese in 1939 as instructors in French and speech, respectively. Miss Benoit received the Alumni President's Cup in 1971, and retired in 1981, the last of the original faculty who had stayed on to teach several generations of area students.

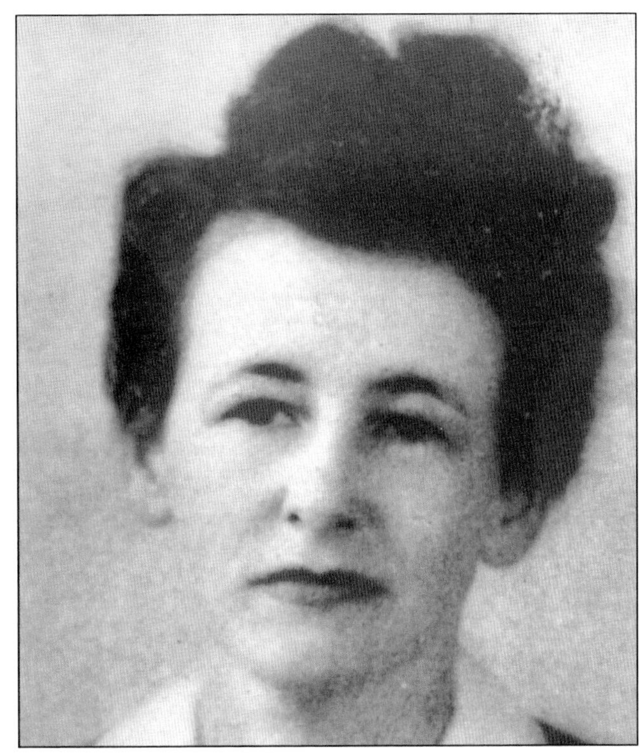

Ada Sabatier. Ada Sabatier was also one of the original 13 faculty, those dedicated and exceptionally able men and women who left their mark on McNeese's history. Sabatier taught history and served as the counselor to women. She was called to active duty in the United States Navy in 1942, resuming her teaching duties at McNeese in 1945. She continued to teach and inspire her students until her retirement in 1968.

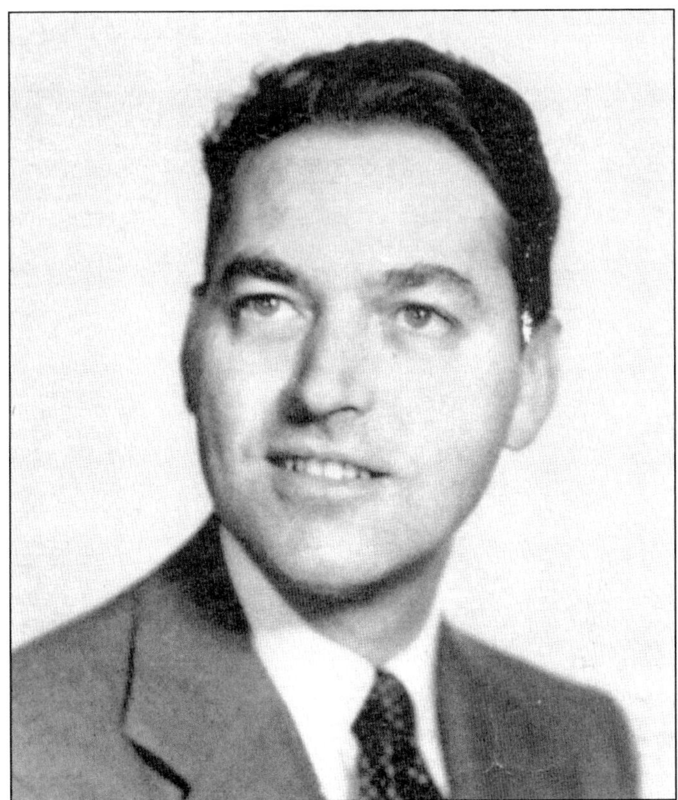

Dr. Clet A. Girard. Dr. Girard was one of the most popular and well-rounded teachers of his day. He had attended the United States Naval Academy at Annapolis, originally studying engineering. He changed his mind and instead studied English literature and philosophy at Loyola, Louisiana State University, and Oxford College in England. Girard was intensely interested in jazz; he spent as much time as possible studying jazz and playing jazz piano. He was called into active duty during the Second World War, but returned to McNeese where he served as Head of the Department of Languages, Dean of Liberal Arts, Head of the Division of Graduate Studies, and Dean of the Graduate School. He retired in 1974, with 34 years of service to McNeese.

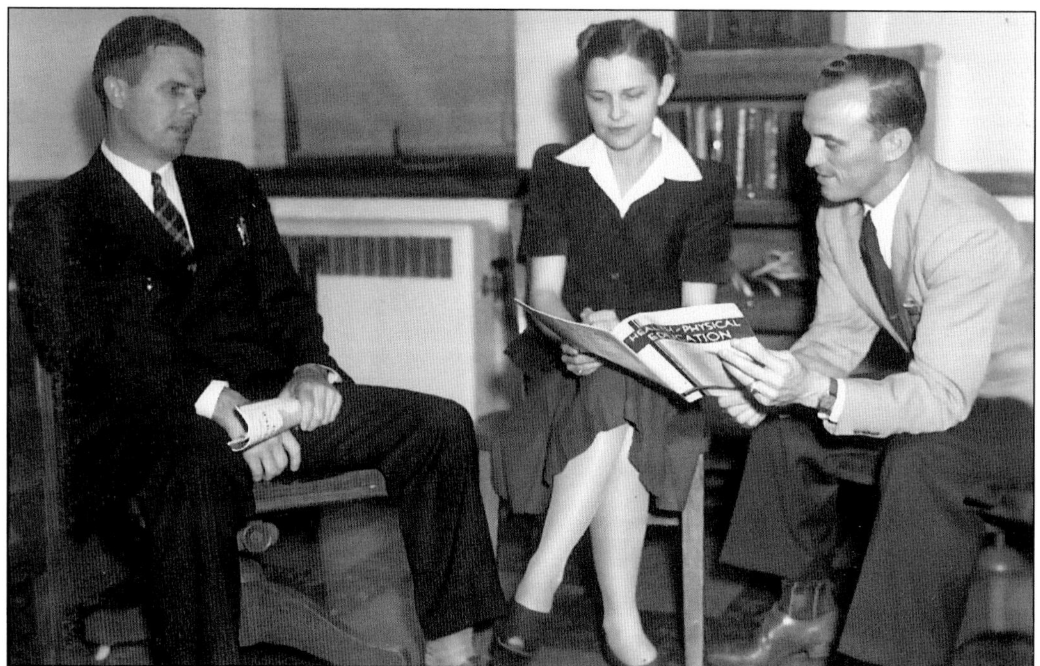

Miriam Callender, Wayne N. Cusic, and Edwin Crews. The original Health and Physical Education faculty consisted of Wayne N. Cusic, left, Miriam Callender, and Ed Crews. Cusic went on to become president of McNeese in 1955. Callender retired in 1978 after 38 years of teaching.

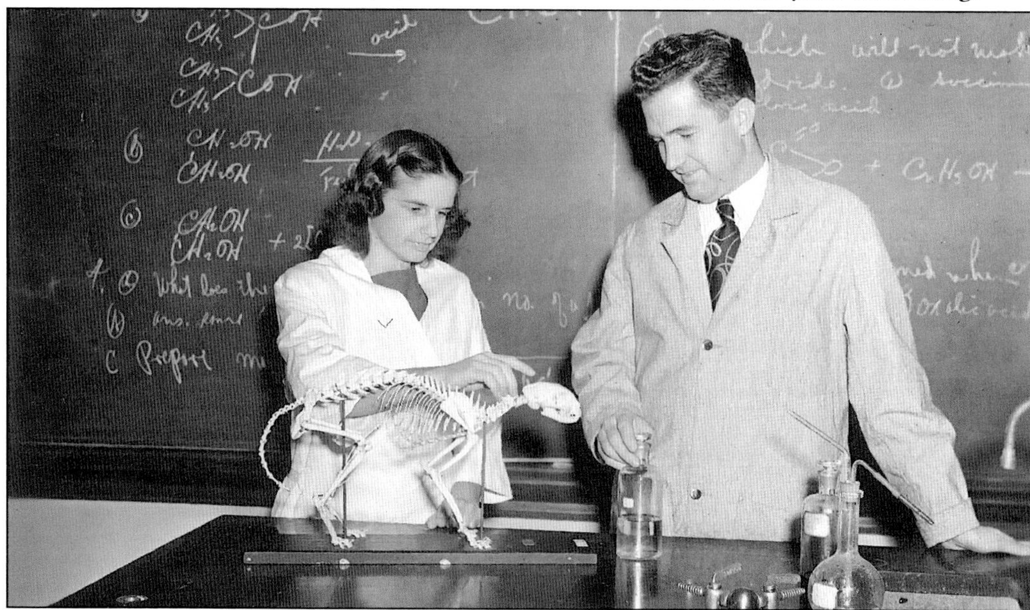

William John Oakley and Clara Louise Jones. William John Oakley, who taught chemistry, and Clara Louise Jones, who taught biology, were part of the original faculty who came to McNeese in the fall of 1939. Jones stayed on to become Head of the Biological Science Department in 1962. Oakley retired in 1973 after working at McNeese for 34 years. After teaching chemistry he had gone to work as purchasing agent and property control officer. He was the recipient of the Alumni President's Cup in 1970.

64

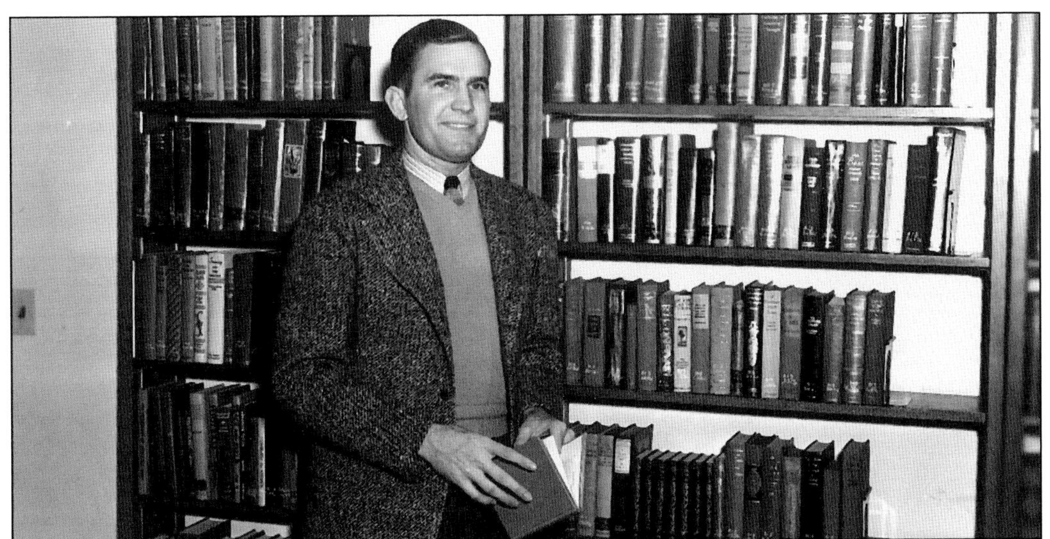

GEORGE JOHNSON. George Johnson was the first librarian at McNeese. Being young and talented as most of the first faculty members were, Johnson was popular with the students. One early student, Kathleen Bordelon, made these comments about the members of the original faculty. "I think they were very proud to be here. Most of them were quite young and felt that there was a real family feeling between students and teachers." Johnson was called to active duty in the United States Marines in April 1942, where he served as a lieutenant. He was killed in the South Pacific the next spring. He was the first faculty member to die in action in World War II.

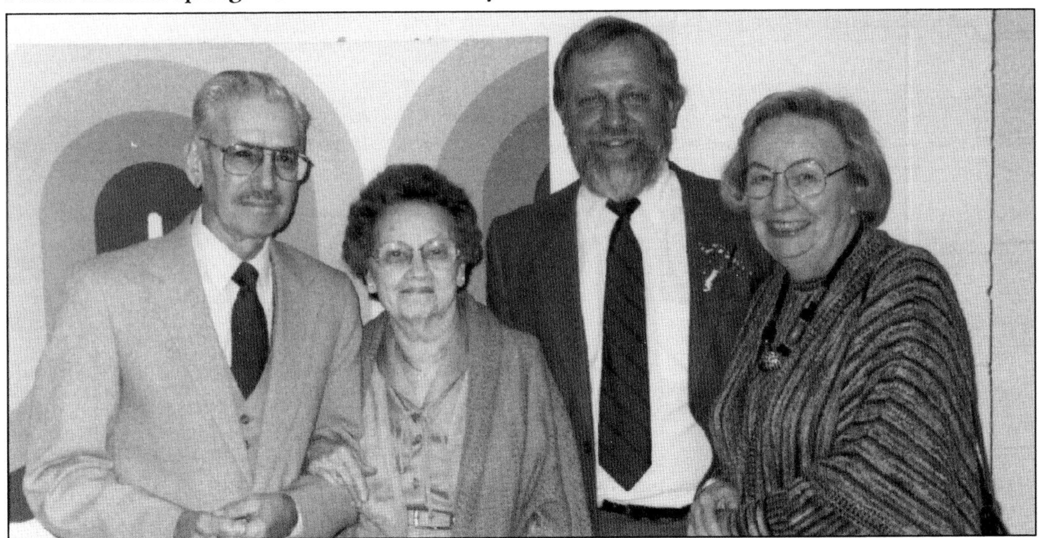

LIBRARY DIRECTORS. Three former directors of the Frazar Memorial Library gathered for the occasion of the 25th anniversary of its dedication. Pictured from left to right are Dr. Samuel Marino, Mrs. Lether E. Frazar, widow of the former president, Mr. Richard H. Reid, and Mrs. Ruth Reedy. Dr. Marino was director of the library when Operation Book Moving transferred the entire library from Kaufman Hall to the new building in 1961. He resigned in 1967, and Dr. Clifford M. Byrne was named as his replacement. Mrs. Reedy took over the responsibilities of running the library in 1972. Mr. Reid became director in 1980, resigning to direct the operations of the foundation in 1989. He currently serves as Vice President of Development and Public Affairs. Mrs. Nancy L. Khoury currently heads the library.

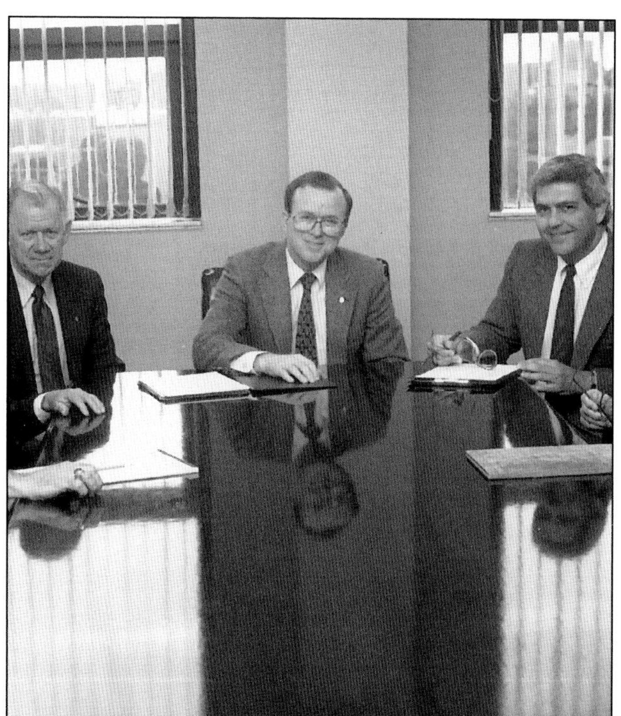

Dr. B.E. Hankins, Dr. Robert D. Hebert, and Dr. Kalil P. Ieyoub. Seated in the President's Conference Room in the Burton Business Center are Dr. B.E. Hankins, left, Dr. Robert D. Hebert, and Dr. Kalil P. Ieyoub. Dr. Hankins came to McNeese in 1959 as an instructor in the Chemistry Department. He served as Dean of the College of Science before being appointed vice president. Dr. Ieyoub attended McNeese as a student in the late 1950s and became a chemistry lab instructor in 1959. After obtaining his doctorate from LSU, he came back to McNeese to teach chemistry, eventually serving as head of that department. He replaced Hankins as Dean of the College of Science, and served in this position until he was named vice president.

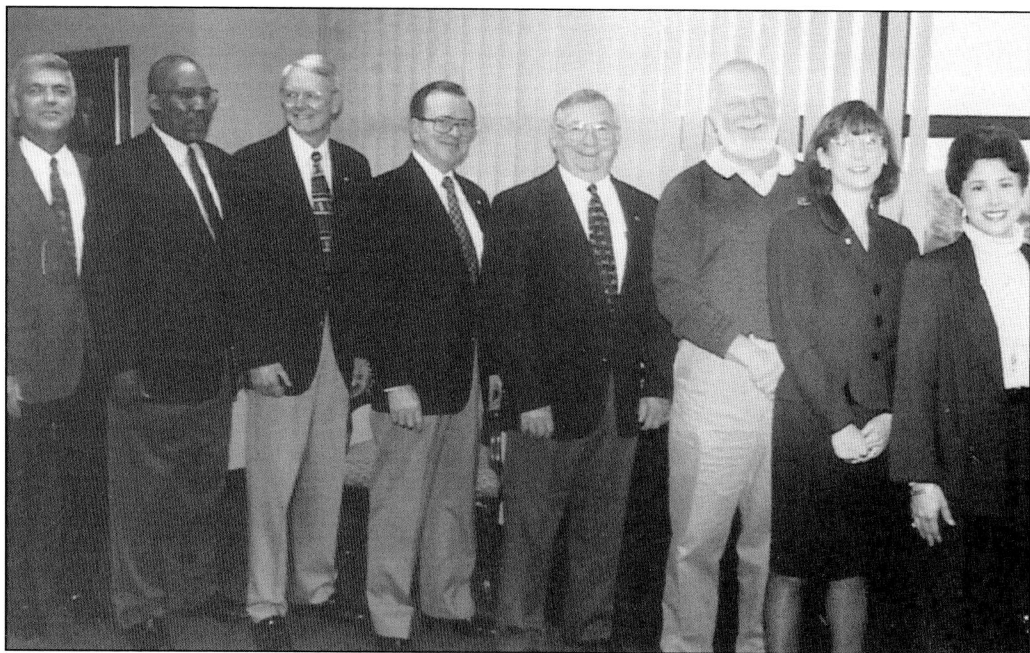

Administrative Leaders. The vice presidents and other administrative leaders join the president of the university in this photograph. From left to right they are Dr. Kalil P. Ieyoub, Dr. Whitney G. Harris, Dr. James M. Brown, Jr., Dr. Robert D. Hebert, Dr. Larry R. DeRouen, Mr. Richard H. Reid, Dr. Jeanne Daboval, and Mrs. Rebecca Mestayer. At the time this photograph was taken, Harris was Executive Director of Human Relations/Social Equity; Daboval was Dean of Enrollment and Institutional Planning, and Mestayer was interim Vice President for Business Affairs.

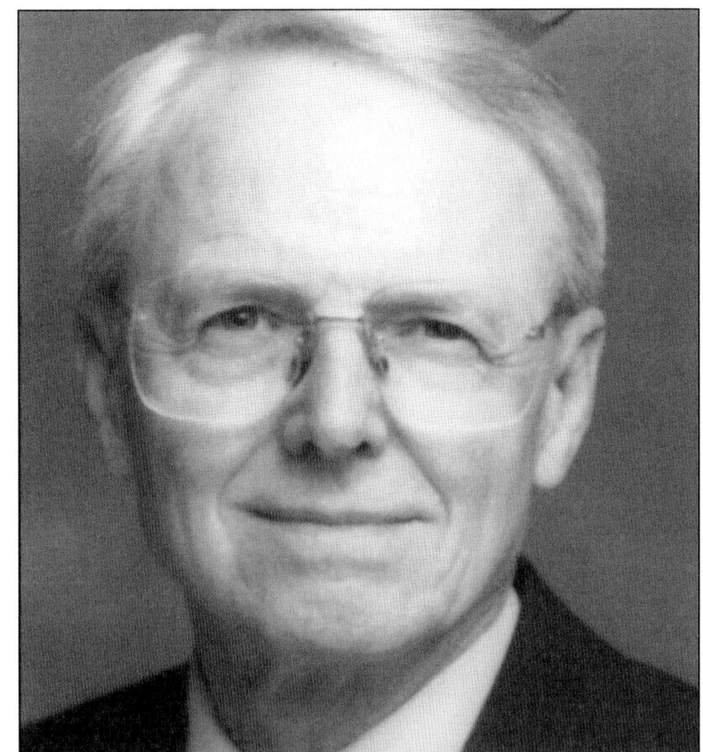

DR. JAMES M. BROWN JR. Dr. Brown retired from McNeese in 2001 after serving as Vice President for Academic Affairs and Provost since 1995. Prior to serving in this capacity, Brown had been Head of the Department of Education and Dean of the College of Education. He received the Alumni President's Cup in 1976.

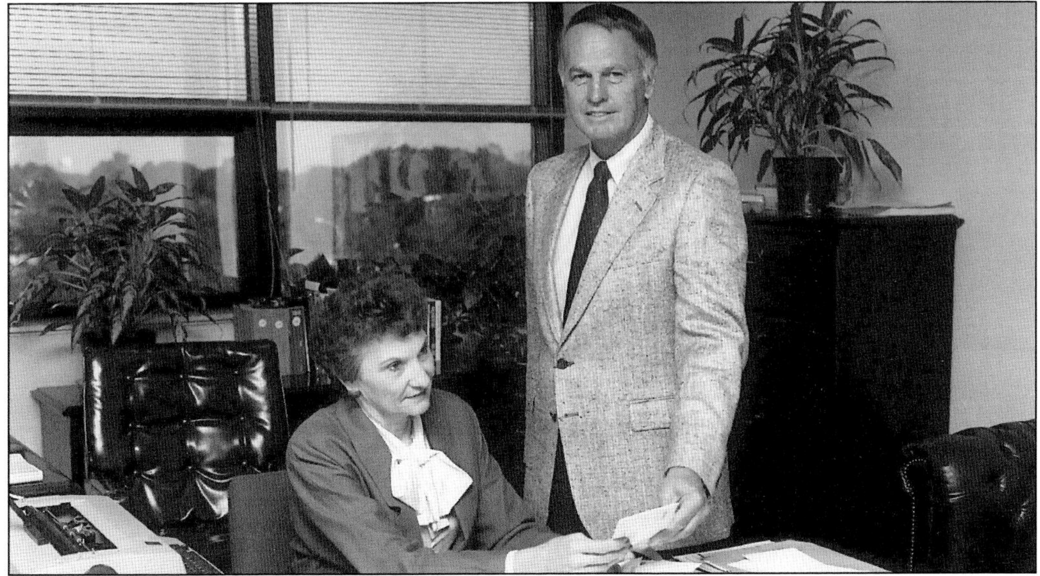

KENNETH SWEENEY. McNeese has been fortunate in that a number of its excellent students have gone on to serve well in faculty and administrative positions. Many have devoted all or most of their careers to McNeese. Among these are, most notably, Kenneth Sweeney, pictured here with his secretary, Barbara McCall. Sweeney served on the Student Council, participated in several sports, taught in the Department of Agriculture, coached the rodeo team, managed the farm, served as Director of Administrative Affairs, and ended his career as Vice President for Administration and Student Affairs. Sweeney received the Distinguished Alumni Award in 1988.

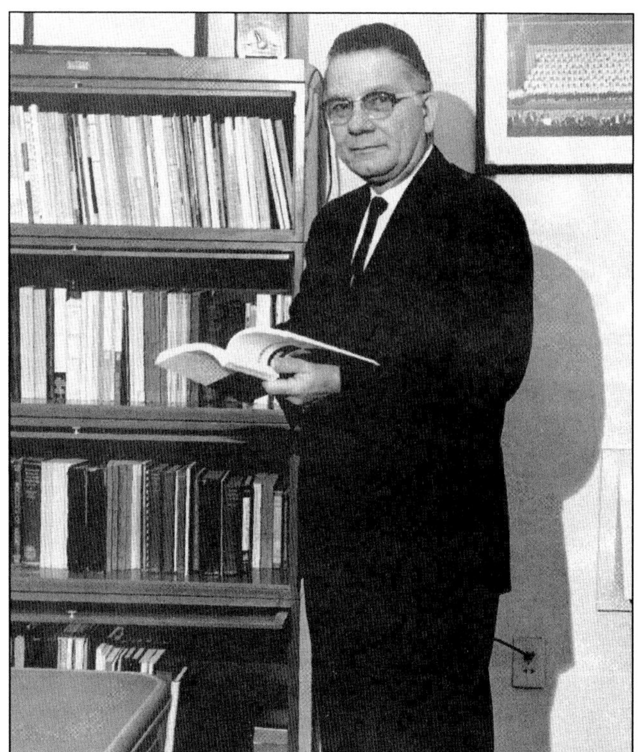

DR. FRANCIS G. BULBER. The McNeese Auditorium was renamed the Francis G. Bulber Auditorium in 1992. There were many tributes paid to Dr. Bulber on the occasion of his retirement in 1974, including Mayor James Sudduth's proclamation that May 19, 1974, should be known as "Francis Bulber Day."

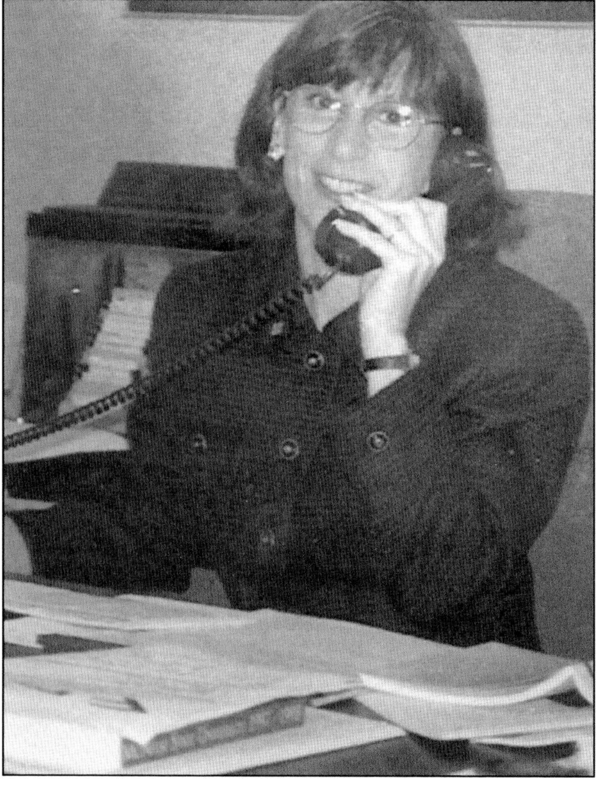

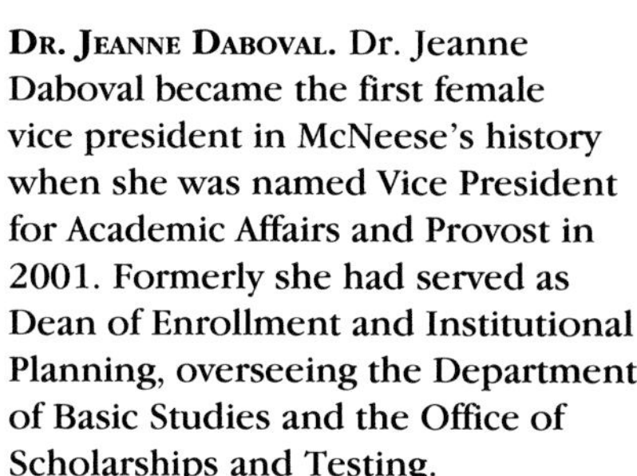

DR. JEANNE DABOVAL. Dr. Jeanne Daboval became the first female vice president in McNeese's history when she was named Vice President for Academic Affairs and Provost in 2001. Formerly she had served as Dean of Enrollment and Institutional Planning, overseeing the Department of Basic Studies and the Office of Scholarships and Testing.

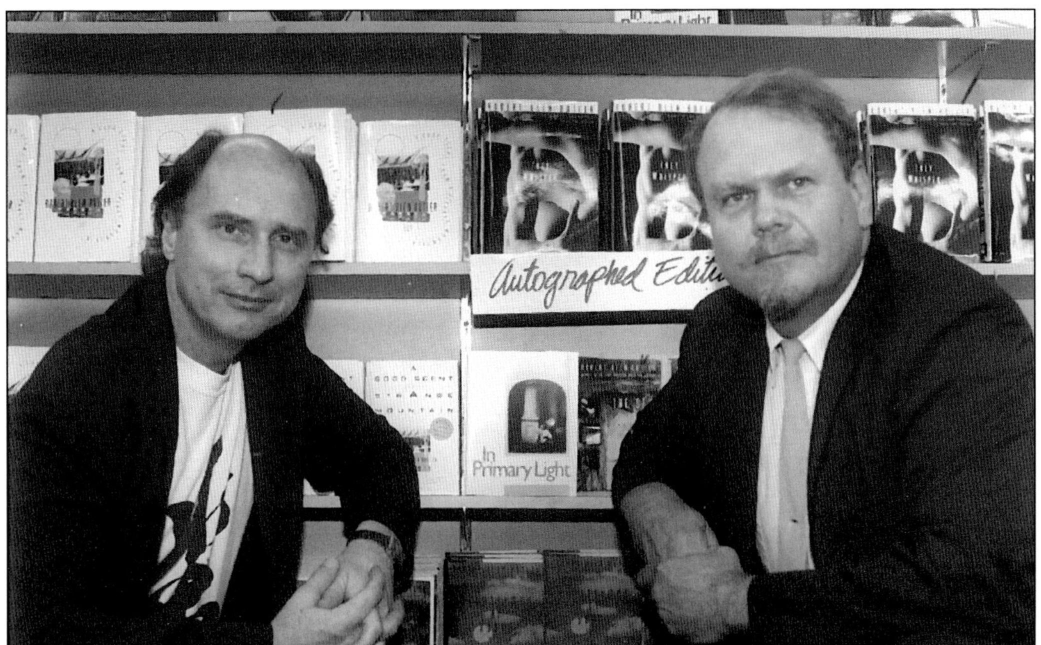

ROBERT OLEN BUTLER AND DR. JOHN A. WOOD. Many of the McNeese faculty are or have been notable and prize-winning authors. Robert Olen Butler, left, received the Pulitzer Prize for fiction in 1993 for his book, *A Good Scent from a Strange Mountain,* while teaching at McNeese. He was the first director of the Master of Fine Arts Creative Writing Program. The current director, Dr. John A. Wood, is an internationally known poet and photographic historian. Another former faculty member and former Head of the Department of History, Dr. Daniel Sutherland, received a Pulitzer Prize nomination for his book, *Confederate Carpetbaggers,* in 1989.

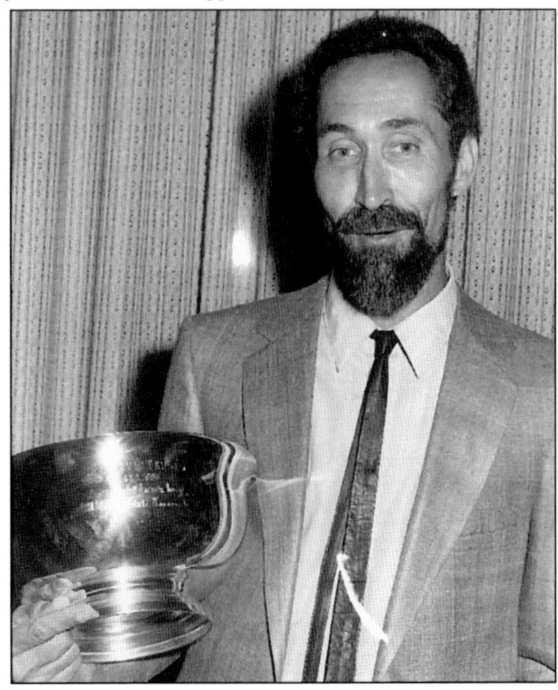

DR. J. DAVID TAUBER. The Distinguished Faculty Award is presented each year to a faculty member who has been selected based on the examination of letters of recommendation, teacher evaluations, faculty member's vita, and other relevant documents. Dr. J. David Tauber, of the Department of Chemistry, is shown here with the award he received in 1985. Other winners include the first recipient, Dr. Joe Gray Taylor, Dr. George V.S. White, Dr. Curtis Whittington, Dr. Fred Sahlmann, Dr. Lise Pederson, Dr. James N. Beck, Heather Ryan Kelley, Dr. John C. Young, Dr. Jess Feist, Dr. Stearns Rogers, Dr. Douglas W. McNiel, Dr. John Wood, Dr. Leo Luke Marcello, Robert Olen Butler, Michelle Martin, Dr. Mark Wygoda, Dr. Linda Brannon, Dr. Mark Paulissen, Gerry Wubben, and Dr. Pankaj Chandra.

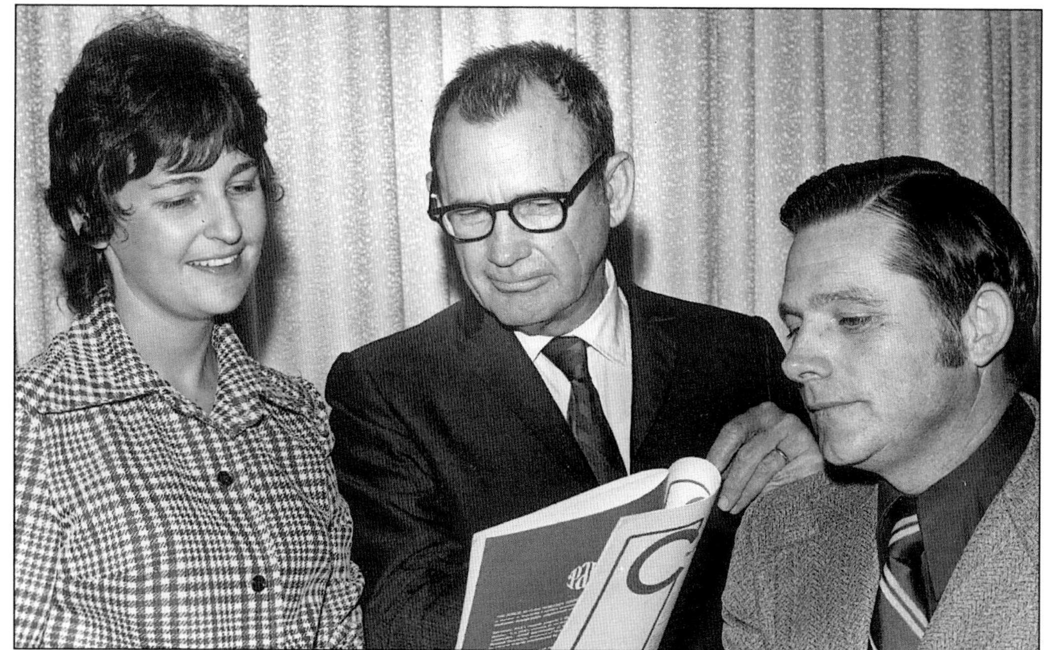

Dr. Joe Gray Taylor. Dr. Joe Gray Taylor, center, was an outstanding teacher and historian. He wrote books on the history of the South, the United States Air Force, and Louisiana, including the bicentennial history of Louisiana and the history of McNeese State University. He received numerous awards including the first Distinguished Teacher/Faculty Award in 1979 and the Louisiana Humanist of the Year Award shortly before his death in 1987. He is pictured here with Mrs. Frances Summars Milburn, Office of High School Relations, and Dr. William P. Greenlee, professor of philosophy.

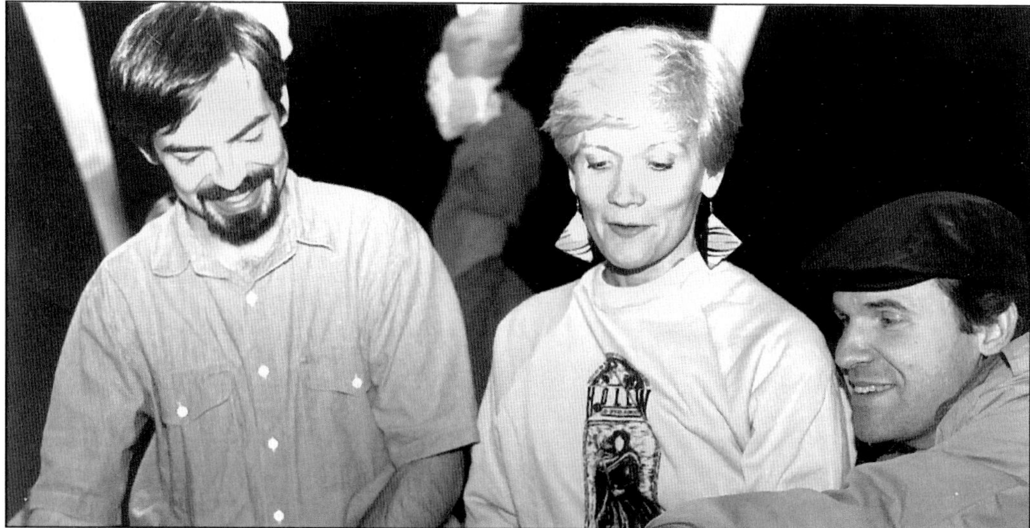

Theatre Department. Looking over the music for their production of *The Hollow* are Dr. Susan Kelso, and Keith Gates, right. Also pictured is conductor Jeffery Bell-Hanson. Kelso currently directs the McNeese Theatre; Gates is a talented member of the Music Department. He has written the music for several original productions, including *The Hollow, Evangeline,* and *Tom Sawyer.* Prior to Kelso, Dan Plato and Jerry Brown directed the theatre productions.

70

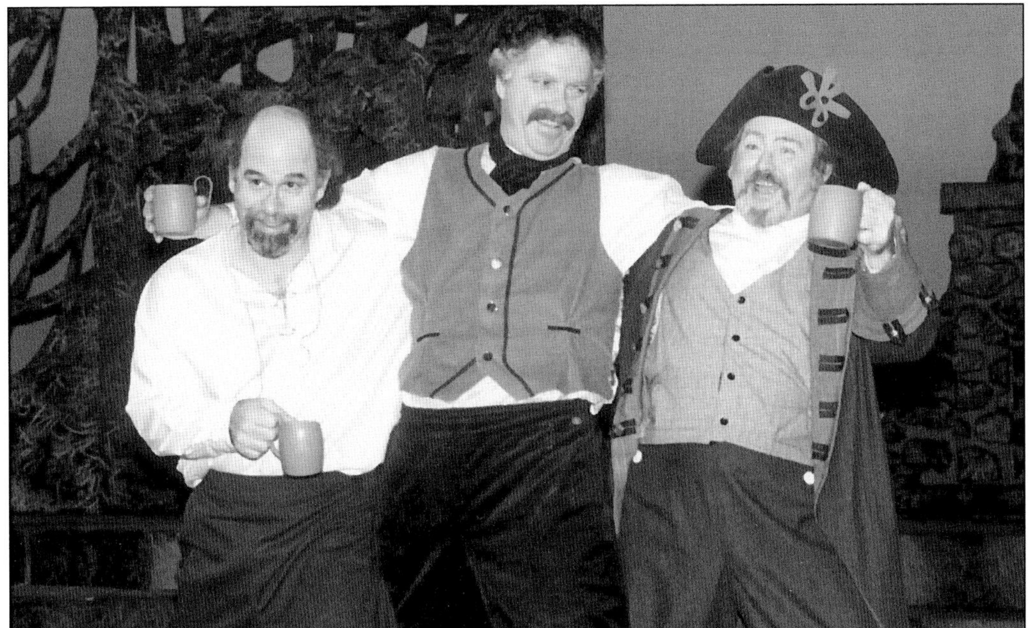

EVANGELINE. Dedicated to the Acadians who have enriched the culture and arts of Louisiana, *Evangeline* premiered at McNeese in 1996. With music composed by Keith Gates, libretto by Jon Robertson, and talented singers such as (left to right) Ross Allured, Blake Whitley, and Ron Brumley, the production was a great success.

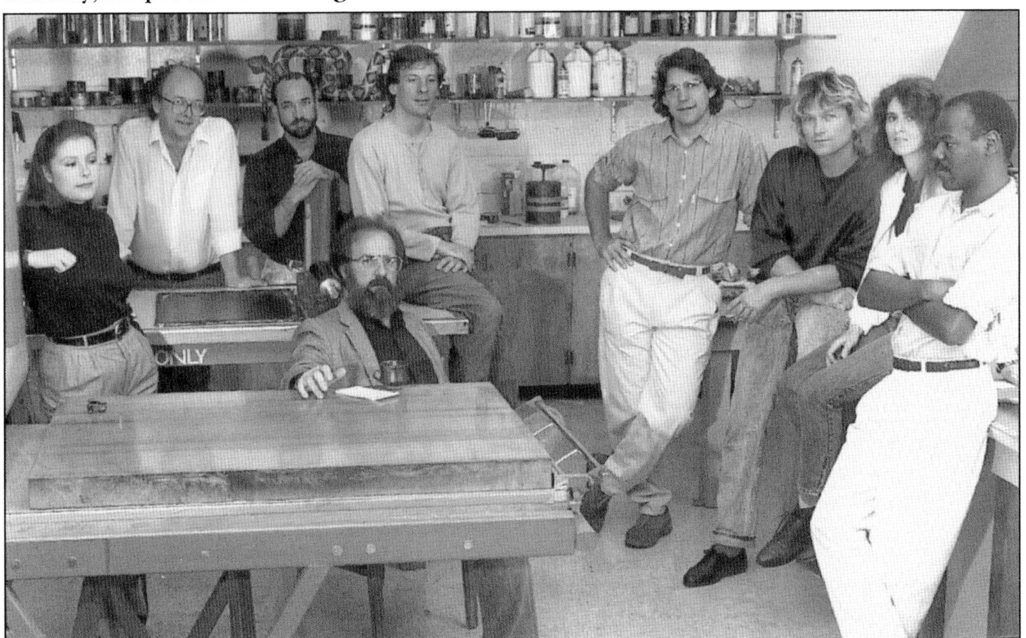

VISUAL ARTS. The faculty members in the Department of Visual Arts in 1989 included Bill Iles (seated) Head of the Department, and, from left to right, Marcie Inman, Marty Bee, Lewis Temple, Todd Turek, Gerry Wubben, Larry Schuh, Heather Ryan Kelley, and Gary Porter. Iles returned to full-time teaching at the end of the spring semester 2000. Lisa Bell Reinauer now heads the department.

71

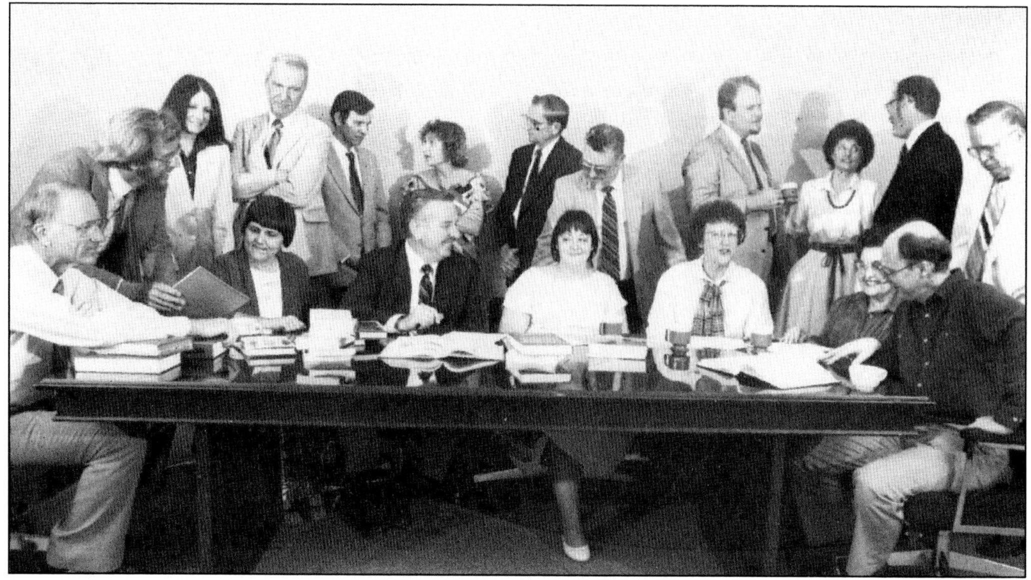

LANGUAGES. The faculty from the Department of Languages got together for a group photograph in 1988. Seated at the table, from left to right, are Dr. Robert M. Cooper, Dr. Judy A. Savoie, Dr. Joe L. Cash (head of the department), Dr. Cheryl Ware, Dr. Stella Nesanovich, Dr. Maria T. Bustillo, and Robert Olen Butler. Standing from left to right are Dr. Russell E. "Gene" Marshall, Dr. Elizabeth Hait, Dr. Clifford M. Byrne, Dr. David B. Eakin, Dr. Carol L. Wood, Curtis S. Nelson Jr., Benjamin C. Harlow, Dr. John A. Wood, Dr. Monique Nagem, Dr. Millard T. Jones (Dean of the College of Liberal Arts), and Loris D. Galford.

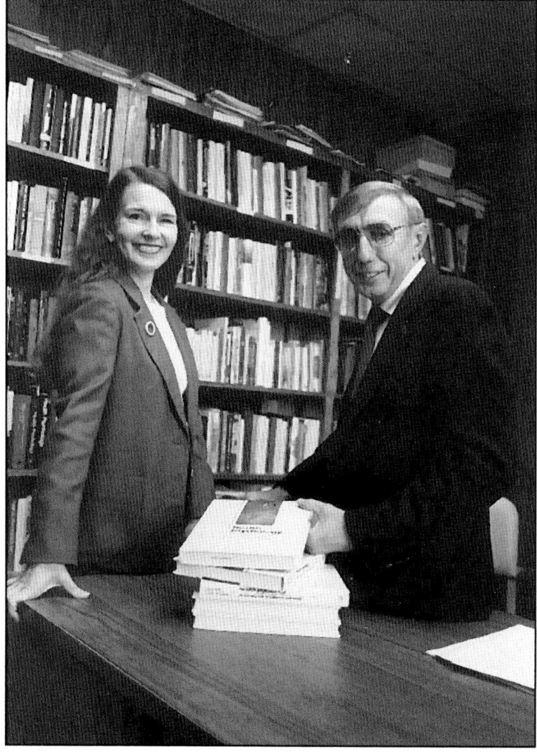

COLLABORATORS. Drs. Linda Brannon and Jess Feist, Department of Psychology, published *Health Psychology* in 1987. Both are winners of the Distinguished Faculty Award, Feist in 1988–1989 and Brannon in 1997–1998.

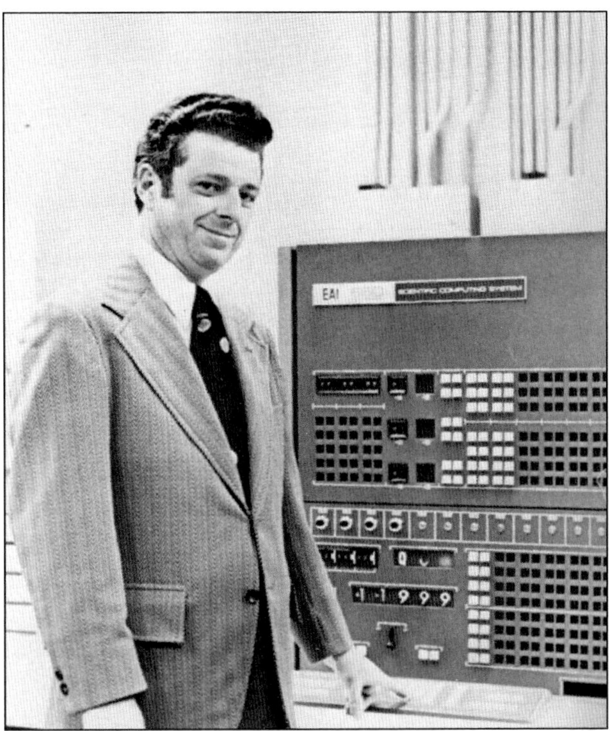

Dr. O. Carroll Karkalits. Dean of the College of Engineering and Technology, Dr. Karkalits has held that position since 1972. In 1975, McNeese was awarded a grant from the Energy Research and Development Administration for the investigation of geothermal geopressured energy stored in hot water reservoirs in Louisiana coastal areas. Principal investigators in addition to Karkalits were Dr. B.E. Hankins, Dr. Russell Ham, Raymond Chavanne, Dr. James W. Batchelor, Dr. V.L. Boaz, and George Copeland.

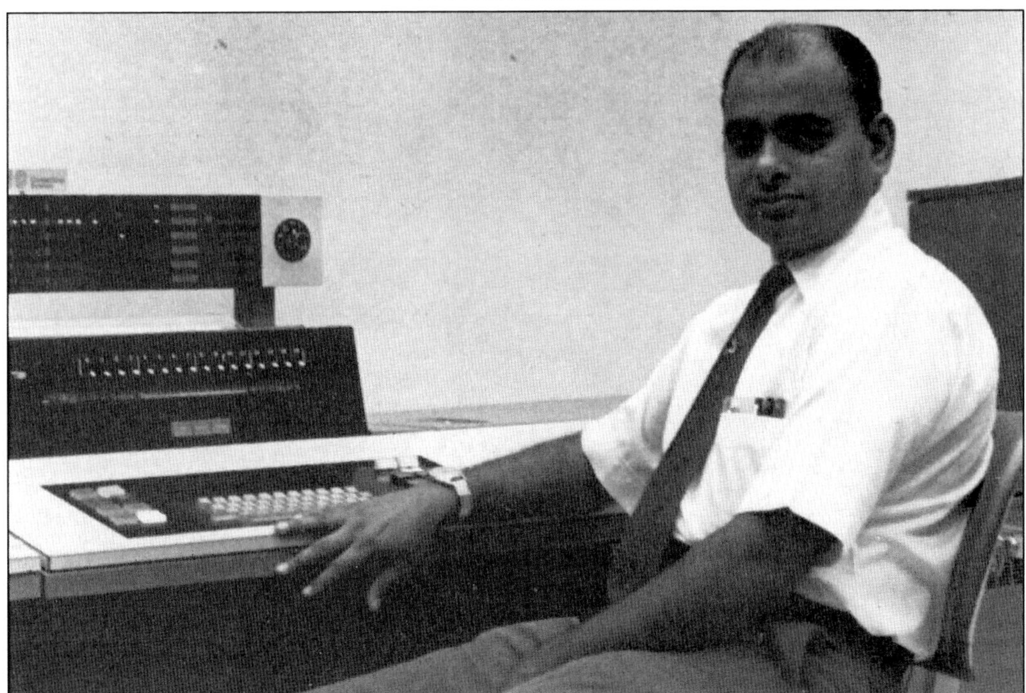

Sundaram Swetharanyam. Much of the credit for bringing McNeese into the computer age goes to the director of the campus computer center, Sundaram Swetharanyam. Affectionately known around campus as "Sweth," he joined the computing science faculty during the 1968–1969 academic year, and was named Director of the Computer Center in 1975–1976.

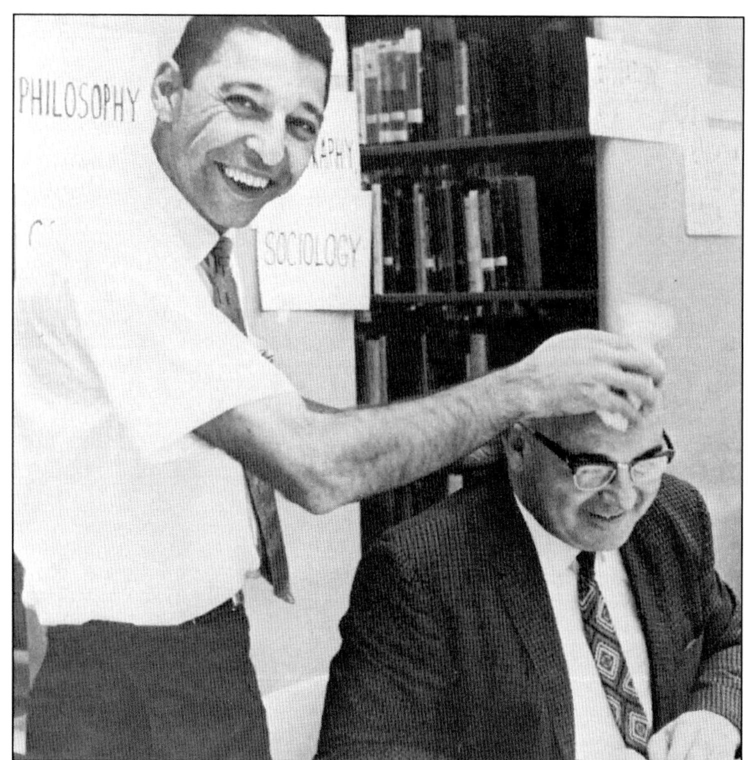

RAYMOND LEBLANC. Raymond LeBlanc joined the Sociology Department in 1964 and was a popular teacher until his retirement in 1995. Easing the tension of registration, LeBlanc, left, clowns around with Dee Newland, also in the Sociology Department, in this 1968 photograph.

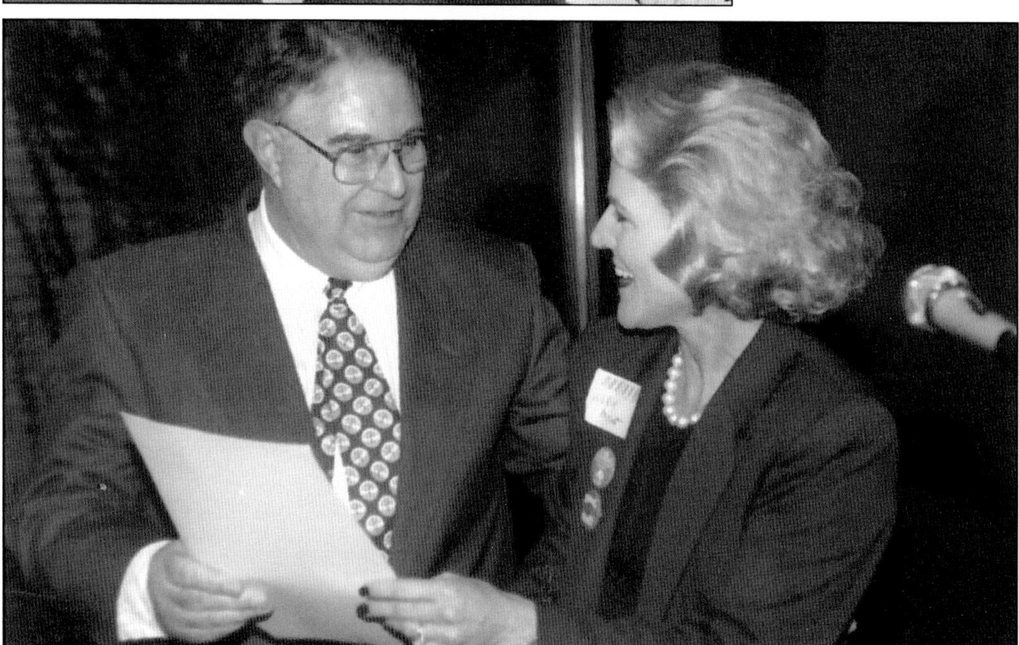

DEAN LOUIS RIVIERE AND MAYOR WILLIE MOUNT. Louis Riviere, left, was a former McNeese student who devoted his life and career to his alma mater. Various offices held by Riviere included Alumni Secretary, Men's Housing Director, Dean of Men, and, at his retirement, Dean of Student Life. He is pictured here with another former McNeese student, former Mayor Willie Landry Mount.

74

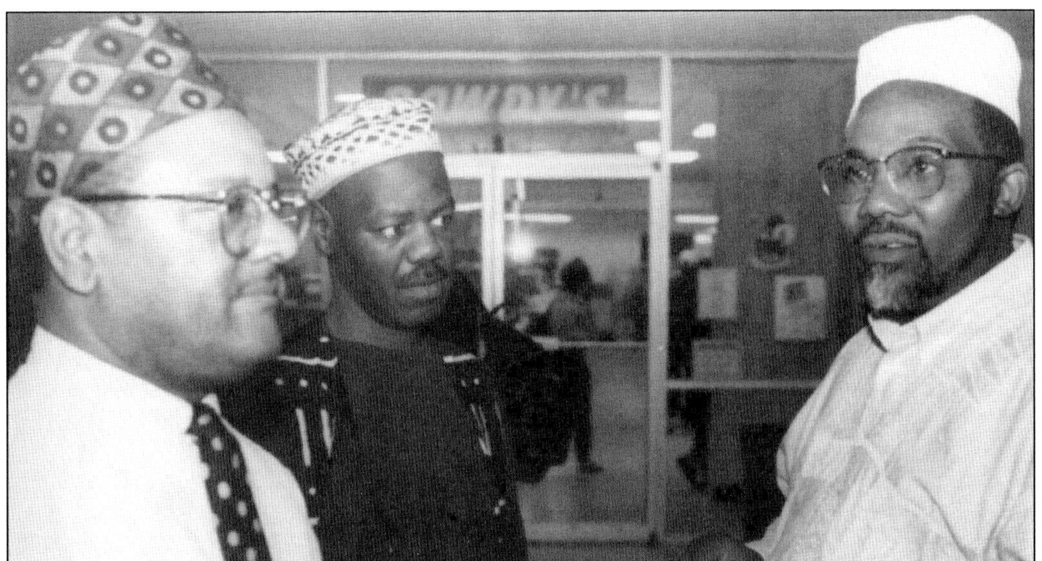

Dean Will Chenier, Gary Porter, and Dr. Whitney G. Harris. Dressed in traditional African attire, these three faculty members participate in African-American Day festivities at McNeese. Pictured from left to right they are, Chenier, Assistant Dean of Student Services; Porter, Art Department; and Harris, Executive Director of Human Relations and Social Equity. Harris had been a student at McNeese and was the first black president of the SGA in 1973.

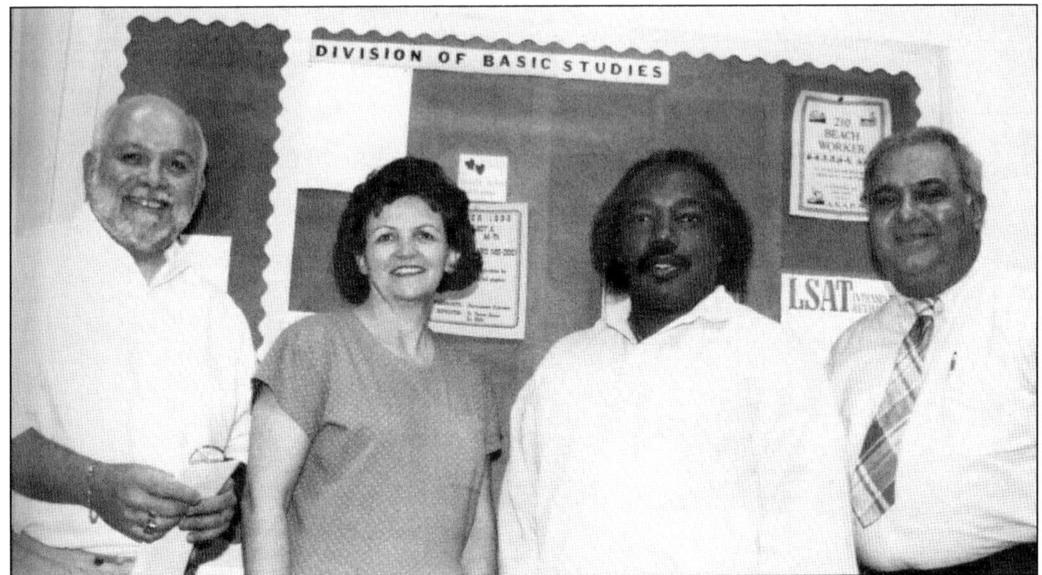

Basic Studies. The Division of Basic Studies was first organized in 1974 with Dr. Robert D. Hebert serving as the first director. In this photograph, current director Ed Khoury, left, poses with advisors Sandra Moore, Alfread G. Mouton, and Daniel P. Ieyoub. The primary purpose of the Division of Basic Studies is to enhance recruitment and retention of students.

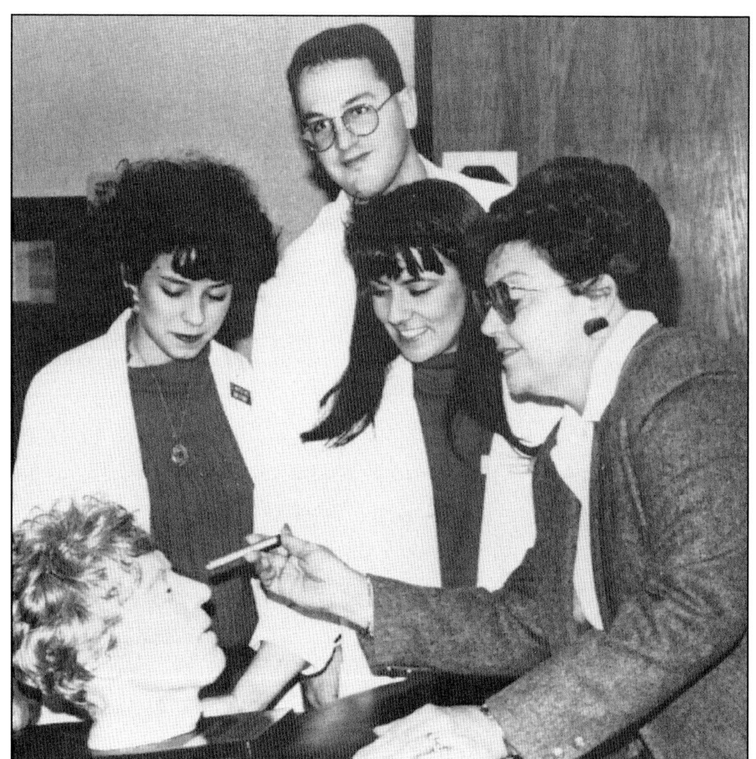

ANITA FIELDS. Dr. Anita Fields, right, was appointed the first Dean of the College of Nursing in 1983, a position she retained until her retirement in 2000. She is seen in this photograph with students, from left to right, Chantel Mayeux, Darren Caillouet, and Rachelle Woods. The College of Nursing was housed in Drew Hall until 2001 when it moved to the newly constructed Hardtner Hall. The College of Nursing received its national accreditation in 1981.

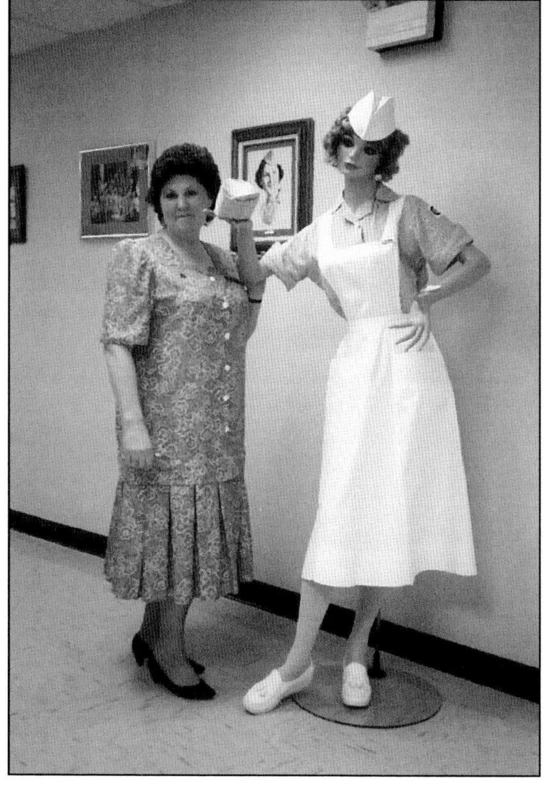

NURSING. Lyndell McGowan Fehl, College of Nursing, poses with a mannequin dressed in the first uniform worn by nursing students to clinicals at St. Patrick Hospital. The College of Nursing was originally a department in the College of Science. Mrs. Fannie L. Sample was the director of the nursing program until 1958, when Mrs. Constance White replaced her. Mrs. White retired during the 1967–1968 academic year. Mrs. Lynda Jane Jones became the new Director of the Department of Nursing until replaced by Dr. Anita Fields during the 1980–1981 academic year.

76

Five

CLUBS AND ORGANIZATIONS

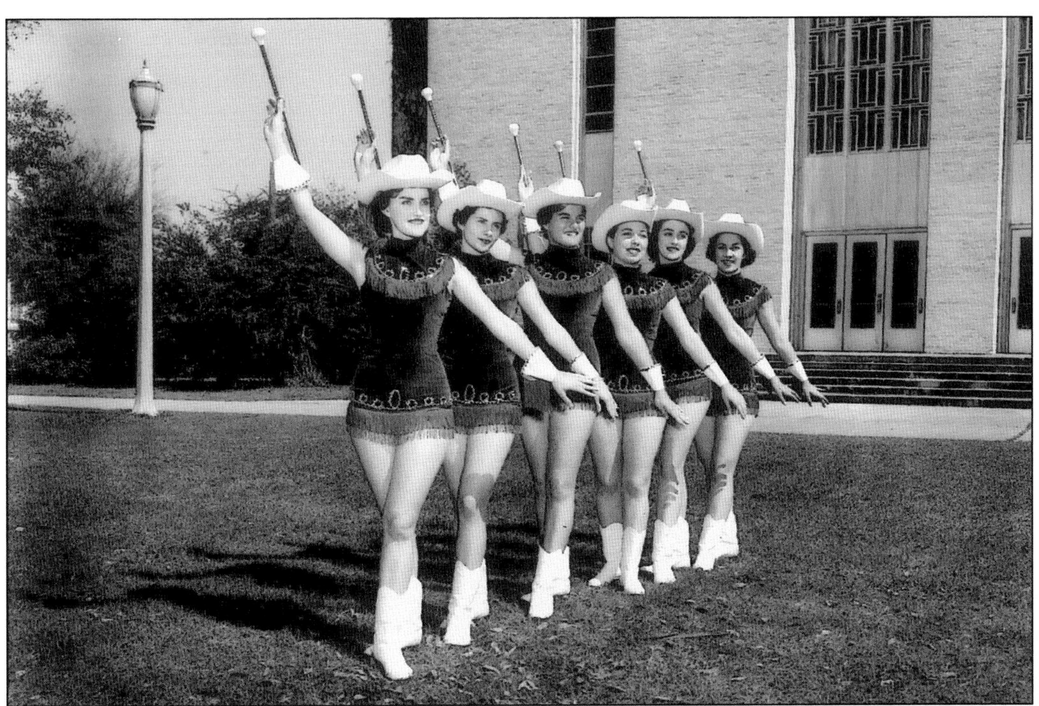

COWBELLES. From left to right are Jackie Bouquet, Sandra Naff, Shirley Castete, Billece Curless, Gwen Gabbert, and Emma Mae Teer who were the Cowbelles in this 1957 photograph. The Cowbelles were a popular baton-twirling group that performed with the marching band.

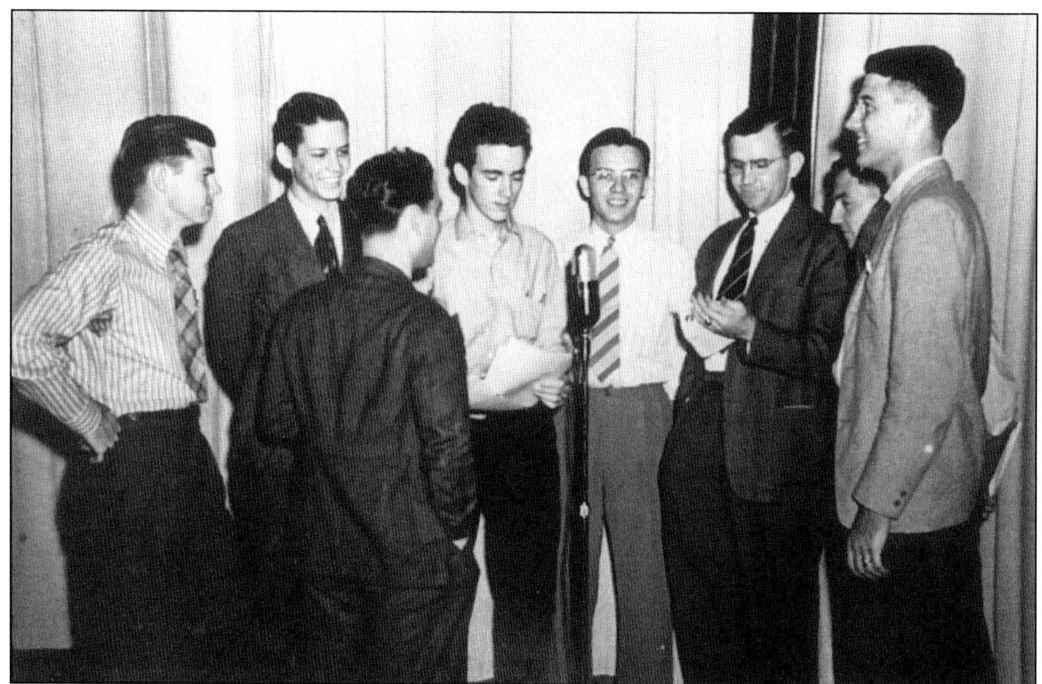

RADIO-DRAMA GUILD. Under the faculty supervision of Mrs. Freda Scoggins Thomas, the Radio-Drama Guild presented a daily five-minute program to the students at McNeese. Each day the program featured a different department, humor, or miscellaneous news items. One day a week a special 15-minute program displayed various talents at McNeese among the students and faculty. Some of the most popular were Quiz-Kids, short skits, and organ music by Miss Kathleen Allums. The Guild is seen performing in this early 1940s photograph. George Johnson, librarian, is third from right.

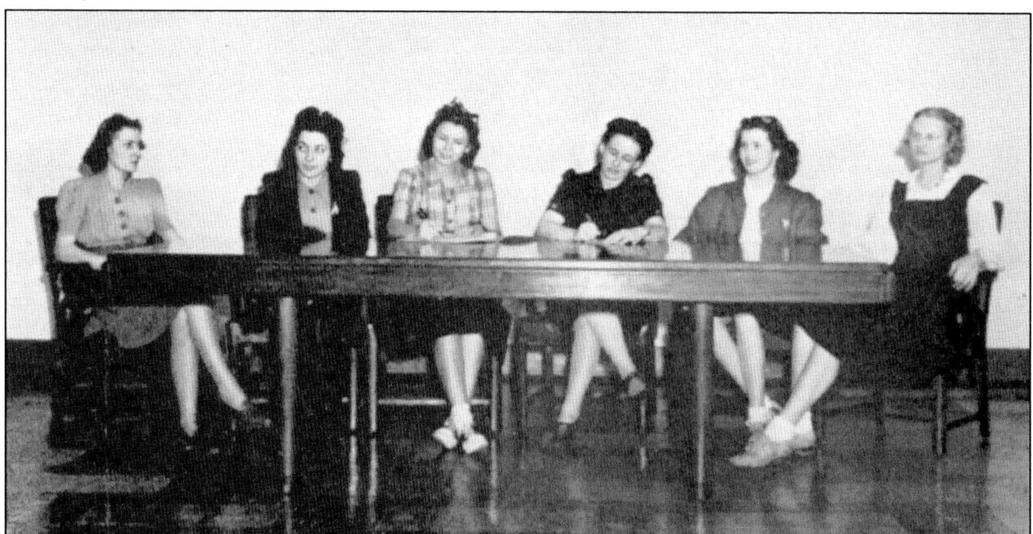

WOMEN'S STUDENT ASSOCIATION. From left to right in this 1941 photograph of the first Women's Student Association are, Aline Smith, Marie Therese LeVeque, Dahlia Cook, Ada Sabatier (advisor), Marjorie North, and Betty Dimmick. The association was established to maintain high standards of conduct and scholarship among women students at McNeese.

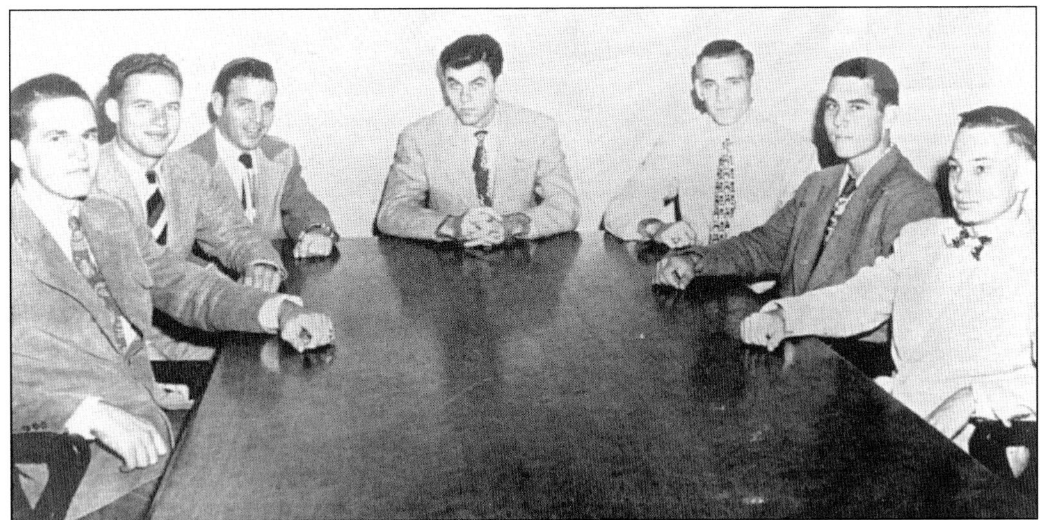

STUDENT COUNCIL. The Student Council was made up of representatives from each class, elected by the students. The main purpose of the organization was to sponsor social activities for the student body. Council members in 1949, shown from left to right in this photograph, are Kenneth Sweeney, Freddie LeBlanc, Buster Crowley, Allen Commander, Bill Dimmick, Gilbert Manuel, and Bill Clarke. Kenneth Sweeney returned to McNeese after graduation, eventually serving as Vice President for Administration and Student Affairs. Commander and Clarke both later served as active members in the Alumni Association.

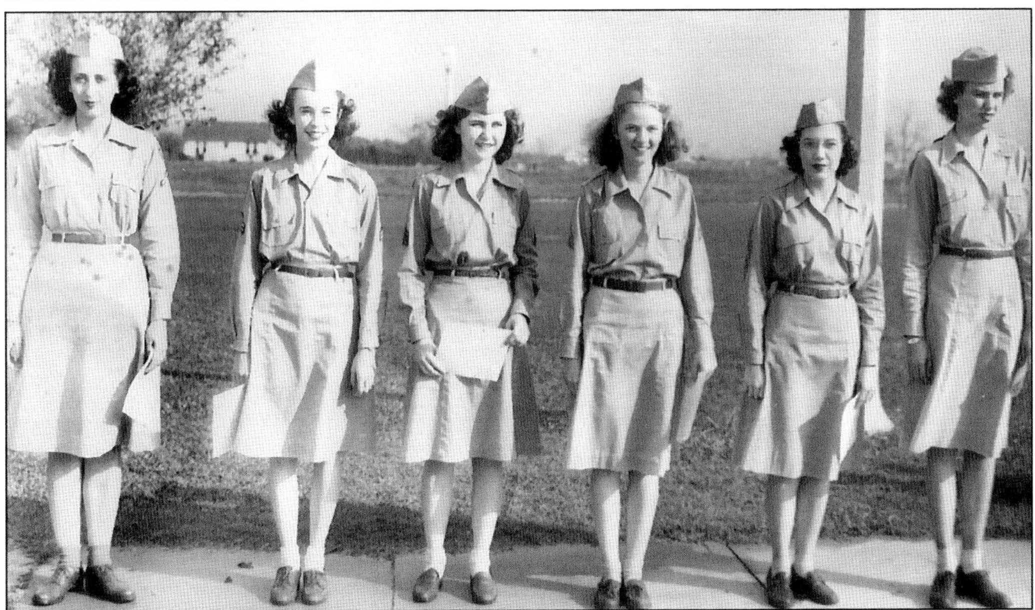

MACs. When the ROTC was formed on campus in 1942, the female students promptly voted unanimously to organize their own training program. Dolive Benoit became the supervisor of the MACs, who drilled regularly, organized a drum and bugle corps, participated in Red Cross activities, and studied ways in which women could help with the war effort. After the war, the organization served the college and the community by assisting in school and civic projects. The young women in this photograph are, from left to right, Lena Basone, Mildred Carleton, Mary Burch, Melda Dietz, Cornell Scoggins, and Jean Goforth.

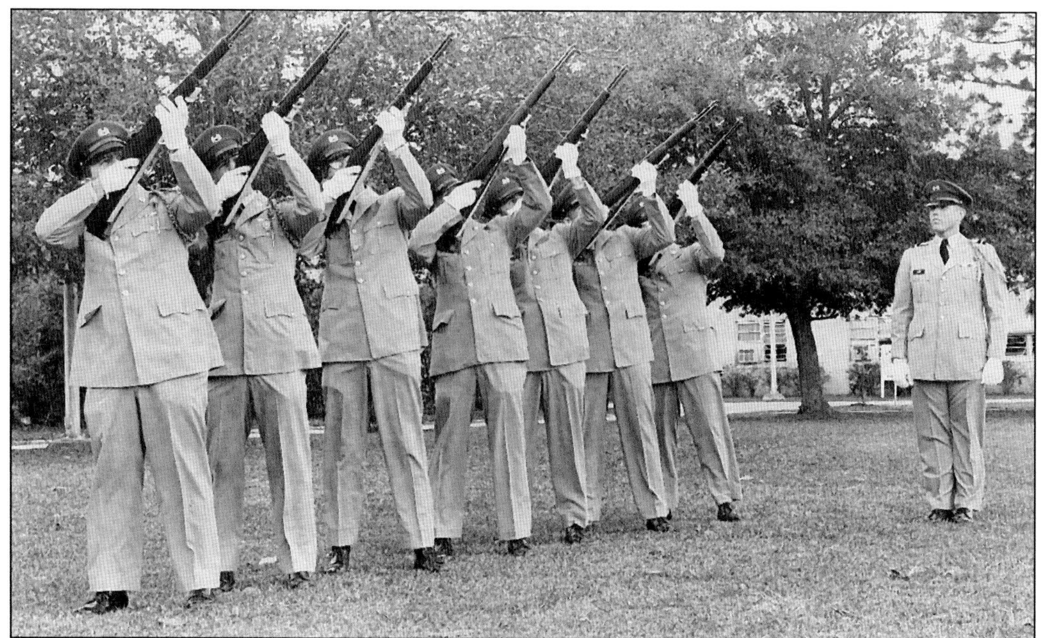

PERSHING-WARE RIFLES. The Pershing Rifles, organized in 1947 at John McNeese Junior College, changed their name in 1952 to honor Col. Charles S. Ware Sr., a popular professor of military science who died in Korea. They performed at special ceremonies, fairs, and exhibitions.

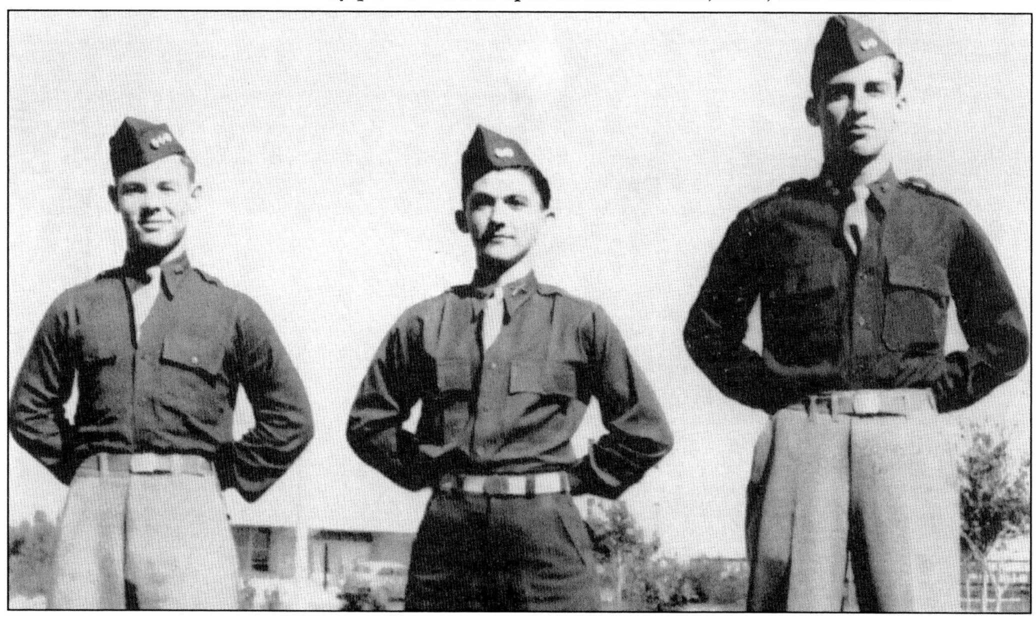

ROTC. The ROTC unit of McNeese State College was established in 1942. The *Catalogue,* in the early days of World War II, stated, "Through classes, through lectures, through club activities, through the military unit, and the Red Cross Guild, students, faculty, and staff are dedicated to meet the great challenges confronting loyal Americans today." Participation in ROTC was required for all male students until 1969, when it became voluntary. The McNeese ROTC program closed in 1997. This 1946 photograph shows, from left to right, Patrick L. Ford, Henry Dudley Doiron, and Bill Traylor.

80

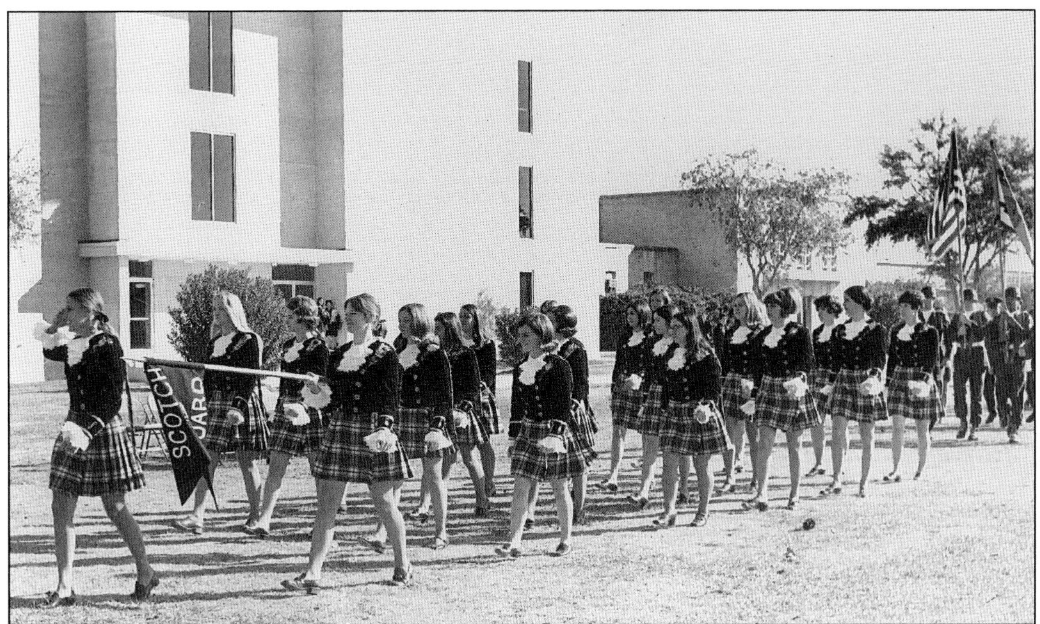

SCOTCH GUARD. The McDuff Clan of the Scotch Guard was established in 1966. The Guard was a women's service auxiliary with the goal of promoting Army ROTC and the military in general. The Guard participated in parades and in various activities, including visiting Fort Polk, participating in field training with ROTC cadets, assisting with the Military Ball, taking part in ROTC Organization Day, holding spring and fall rush, and attending social get-togethers with ROTC cadets. In addition, the Guard members sent goodie boxes to Veteran's Administration Hospital nursing home patients in Alexandria.

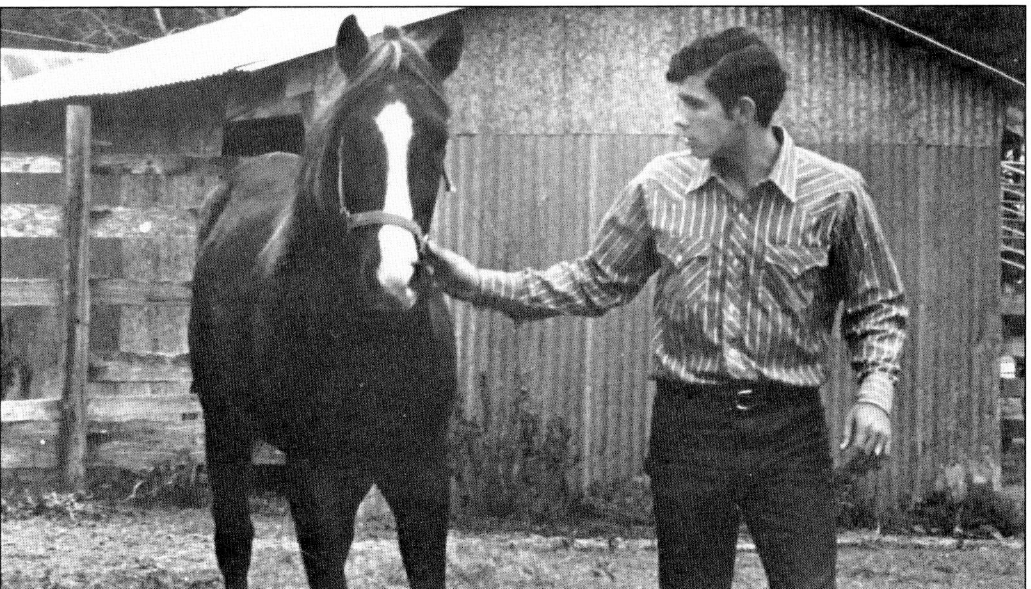

BLOCK AND BRIDLE. A national organization of animal husbandry students, the Block and Bridle Club was established at McNeese during the 1956–1957 school year. A similar club existing during this same time was the Hoof and Horn Club, whose objectives were centered on the agriculture curriculum. The Rodeo Team was also very active during the 1950s at McNeese.

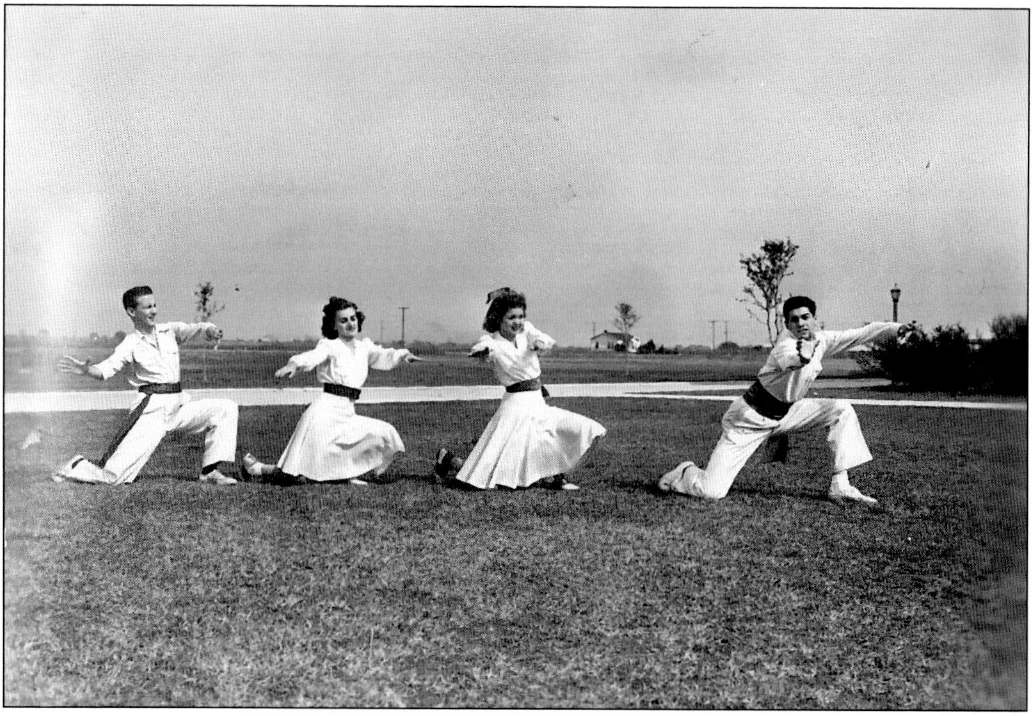

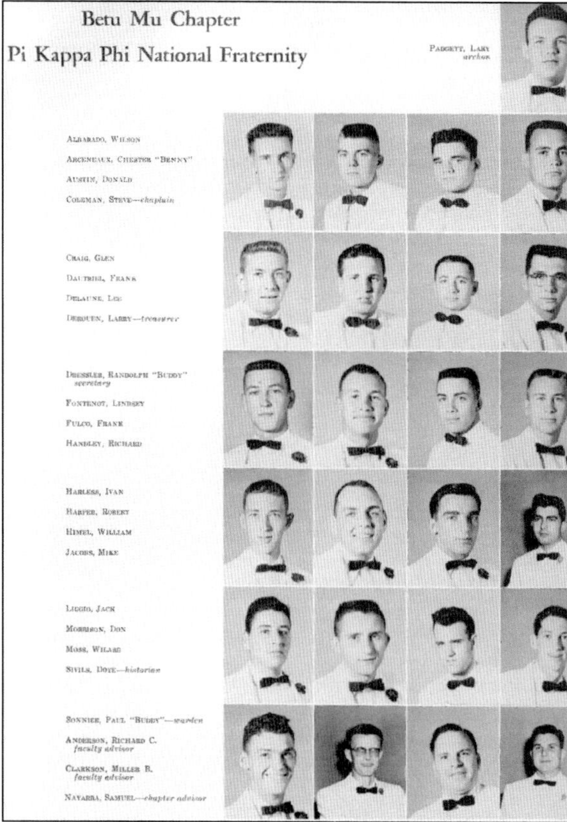

Betu Mu Chapter
Pi Kappa Phi National Fraternity

PADGETT, LARRY
archon

ALBARADO, WILSON

ARCENEAUX, CHESTER "BENNY"

AUSTIN, DONALD

COLEMAN, STEVE—*chaplain*

CRAIG, GLEN

DAUTHIEL, FRANK

DELAUNE, LEE

DEROUEN, LARRY—*treasurer*

DRESSLER, RANDOLPH "BUDDY"
secretary

FONTENOT, LINDSEY

FULCO, FRANK

HANDLEY, RICHARD

HARLESS, IVAN

HARPER, ROBERT

HIMEL, WILLIAM

JACOBS, MIKE

LIGGIO, JACK

MORRISON, DON

MOSS, WILLARD

SIVILS, DOYE—*historian*

SONNIER, PAUL "BUDDY"—*warden*

ANDERSON, RICHARD C.
faculty advisor

CLARKSON, MILLER B.
faculty advisor

NAVARRA, SAMUEL—*chapter advisor*

CHEERLEADERS. Cheerleaders are always an important component of school spirit. The first cheerleaders at McNeese were, from left to right, John William Eggers, Doris Drost, Bettye Sue Moore, and Willis Stone. The cheerleaders were always in action at pep rallies and at the games. Another pep squad in the 1940s was called the Rangerettes, again keeping the cowboy/cowgirl theme.

PI KAPPA PHI. The first nationally chartered fraternity at McNeese was Pi Kappa Phi, organized in 1955. The Beta Mu Chapter was dedicated to the promotion of loyalty, honor, and friendship, and encouraged excellence in scholarship. Larry DeRouen was treasurer of this first fraternity chapter. He later returned to McNeese to teach in the Department of Languages and to serve as Director of Research and later as Director of Facilities and Planning. The first social fraternity for men on campus was the Deacons, organized in 1940–1941. The first national sorority was Chi Omega, organized in 1958.

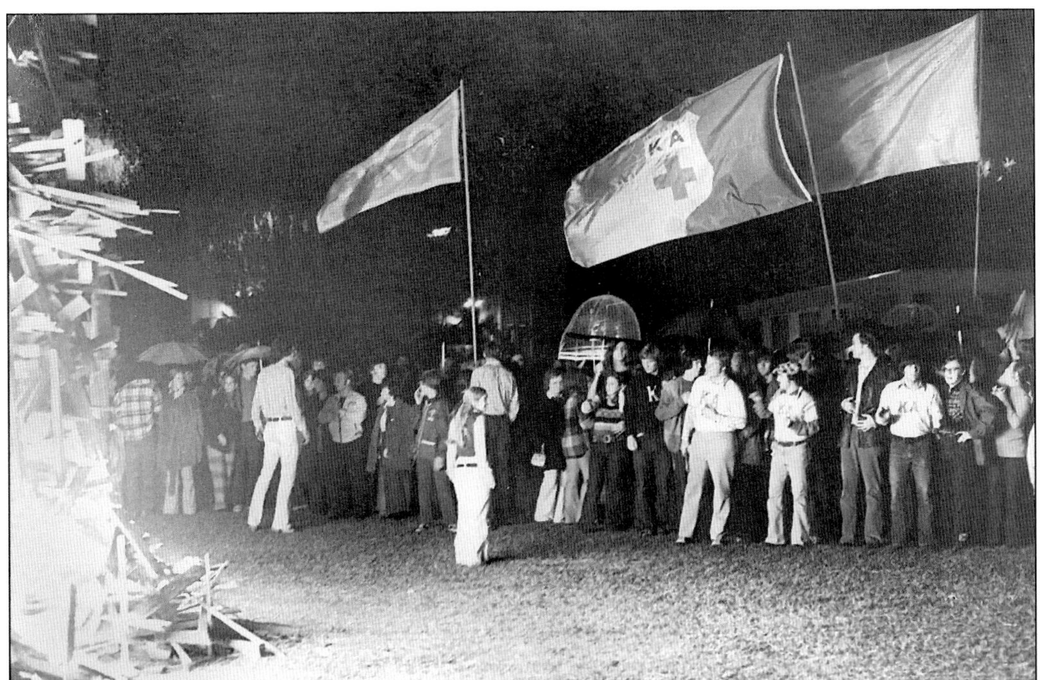

HOMECOMING FIRE. The traditional bonfire was lit at the end of the festivities surrounding Homecoming. In this photograph, fraternities hoist their banners as the bonfire begins to burn.

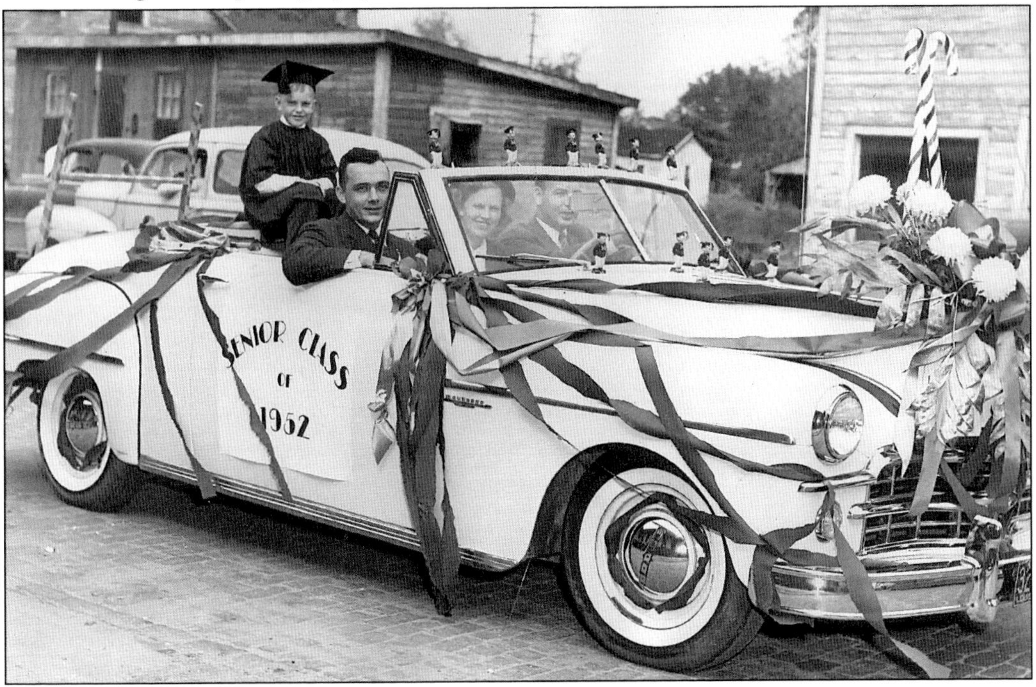

SENIOR CAR. This unidentified photograph came from a scrapbook belonging to Lether E. Frazar, the first president of McNeese. When McNeese became a four-year institution the class of 1952 was the first class to receive the four-year degree. No doubt this parade entry reflected that achievement.

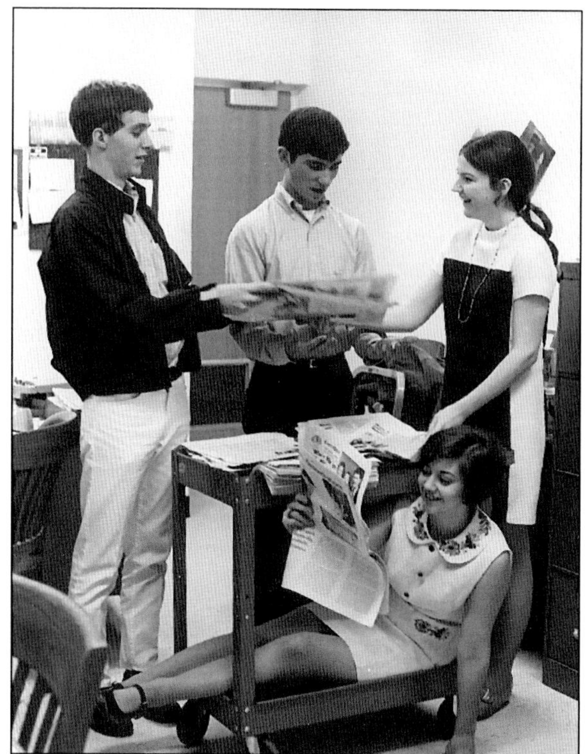

CONTRABAND STAFF. The 1969–1970 *Contraband* staff checks out a hot-off-the-press issue. Seated is student Cheryl Ware, currently a professor in the Department of Languages at McNeese. Standing from left to right are Mike Boudreaux, Chick Hawsey, and Patsey Carlberg. Brett Downer, *Contraband* editor during the late 1980s, currently holds the position of executive editor of the *Lake Charles American Press.*

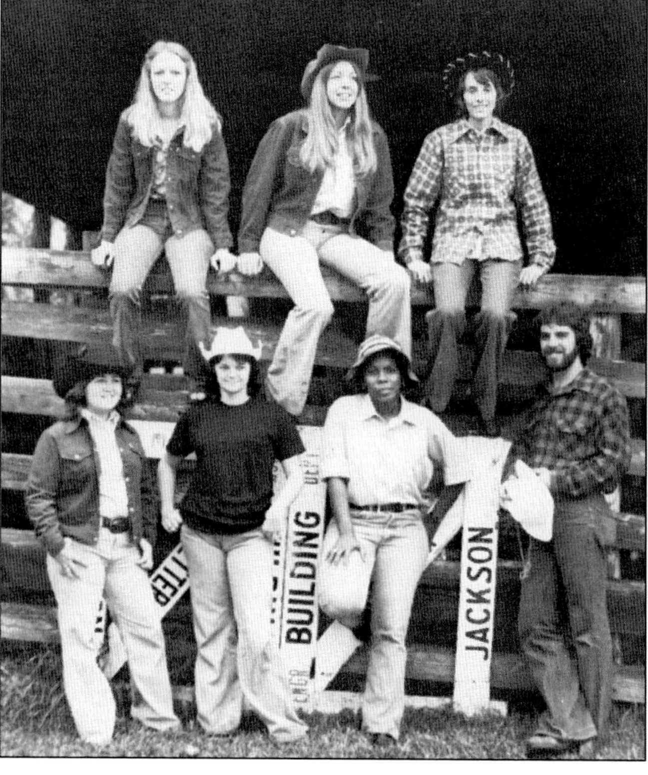

LOG STAFF. The 1975–1976 *Log* staff dresses the part of cowboys and cowgirls as they pose for this photograph. On the ground from left to right are Ivette Honeycutt, Tina Thibodeaux, Geralyn Simon, and Russell Duplechain. Sitting atop the fence are Sheron Faulk, Mary Stewart New (*Log* editor), and Ann Lipre.

BLUE KEY. Blue Key was founded on the McNeese campus in 1956. It is composed of junior and senior men who have shown outstanding leadership and scholarship. As a service to the college, the club publishes the *Blue Key Student-Faculty Directory* at the beginning of each academic year. This page from the student yearbook, the *Log,* shows members Kalil Ieyoub, Raymond Chavanne, and Larry DeRouen, all students who returned to teach at McNeese and to serve in other administrative positions.

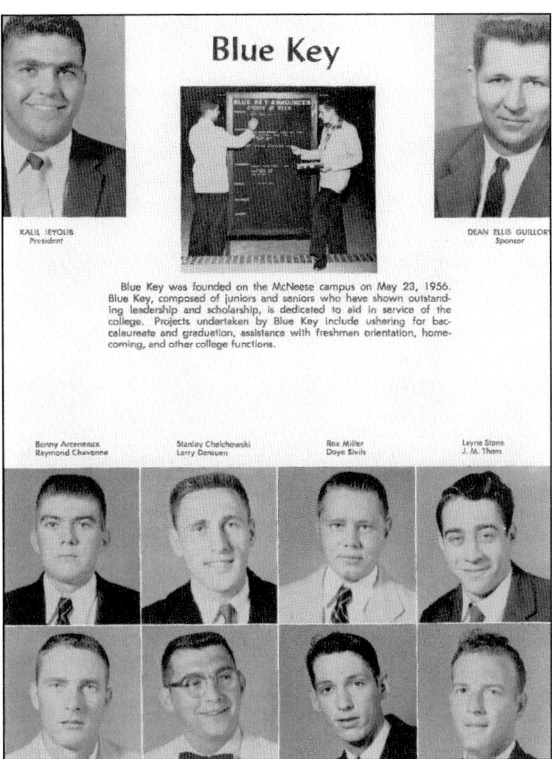

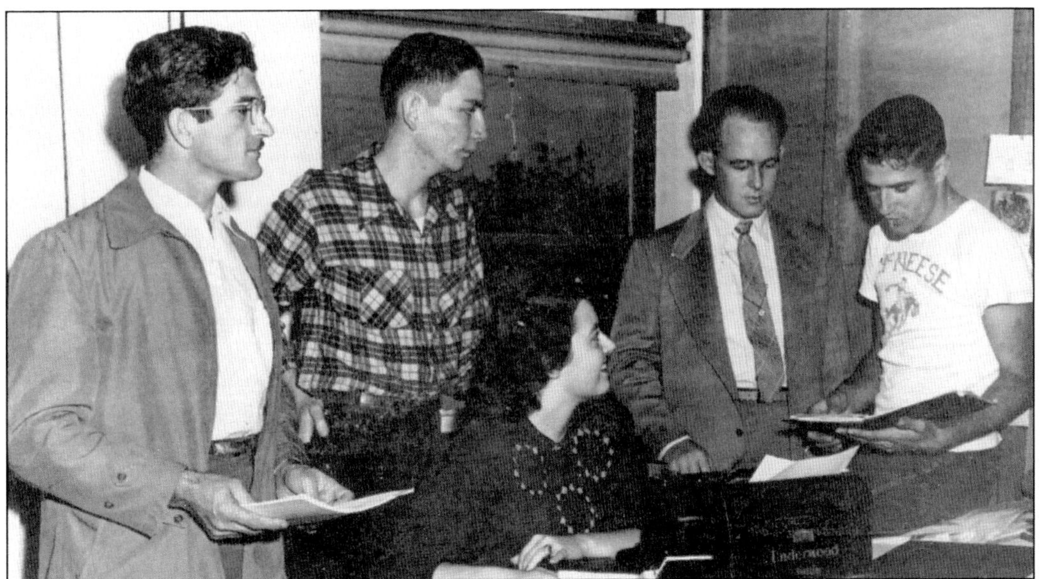

DEBATE CLUB. Led by Dr. W.J. "Bill" Casey, McNeese's outstanding debate team won numerous awards in major regional and national tournaments. The team challenged the Harvard University debate team many times over the years and won more than half of the debates. In this 1949 photograph, debate team members Ludon Angelle, Bill McLeod, Betty Harden, Earl McCoy, and Joe Kelly organize material for their next competition. Bill McLeod, in later years, used the talent he perfected on the debate team to his advantage. He was a prominent attorney, state senator, and 14th Judicial District Court Judge until his recent retirement.

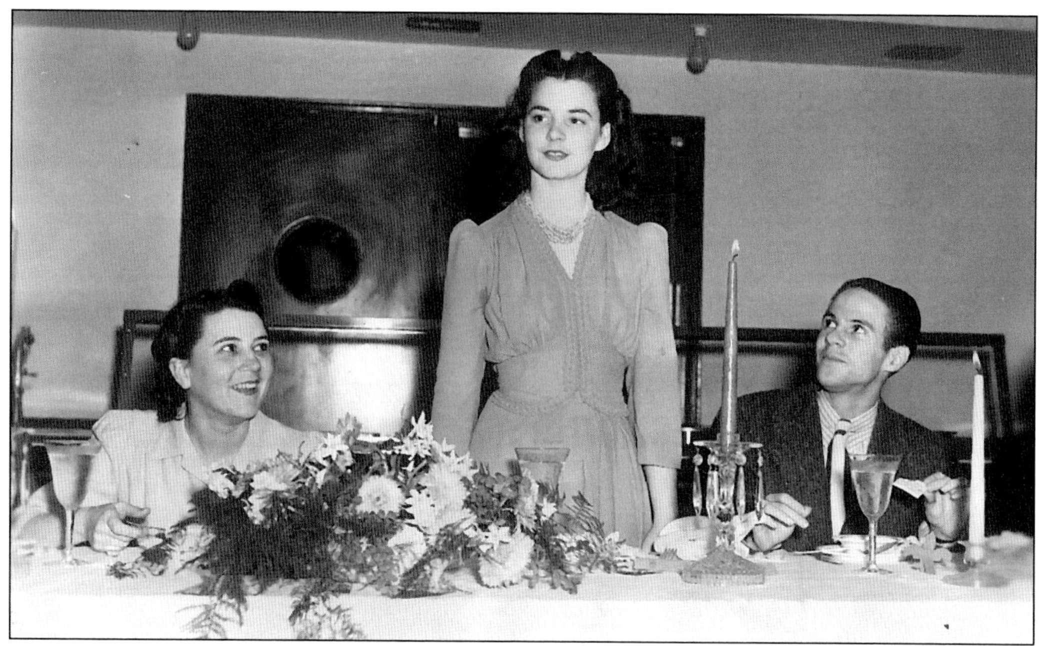

LA JEUNESSE. The first French Club organized on campus was La Jeunesse in 1939–1940. Speaking at a banquet is Kathleen Bordelon. Seated to the left is Dolive Benoit, the club advisor and first French teacher. To the right is K.D. Jones. In a recent interview, Kathleen Bordelon Levingston said, "I loved the French Club. We gave little French plays and learned songs and entertained each other. Miss Benoit at that time was young herself and very active with her students." The purpose of this club and later French clubs was to encourage French conversation and to appreciate the French culture, especially in Louisiana.

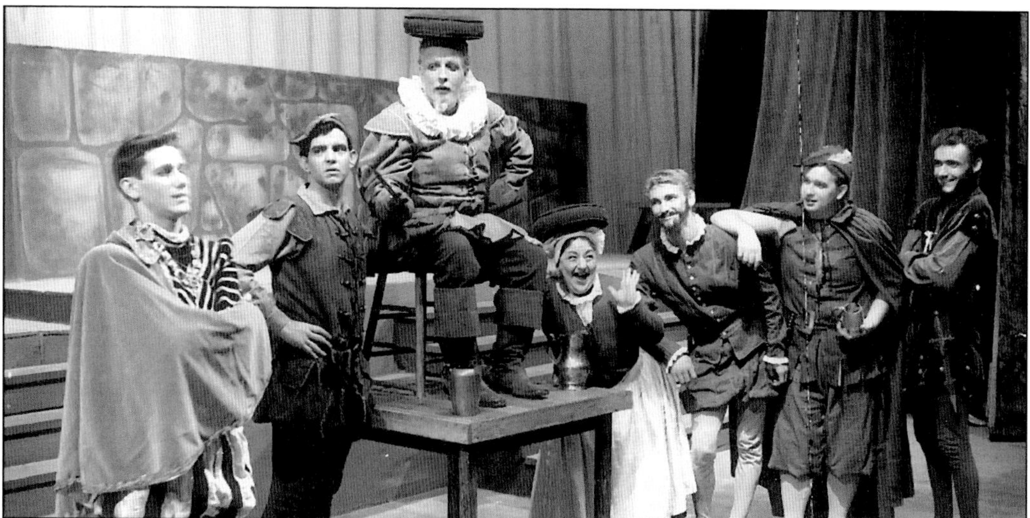

BAYOU PLAYERS. The Bayou Players was the drama group formed by Margery Parsons Wilson when she came to McNeese in 1944. This production of *King Henry IV, Part I* was a joint effort on the part of the Bayou Players and the Lake Charles Little Theatre. The Bayou Players staged productions in the auditorium and later in the Ralph Squires Theatre in the Fine Arts Building. Left to right in this 1954 production are Larry Guillory, Davey Lee Hebert, Ed Daugherty, Rosa Hart, Bill McMahon, Don Goss, and Herman Brewer.

86

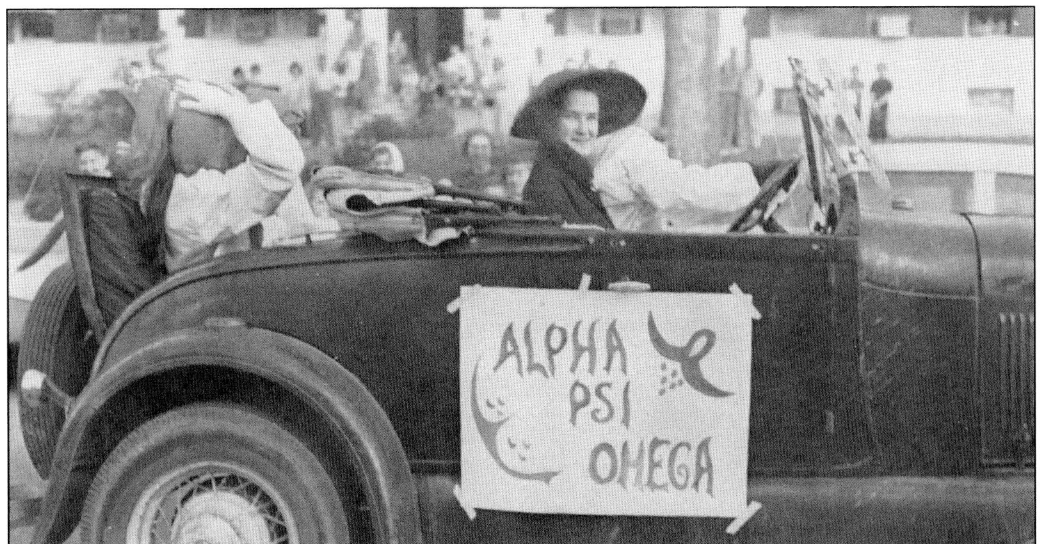

ALPHA PSI OMEGA. The chapter charter of the dramatic fraternity Alpha Psi Omega was signed in 1955. The fraternity offers fellowship to students who are interested in drama, play production, and acting. Charter members included Daniel Ieyoub, Betty Jean Singleton, Tasca Dickerson, Bruce B. Brown, Joan Adams, Carol Ashburn, Larry G. Guillory, Bill McMahon, Charles Burrows, William Himel, Carolyn Piel, Eva Jo Ward, JoAnn Medrano, and Herman Brewer. This photograph shows Joan Adams riding in Alpha Psi Omega's entry in the 1958 Homecoming parade.

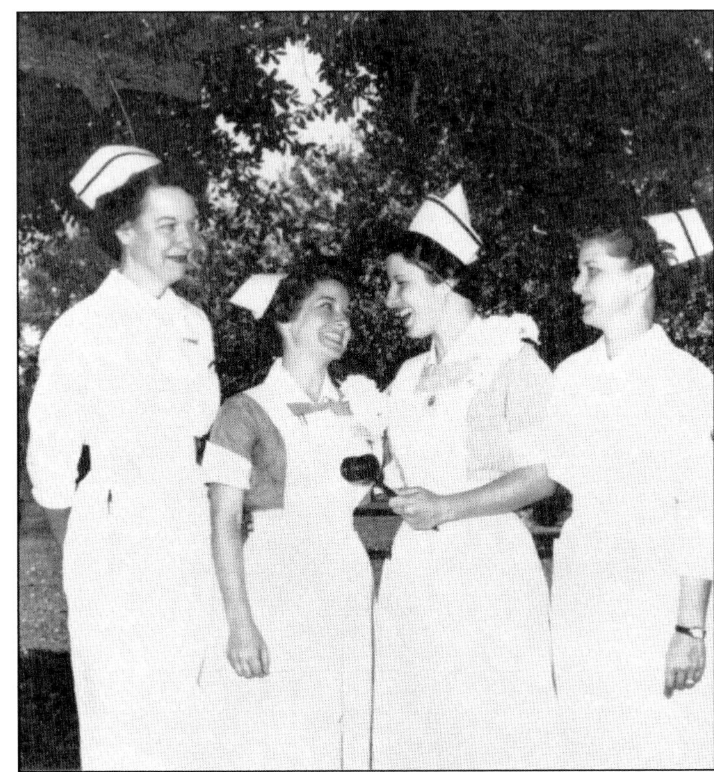

STUDENT NURSES. The Student Nurses Association was established to encourage interest in the nursing profession and to understand its service at the community, local, state, and national level. Black-banded caps were placed on the heads of senior nurses during the capping ceremony. Today, pinning has replaced capping in the traditional ceremony marking the graduation of the student nurses.

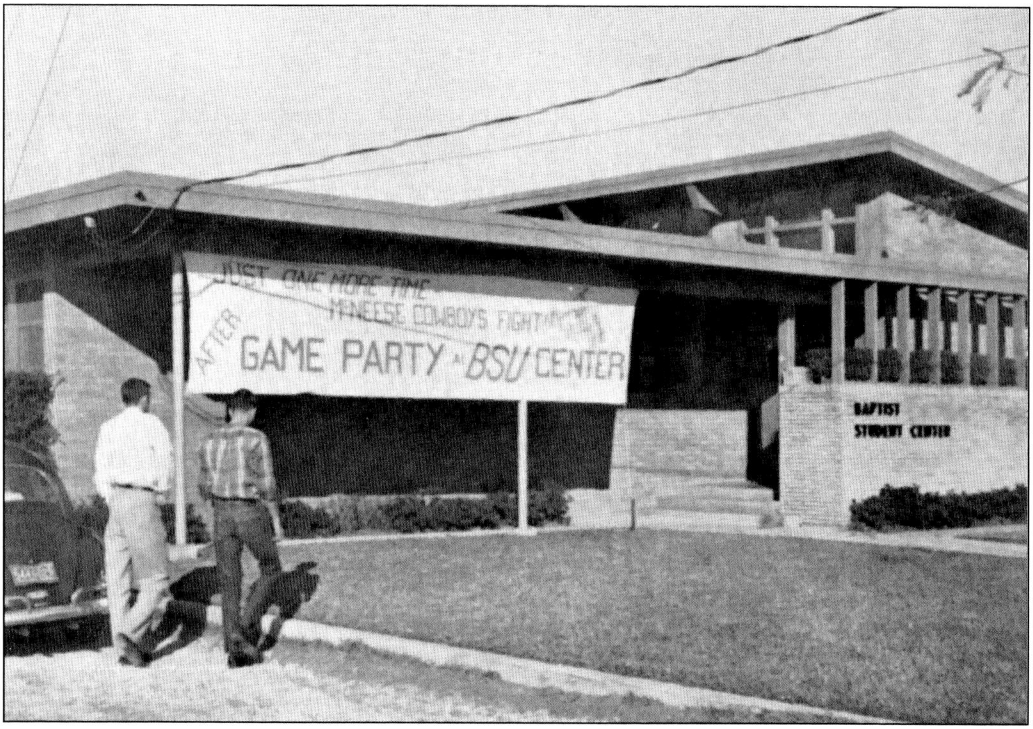

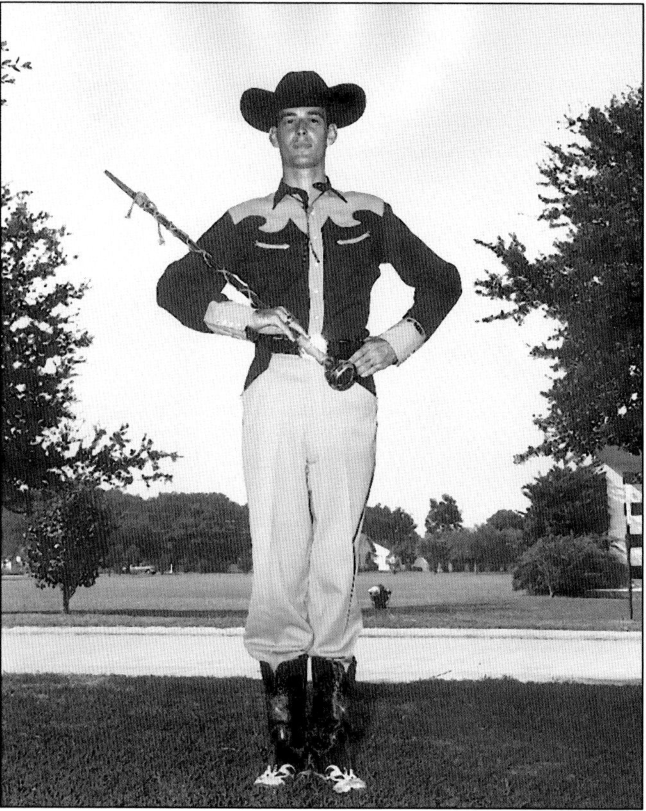

BAPTIST STUDENT UNION. Located across Ryan Street from Frasch Hall, the Baptist Student Union was one of the first religious centers on campus. Others include the Canterbury Association, the Wesley Foundation, Campus Outreach, and the Catholic Student Center. The clubs associated with these religious centers sponsored worship periods, after-game parties, weekly lunches, and other activities. Tom Lutner became the director of the Baptist Student Union during 1957–1958 and served in that position for 30 years.

DRUM MAJOR. Drum Major Fred Patterson sports one of several band uniforms worn by the McNeese Marching Band through the years in this 1961 photograph. The drum major led the band onto the football field and in the parades.

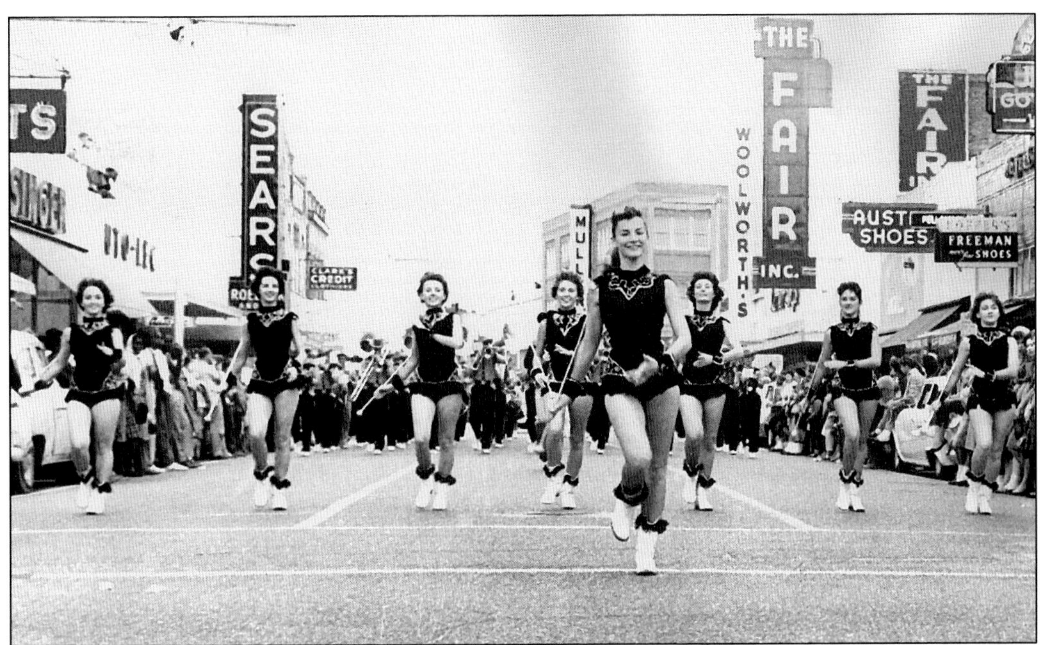

COWBELLES AND THE MARCHING BAND. Entertaining a crowd on Ryan Street in the early 1960s, the Cowbelles and the marching band lead the Homecoming Parade.

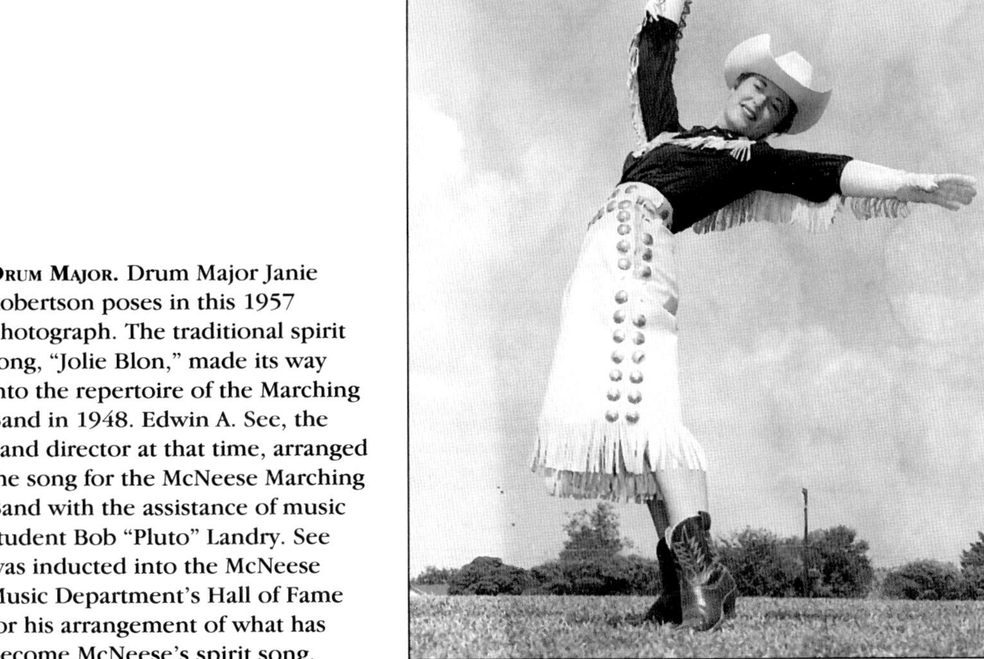

DRUM MAJOR. Drum Major Janie Robertson poses in this 1957 photograph. The traditional spirit song, "Jolie Blon," made its way into the repertoire of the Marching Band in 1948. Edwin A. See, the band director at that time, arranged the song for the McNeese Marching Band with the assistance of music student Bob "Pluto" Landry. See was inducted into the McNeese Music Department's Hall of Fame for his arrangement of what has become McNeese's spirit song.

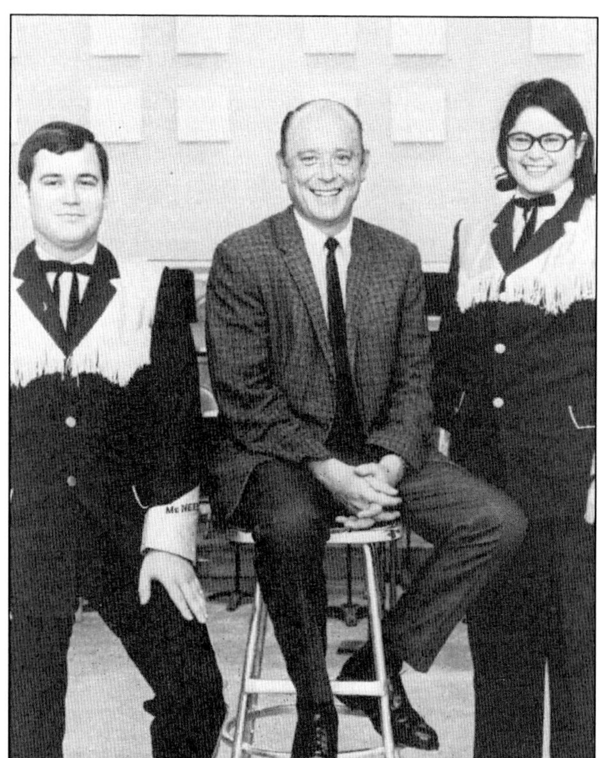

KELLY LOVE. Band director Kelly Love impressed audiences with his marching band's prowess in the 1970s. The "Sound of the Seventies," the McNeese State University Marching Band, gained acclaim for its excellent performances, both on and off the football field. Attired in striking red, white, and blue uniforms, members of its marching units presented sparkling maneuvers. Performing at home football games and parades, the show featured the Twirling Corps, the Rifle Corps, and the Flag Corps. Later the band wore distinctive blue and gold uniforms to match the school colors. Pictured here, from left to right, are Greg Danigole, Kelly Love, and Rose Fournet.

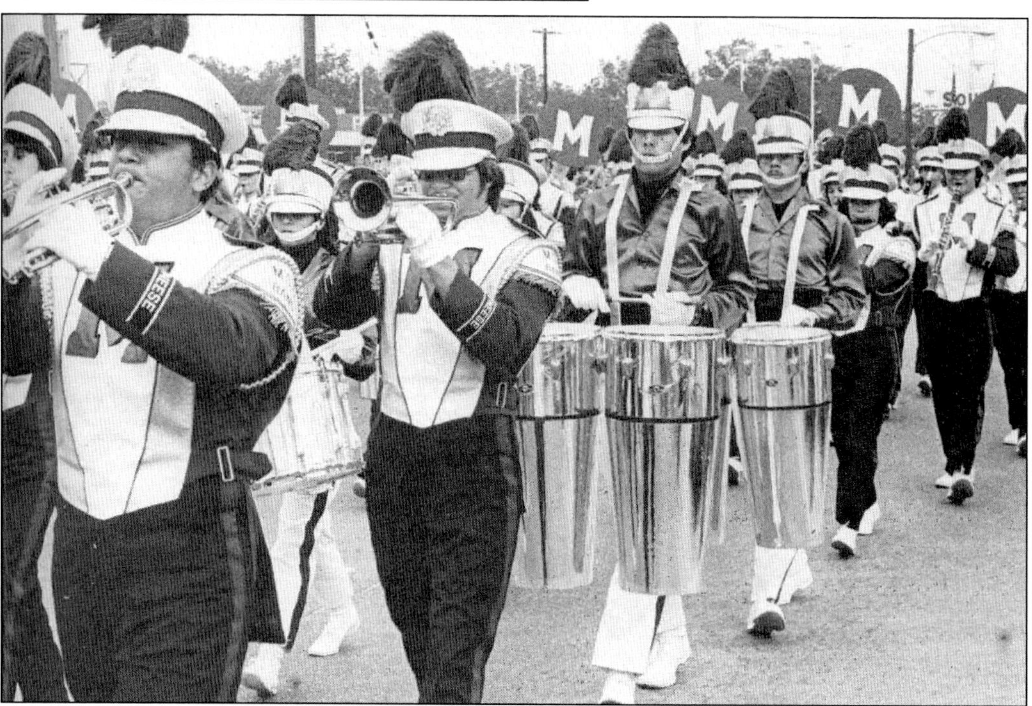

BROTHER LOVE'S TRAVELIN' SALVATION SHOW. Nicknamed Brother Love's Travelin' Salvation Show, the McNeese Marching Band won many awards and appeared in bowl games and on national television. Kelly Love became band director in 1970; he left McNeese in 1973.

Six

ATHLETICS

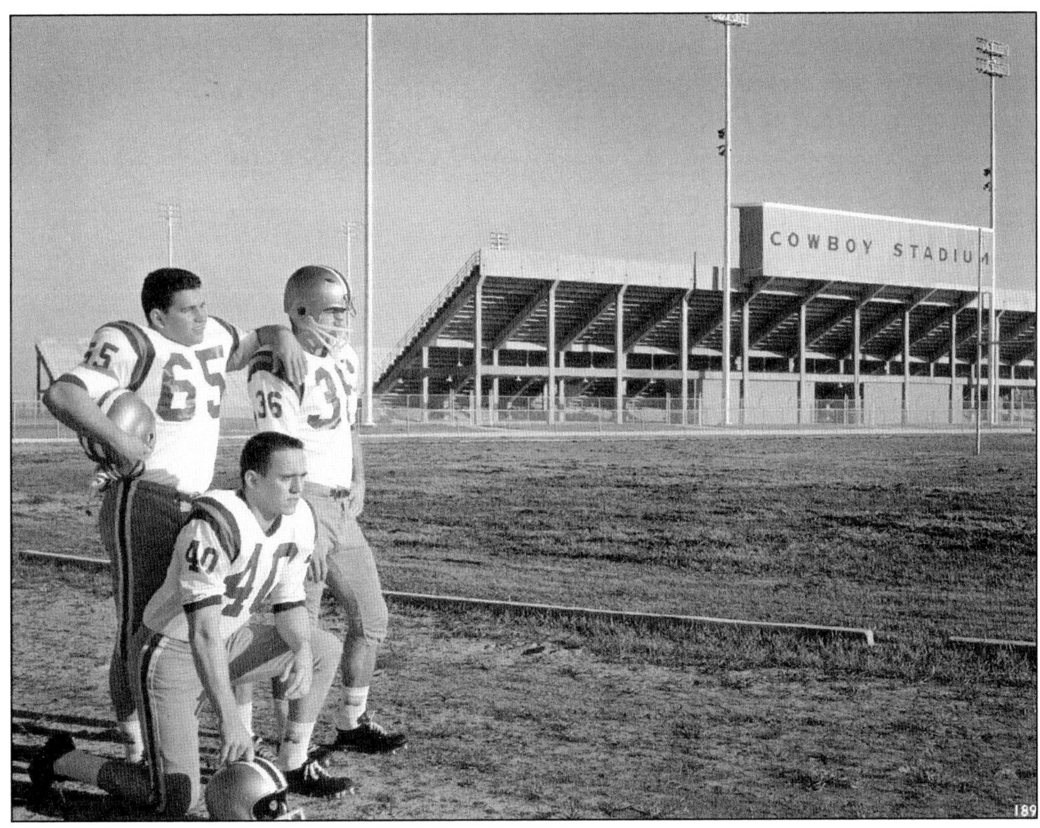

COWBOY STADIUM. This is the way the stadium looked in 1965. The seating capacity was just over 12,000. In 1975 it was expanded to seat over 17,000; a three-tier press box known as the Sky Ranch, a new scoreboard, and a sound system were added in 1998. Kneeling in this photo is Tony Ber. Standing from left to right are Steve Meaux and Felix Simon.

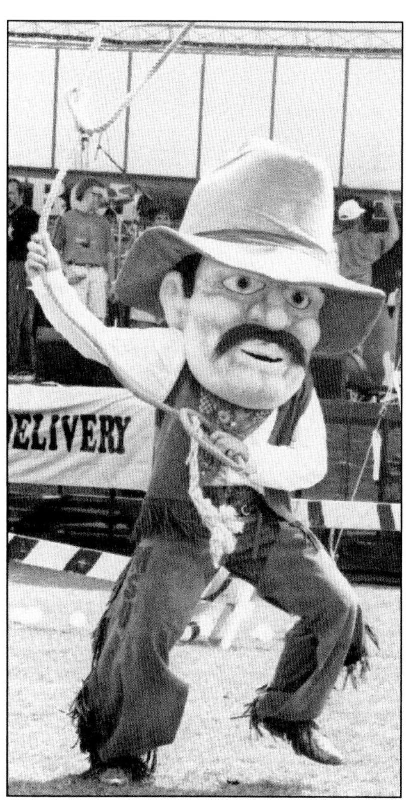

ROWDY. The current Cowboy Team Mascot is known as Rowdy, again following the cowboy theme used by McNeese since the beginning of the school. The Cowboys are also sometimes called the "Pokes," a variation of cowpokes. The name Rowdy comes from the character Clint Eastwood played on the television show *Rawhide*. At one time in the school's history the mascot was a pony called "Mac."

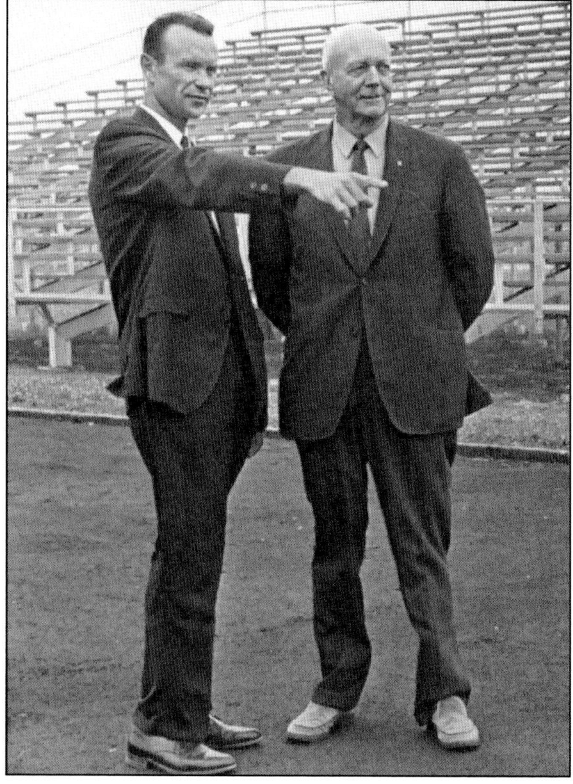

ALBERT I. RATCLIFF AND BOB HAYES. Albert I. Ratcliff was hired in 1946 to coach the McNeese Cowboy Football Team. During Ratcliff's nine coaching years, the team gained admission to the Gulf States Conference and participated in four bowl games. He became athletic director in 1954, holding this position until he retired in 1973. He won the Alumni President's Cup (the first) in 1958, and was inducted into the McNeese Sports Hall of Fame in 1981. Bob Hayes was hired as track coach in 1967, holding this position for many years. He coached the track and cross-country teams through many conference titles, earning Track Coach of Year titles himself. Hayes served as athletic director from 1987 till 1994, and was inducted into the McNeese Sports Hall of Fame in 2000.

CHARLES KUEHN. Charles Kuehn, one of many football luminaries throughout the years, was selected to enter the McNeese Sports Hall of Fame in 1981. He and David Poche are the only McNeese football players to have their numbers retired. Poche was inducted into the Hall of Fame in 1989. Other inductees into the football Hall of Fame include Don Breaux, Desmond Jones, Carroll Neely, Stephen Starring, Tom Sestak, Jesse Castete, Glenn Kidder, Jules DeRouen, and Johnnie Thibodeaux. Kuehn also served McNeese as a football scout, assistant football coach, and track coach.

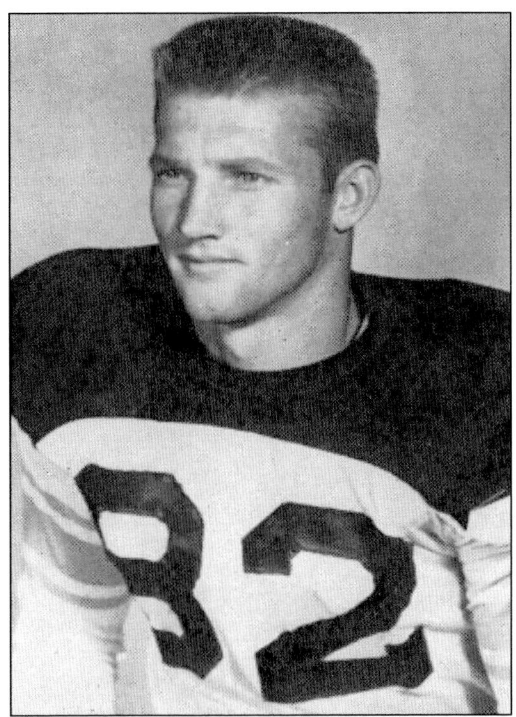

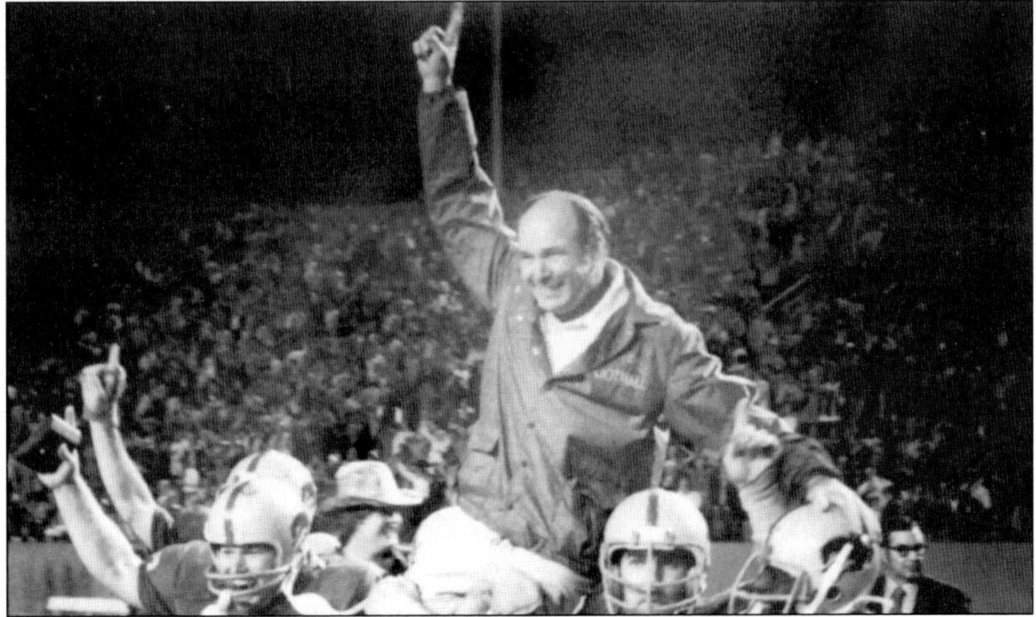

JACK DOLAND. Jack Doland became the head coach of the McNeese Cowboys Football Team in 1970. The next year the Cowboys were ranked number one in the NCAA's small college division, and participated in the Grantland Rice Bowl against Tennessee State. This photograph was taken after the team won the conference championship in 1971. During the 1976 season, Doland was named SLC Coach of the Year and the team won the first Independence Bowl. Ernie Duplechin became coach in 1979 when Doland became university president. His winning season was also followed by a return to the Independence Bowl.

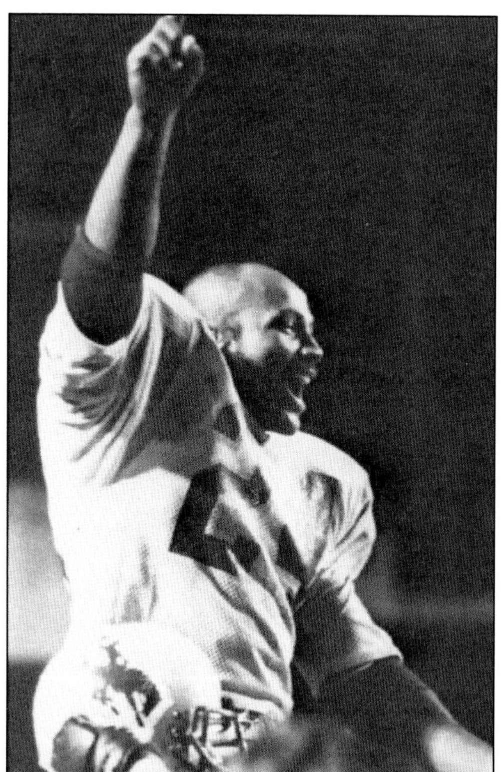

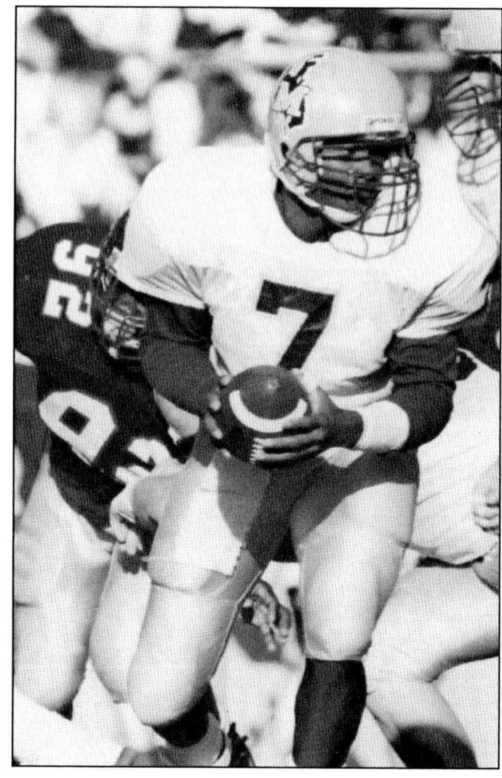

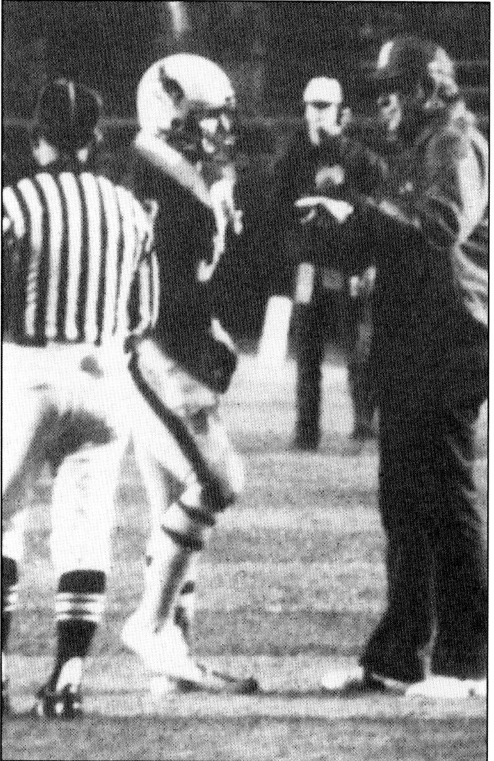

(*Above left*) **BUFORD JORDAN.** Since the 1950s, McNeese has sent their share of athletes to the professional ranks. Both Leonard Smith and Buford Jordon were first-round professional football draft picks in the 1980s. Jordan still holds the team record for touchdowns scored; he was SLC Player of the Year in 1981.
(*Above right*) **KERRY JOSEPH.** Kerry Joseph, playing for McNeese in the early 1990s, holds team records for total offense, passing yardage, passes completed, and touchdown passes. He was SLC Player of the Year in 1995.

INDEPENDENCE BOWL. In 1976, McNeese played in the first Independence Bowl, defeating Tulsa. McNeese returned to the bowl in 1979 and 1980, but lost to Syracuse University and Southern Mississippi, respectively. In this photograph, Coach Duplechin encourages a member of the team. Other bowl games McNeese played in were the Cosmopolitan Bowl in 1951, the Oil Bowl in 1949, the Cajun Bowl in 1947, and the Tung Bowl in 1946. The only NCAA 1-AA championship game McNeese has played was in 1997 against Youngstown State.

SHONZ LAFRENZ. In this photograph, Shonz LaFrenz prepares to kick what will be the winning point needed to send the Cowboys to the NCAA championship game in Chattanooga, Tennessee in 1997. During the preliminary playoff games and the last game of the season in Cowboy Stadium, McNeese fans tore down the goalposts for the first time in school history.

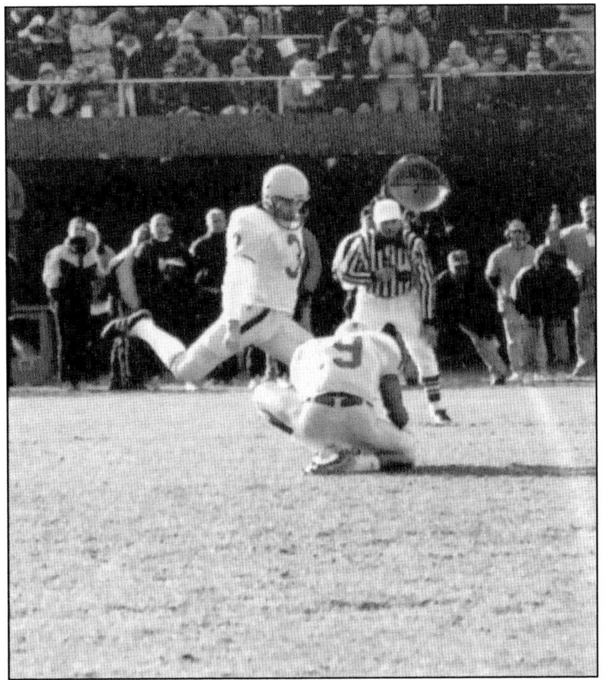

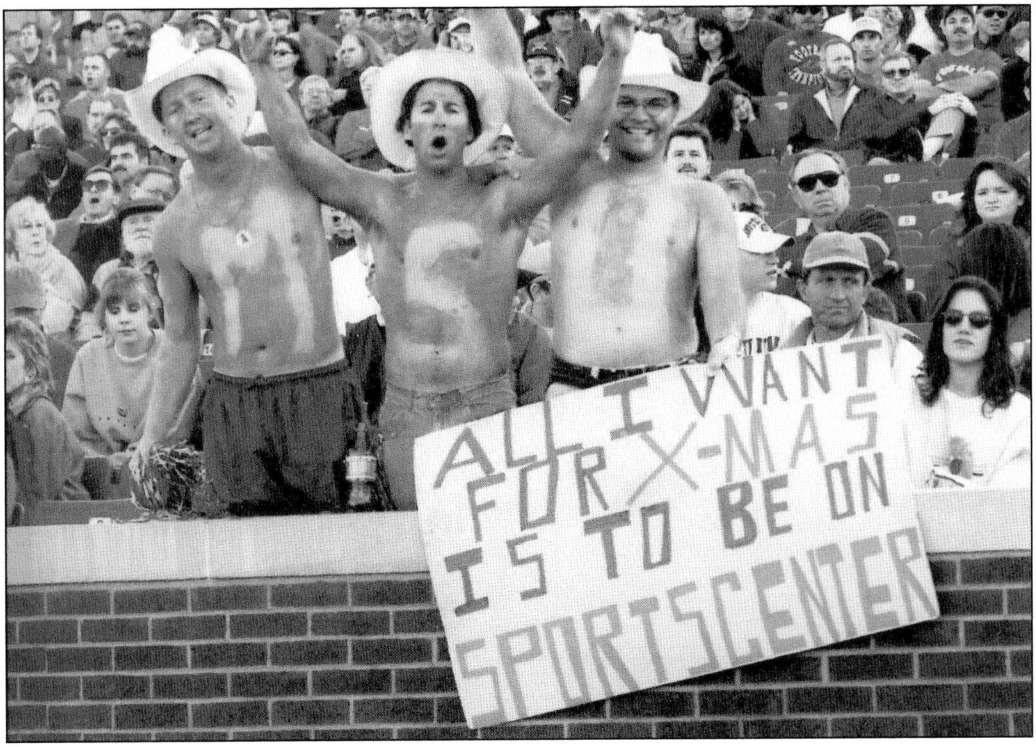

MSU BOYS. An example of student pride was demonstrated at the NCAA championship game in 1997. More than 9,000 fans made the trip to see the "Cardiac Cowboys," a nickname given the team because of so many last-minute saves. The fans never faltered in their support of the team even though McNeese lost the game by one point in the last quarter.

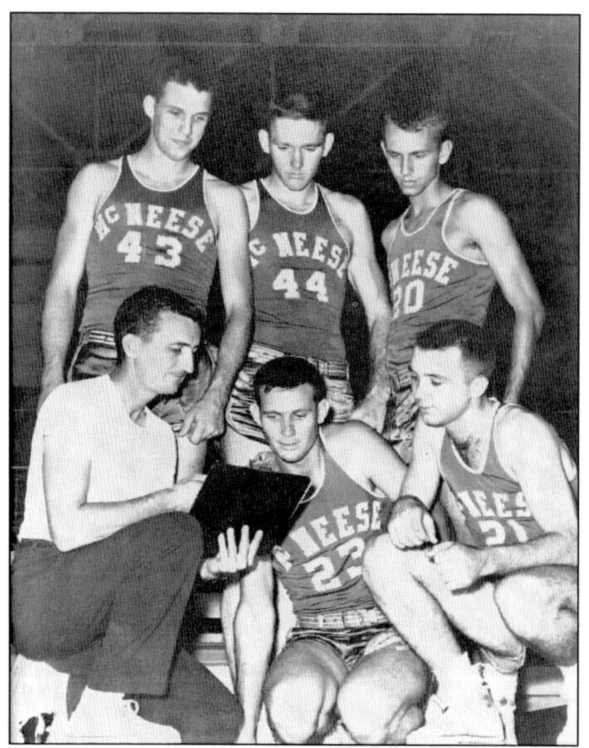

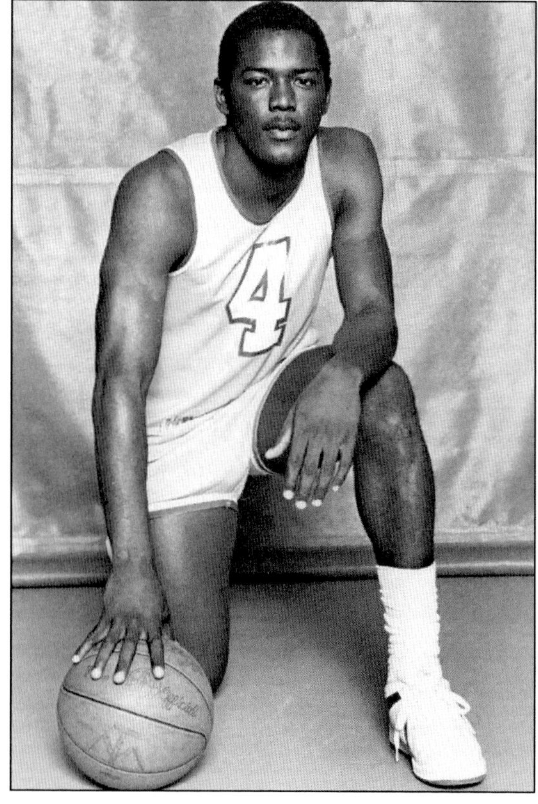

RALPH O. WARD. The longest held coaching record in McNeese history goes to Ralph O. Ward, who coached the basketball team from 1952 until 1971. During his 20 years in the head coaching position, he led the team to several conference titles as well as being named Gulf States Conference Coach of the Year many times. Ward received the Alumni President's Cup in 1961, and was inducted into the McNeese Sports Hall of Fame in 1982. Ward earned the respect of the school and the community for many reasons over the years, including the fact that twice, once in 1950 and again in the 1967–1968 season, he coached a game by telephone from his sickbed.

JOE DUMARS. McNeese MVP, Southland Conference and Louisiana Sports Writers' Player of the Year, the Sporting News All-American, First Team All-Conference, Southland Conference All-Tournament, McNeese Sports Hall of Fame 1994, first round draft pick by the Detroit Pistons 1985—no other player in the history of McNeese basketball has accumulated as many honors as Joe Dumars. In addition to the honors associated with his basketball talent, Joe was elected Mr. McNeese in 1985, indicating his popularity with other students on campus. He also retains his popularity with the entire city, returning each year for the Joe Dumars Golf Classic.

JOE'S NUMBER RETIRED. Joe Dumars' #4 jersey was retired in 1985. The only other numbers retired in the history of McNeese basketball are Bill Reigel's #33, Frank Glenn's #34, and Stan Kernan's #25. Glenn and Kernan were inducted into McNeese's Hall of Fame in 1981 and 1983, respectively.

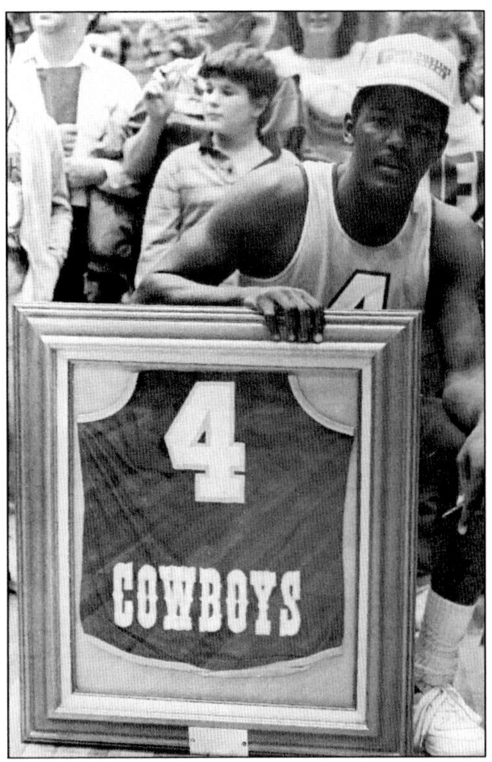

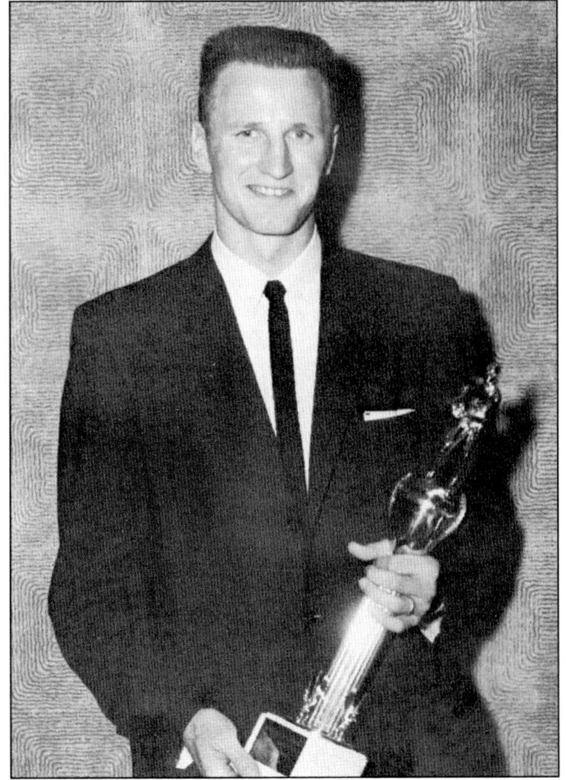

BILL REIGEL. Bill Reigel led the 1955–1956 basketball team to the National Association of Intercollegiate Athletics (NAIA) championship in 1956. He was named the NAIA Most Valuable Player, in addition to Gulf States Conference Player of the Year, NAIA and UPI All-American, and McNeese MVP. He still leads McNeese statistics in several scoring categories. Bill Reigel was named to the McNeese Sports Hall of Fame in 1980. In 1986, he was inducted into the Louisiana Sports Hall of Fame, the first McNeese athlete to be so honored. After graduation, he played for the Minneapolis Lakers.

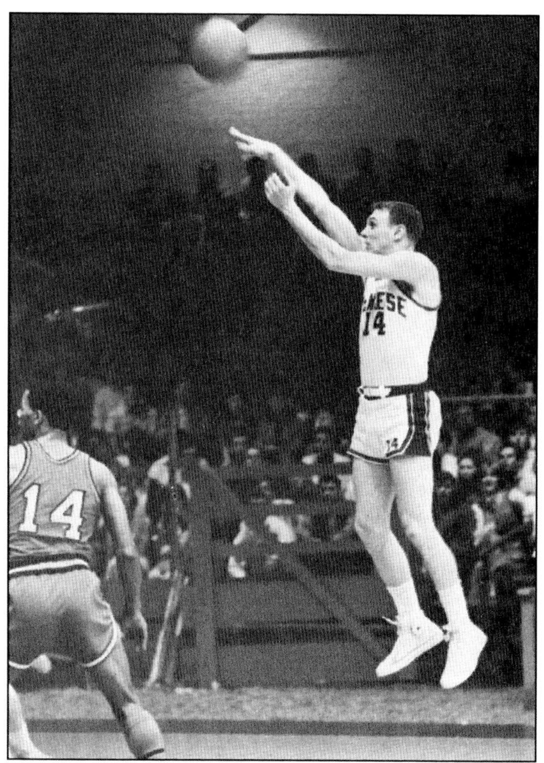

KENT ANDREWS. Inducted into the McNeese Sports Hall of Fame in 1998, Kent Andrews was the national free throw champion in 1967–1968. He scored 85 out of 90 free throws for a percentage of 94.4. Other outstanding basketball players who have been inducted into McNeese's Hall of Fame include Clyde Briley, Charles Decker, Ed Green, Wayne Kingrey, Dick Miller, Roy Moore, George Murphy, and Jimmy Shields.

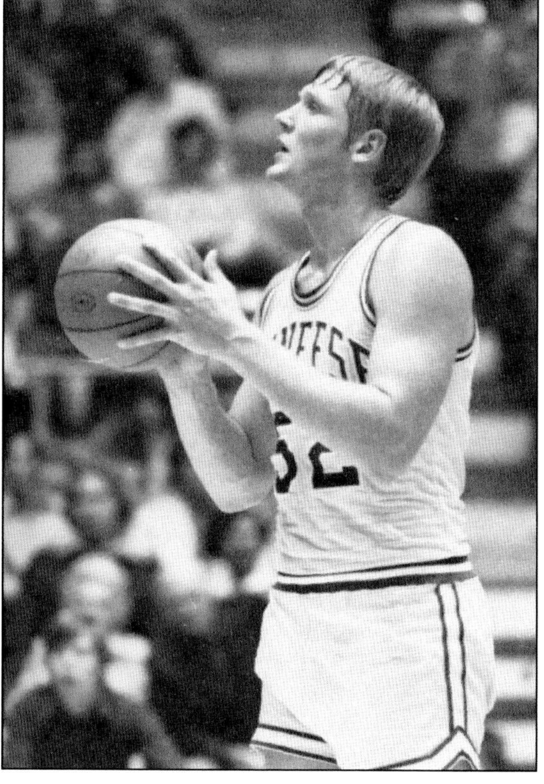

JOHN RUDD. John Rudd was named to the All-Conference First Team in the Southland Conference, and named McNeese MVP in 1977 and 1978. He was inducted into the McNeese Sports Hall of Fame in 1986. Rudd led the Southland Conference three straight years in rebounding, and holds the McNeese record for rebounds per game for a season and for a career. He went on to play for the New York Knicks. Other McNeese basketball players to play for the pros include Michael Cutright, Jerome Batiste, Chris Faggi, David Lawrence, and Henry Ray.

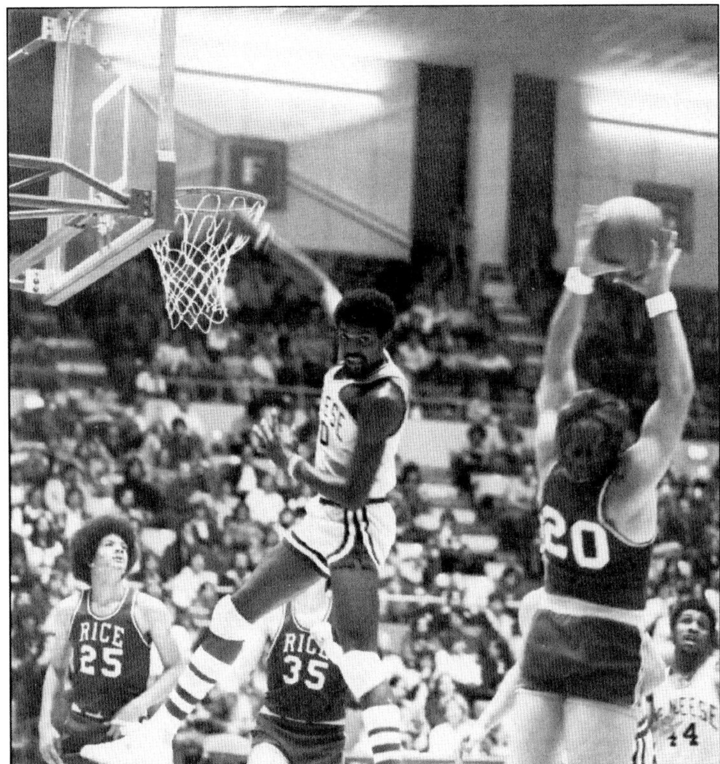

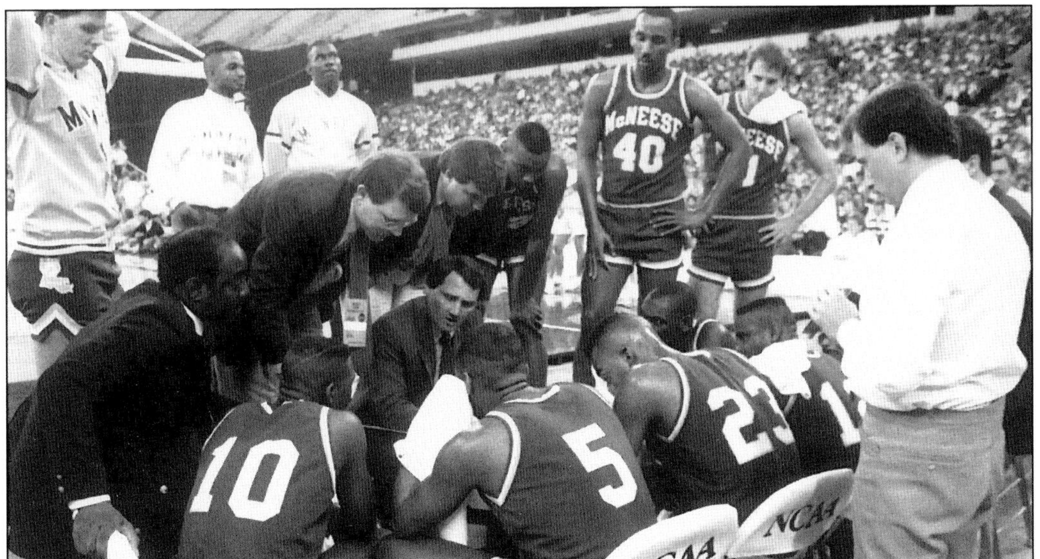

STEVE WELCH AND THE NCAA. The Cowboy Basketball Team made it all the way to the NCAA Division I tournament in 1989, playing before a crowd of over 30,000 in Indianapolis. Coach Steve Welch led the team through an exciting game, eventually losing 77-71. Team standouts included Michael Cutright, #5, and Anthony Pullard, #23. Coaches seen in this photograph are, from left to right, Dave Simmons, Bill Peterson, Jim Armstrong, and Steve Welch, kneeling center. Other team members in this photograph include #10 Dwayne Davis, #12 Terry Griggley, #40 Mark Thompson, and #11 Tab Harris.

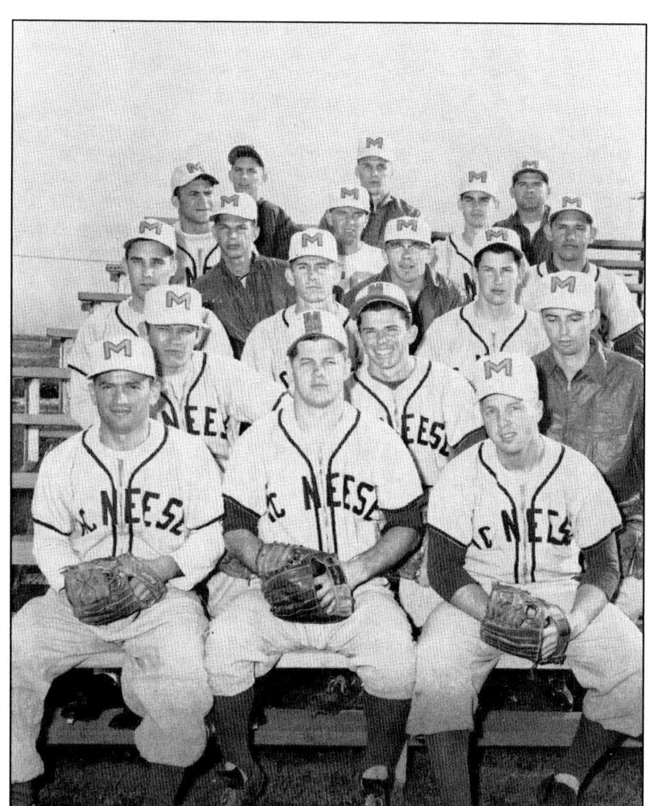

1959 Baseball Team. The 1959 McNeese Cowboy Baseball team included Amos Ivey, who played from 1957 to 1960. He was inducted into the Sports Hall of Fame in 1986. From left to right, bottom to top, the team members are Frank Calloura, Roland Barras, Henry Meachum, Amos Ivey, Ronney Breaux, Billy Johnston, Clive Gustin, Charles Stevenson, Barney Bridges, Benny Augustine, Guy Harvard, Mike Mirelez, Frank Glenn, Ed Melton, Ronnie Sheehan, Carlton Cormier, John Riddile, and Coach Reed Stephens.

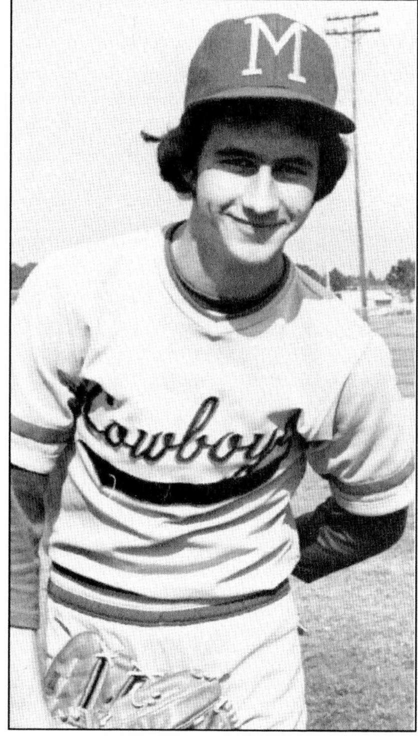

Ray Fontenot. Ray Fontenot pitched for the McNeese Cowboys from 1976 to 1979. He went on to pitch for the New York Yankees, the Chicago Cubs, and the Minnesota Twins. He was included in the McNeese Sports Hall of Fame in 1989. Fontenot still holds the record for pitching victories, pitching shutouts, and strikeouts. Other Cowboys who played in the major leagues are Terry Burrows, John Thomson, and Bob Howry.

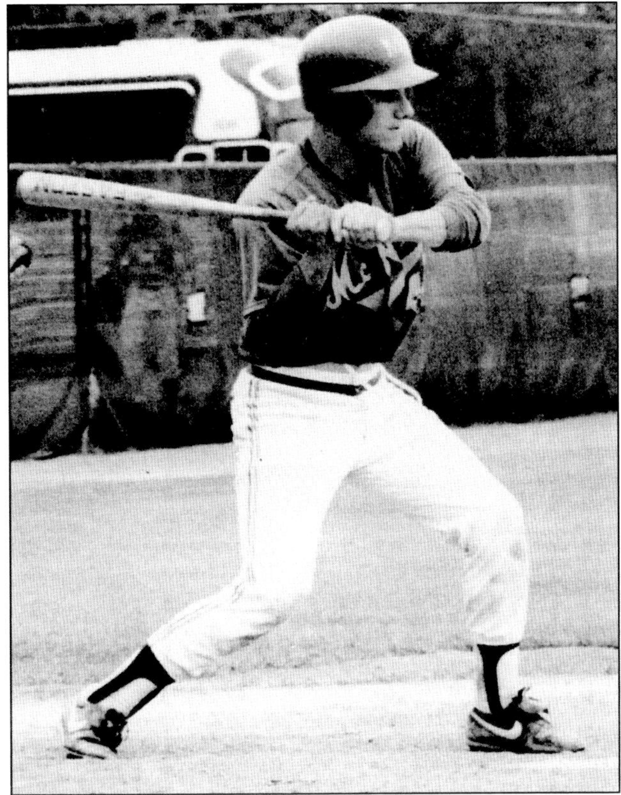

1988 BATTER. The McNeese Cowboy Baseball Team won its first Southland Conference championship in 1988 under the direction of head coach Tony Robichaux. The team also played in the NCAA tournament this year. Ferral Manuel is the batter in this photograph. The team would not win the Southland Conference championship again until 2000, using the coaching talents of Mike Bianco.

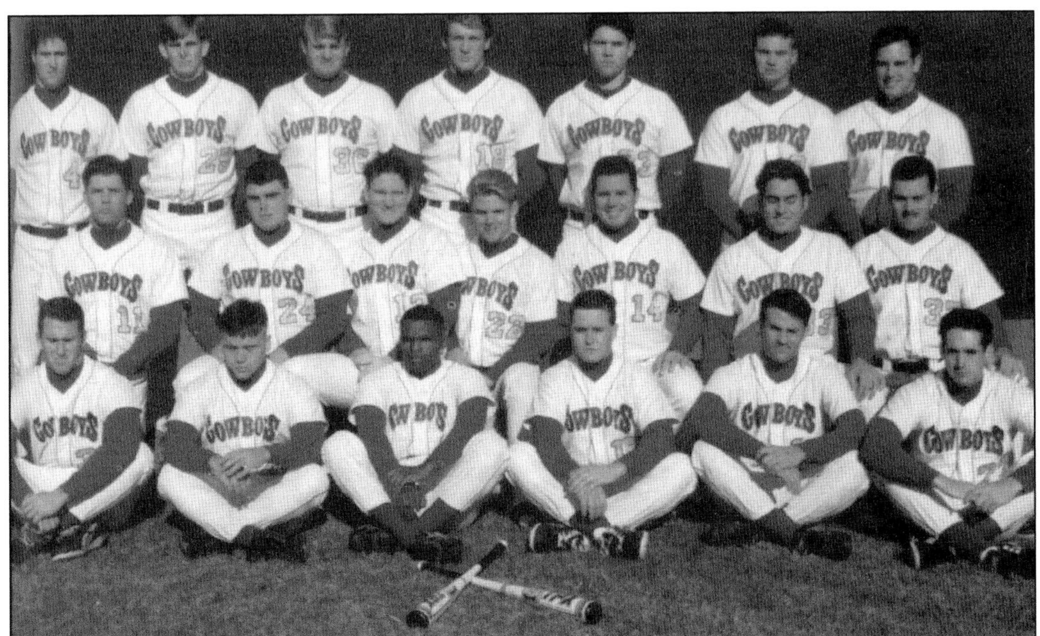

1993 BASEBALL TEAM. The 1993 team included all-conference picks Deron Hofstetter and Clint Gould. Coach Tony Robichuax once again led the team to the NCAA tournament. Hofstetter was chosen SLC Player of the Year in 1994.

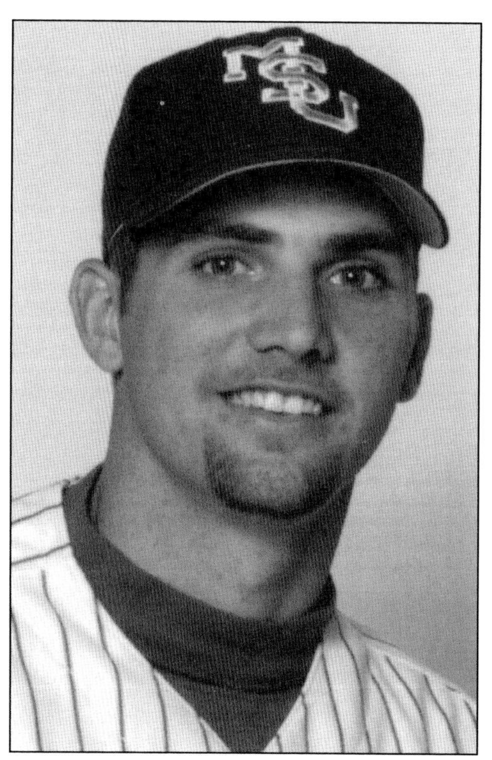

BEN BROUSSARD. Only four players in the history of McNeese baseball have batted over .400 for the year. Amos Ivey batted .407 in 1958 and .431 in 1959, Deron Hofstetter batted .403 in 1994, Ben Broussard batted .438 in 1999, and Kevin Mitchell batted .415 in 2001. Ben Broussard's number 23 was retired in 2000, and is displayed on the centerfield fence at Cowboy Diamond. This is the first baseball player's number to be retired in McNeese baseball history. Broussard was SLC Hitter of the Year in 1998 and 1999 and received McNeese's 1998–1999 Athlete of the Year Award.

(far right) **FANAHAN MCSWEENEY.** The star of the track team in the early 1970s was Irish-born Fanahan McSweeney. Inducted into the McNeese Sports Hall of Fame in 1997, McSweeney won two United States (USTFF) national indoor titles and represented Ireland in the 1972 Summer Olympics in Munich. He wrote *Living and Loving With Cancer,* published in 1994. Other outstanding track and cross-country individuals at McNeese were Brian Cooper, Fred Norris, Craig Henry, and Dicky Morgan.

(right) **BILL JONGBLOED.** Under coaches Charles Kuehn and Bob Hayes, the McNeese Track Team during the late 1960s–early 1970s featured several excellent runners. Bill Jongbloed, seen in this photograph, was MVP for 1967 and was named to the McNeese Sports Hall of Fame in 1994.

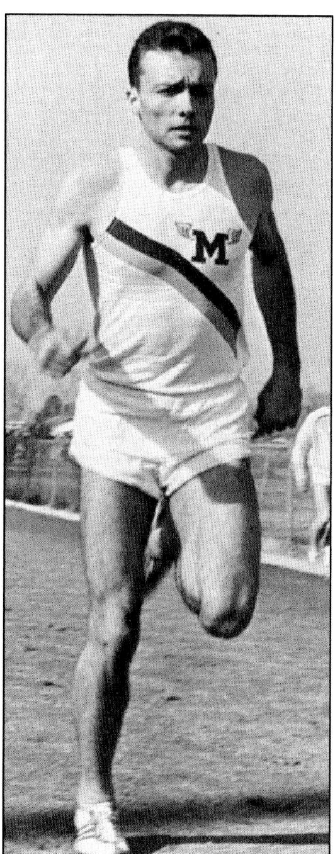

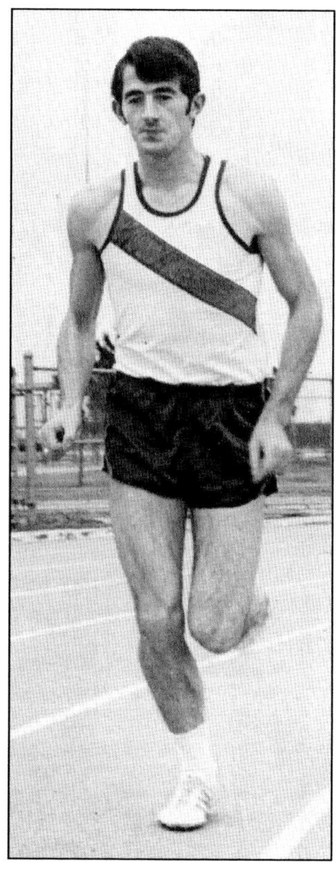

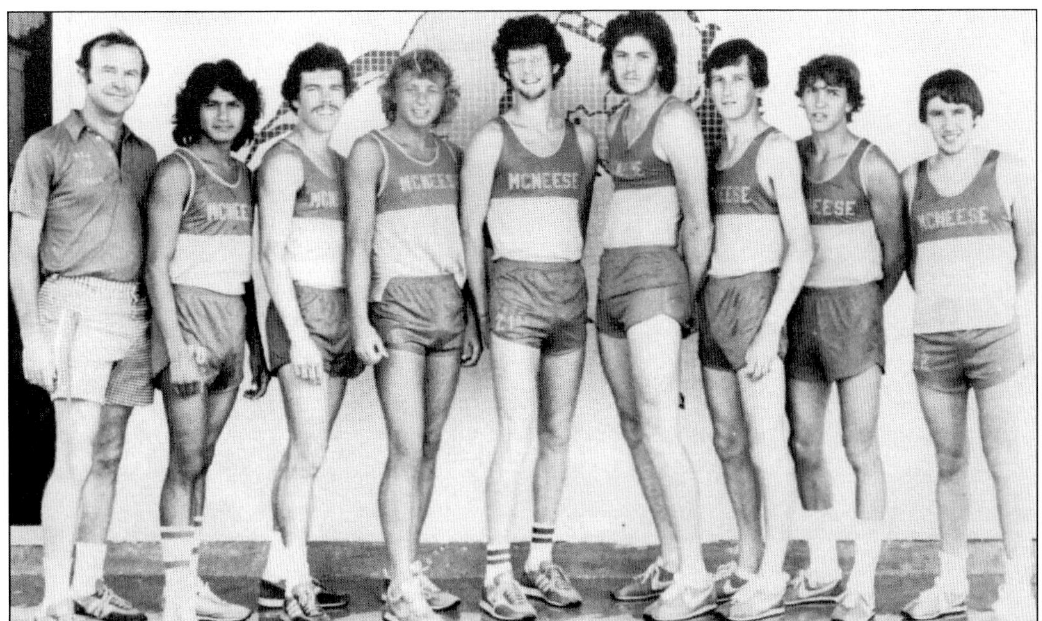

THE 1978 CROSS COUNTRY TEAM. Coached by Bob Hayes, the 1978 Cross Country Team won the Southland Conference Cross Country competition. In this photograph, Bob Hayes is seen on the left. Other team members are, from left to right, John Reyes, Gary Barrow, Tim Riley, David Kohrs, Phil LaHurt, Kevin Darcy, Lyle Van Horn, and Noel McCarron. David Kohrs currently serves McNeese as Human Resource Manager. The Cross Country Team also won conference titles in 1973, 1975, and 1976. Sita Ward, an outstanding female runner, was named SLC Player of the Year in 2000.

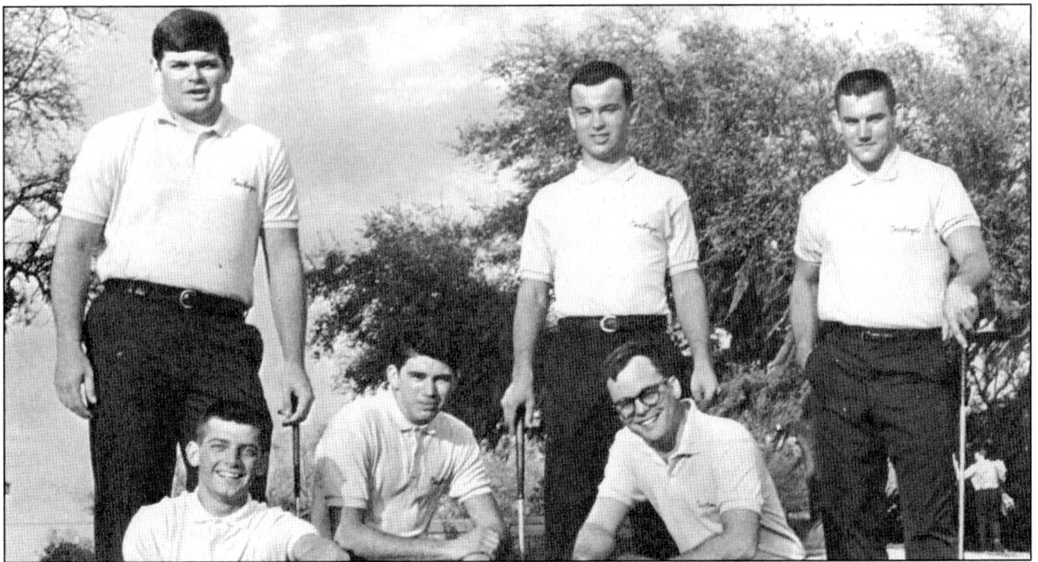

PAT O'BRIEN. The McNeese Golf Team has won several conference championships under the direction of coaches such as Ralph Ward, Ellis Guillory, and Moe O'Brien. The 1966–1967 team included, from left to right, (front row) Ronald Murphy, Frank DiGeorge, and Pat O'Brien; (back row) Tommy Burbank, David Doyle, and Sammy Kuehn. Team member Pat O'Brien was selected to the McNeese Sports Hall of Fame in 1981.

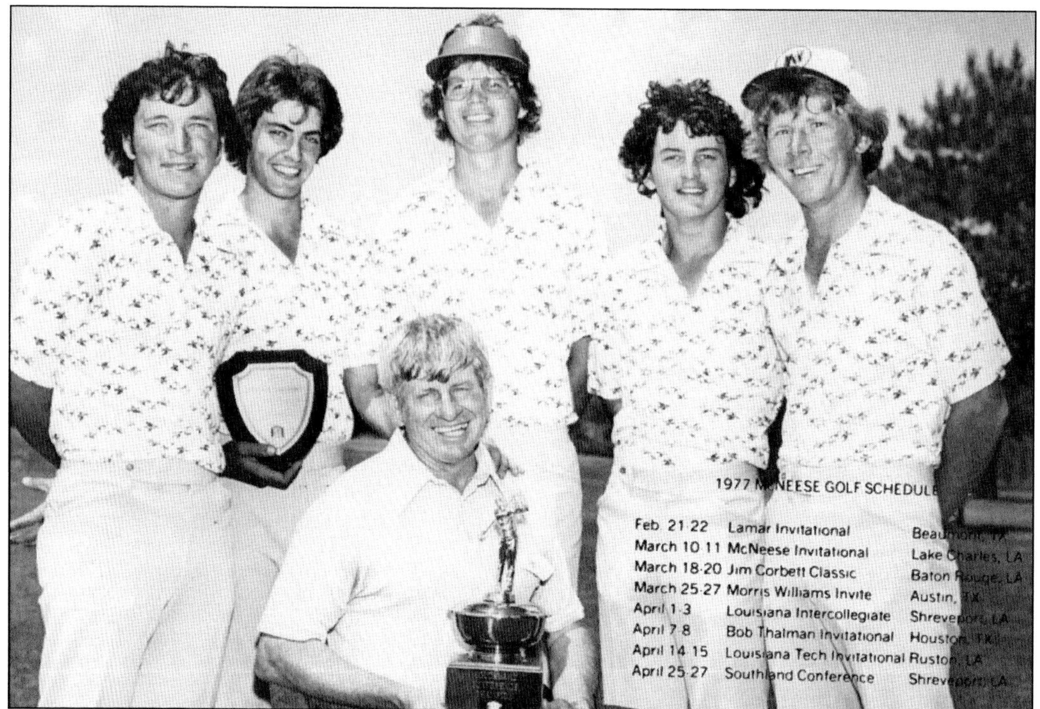

TIM GRAHAM. Tim Graham, named to the McNeese Sports Hall of Fame in 1995, is pictured here with the 1977 SLC Championship Golf Team. Shown are Coach Moe O'Brien, kneeling, and standing from left to right behind him, Billy Trent, Tim Graham, Larry Marshall, Scott Smith, and Mac Blanchard. The McNeese Golf Team also won conference titles in 1978 and 1979. Graham later played on the PGA tour.

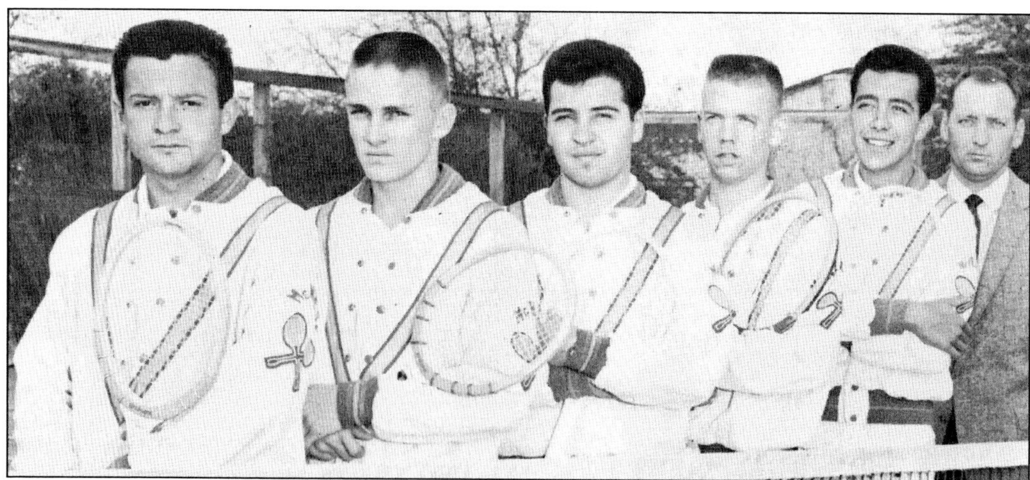

1959 TENNIS TEAM. McNeese's tennis team won the Gulf States Conference championship in 1953, 1958, 1959, 1960, and 1961. Coached by Arthur Lee and Lee Hayley, the team included, from left to right, Fredrico Zarazua, Eddie Watkins, Carlos Perez, Jim Brown, Vicente Hernandez, and Coach Arthur Lee. Lee was named to the McNeese Sports Hall of Fame in 1999. Brown played tennis for McNeese from 1959 until 1961, returning in 1966 to coach. Zarazua was inducted into the McNeese Sports Hall of Fame in 1981. Perez was named Distinguished Alumnus of the Year in 1993.

104

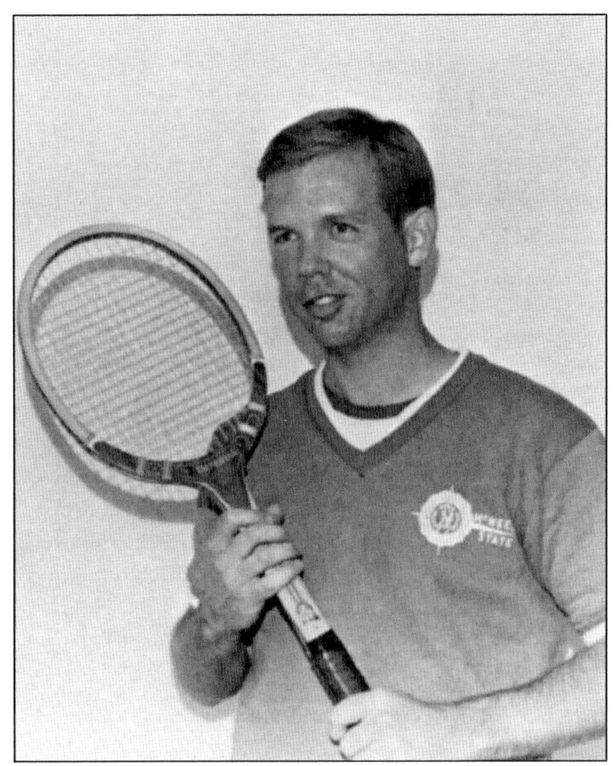

Coach Jim Brown. Jim Brown joined the McNeese Health and Physical Education Department in 1966. He was named tennis coach and coached the team to three straight Gulf States Conference championships in 1968, 1969, and 1970. He gave up coaching in 1971 after earning his Ph.D. and spent the remainder of his time at McNeese teaching and writing. He was inducted into the McNeese Sports Hall of Fame in 1991.

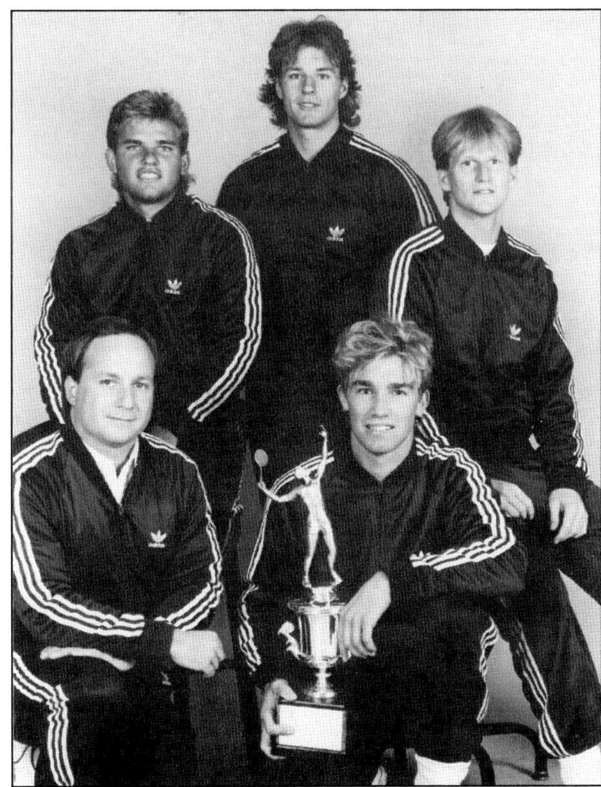

1988 Tennis Team. Lee Holland, one of the most successful McNeese tennis coaches, won the Southland Conference Coach of the Year Award in 1987. The tennis team won two conference titles during his eight seasons as coach. Named All-SLC champions on the 1988 team were (kneeling with trophy) Johan Kjellsten, (standing from left to right) Axel Reich, Pontus Lautgalk, and Ulf Persson. At bottom left is Coach Lee Holland. The tennis program was discontinued following the 1988 season.

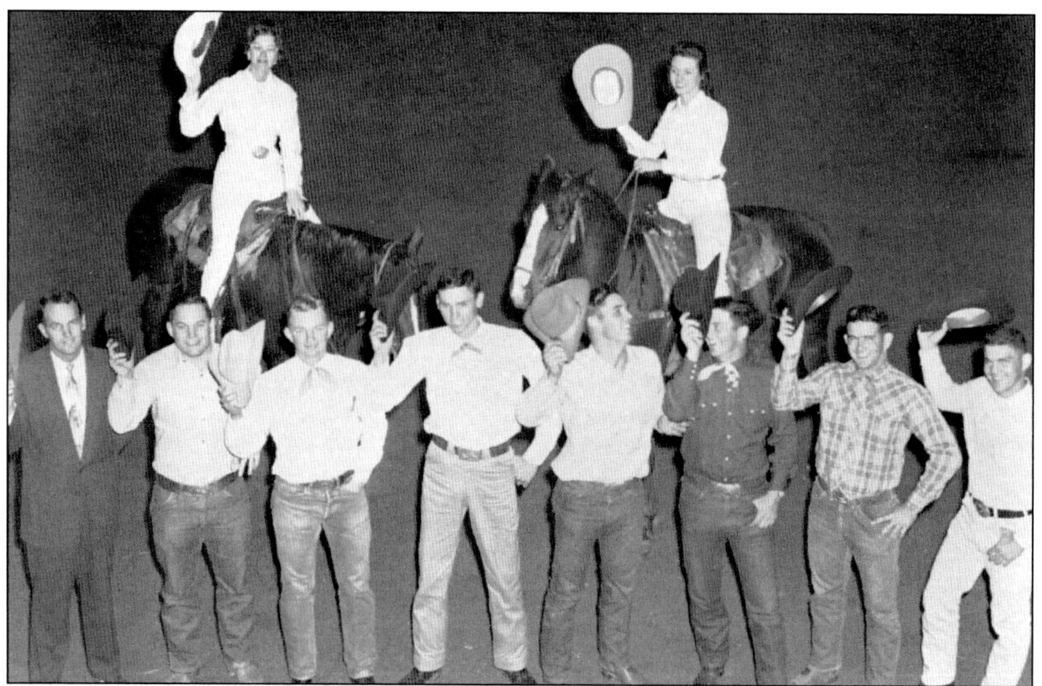

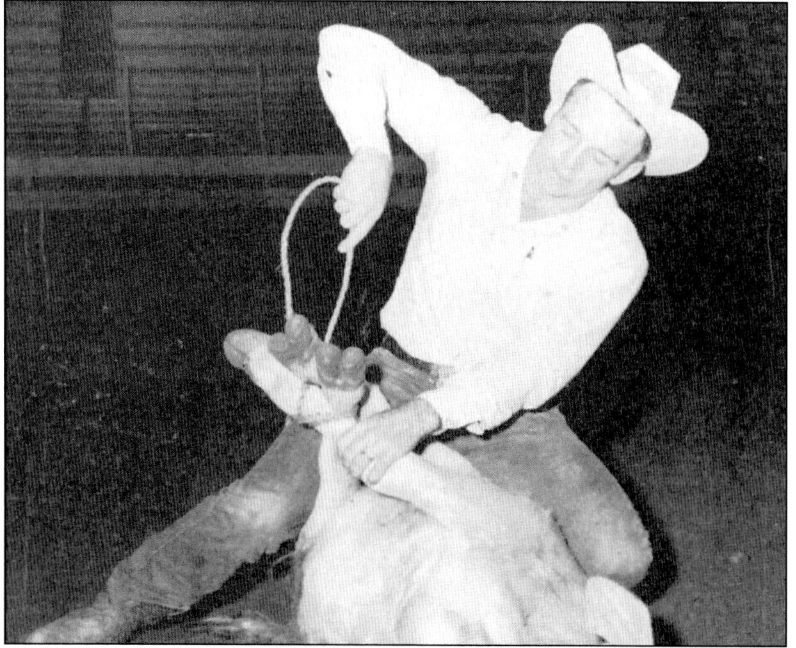

COTTON KINNEY. The impetus to form the rodeo team came from Henry "Cotton" Kinney, an outstanding high school rodeo talent, who entered McNeese in 1953. The Kinney family, from Sulphur, Louisiana, contributed several exceptional students to McNeese and the rodeo team.

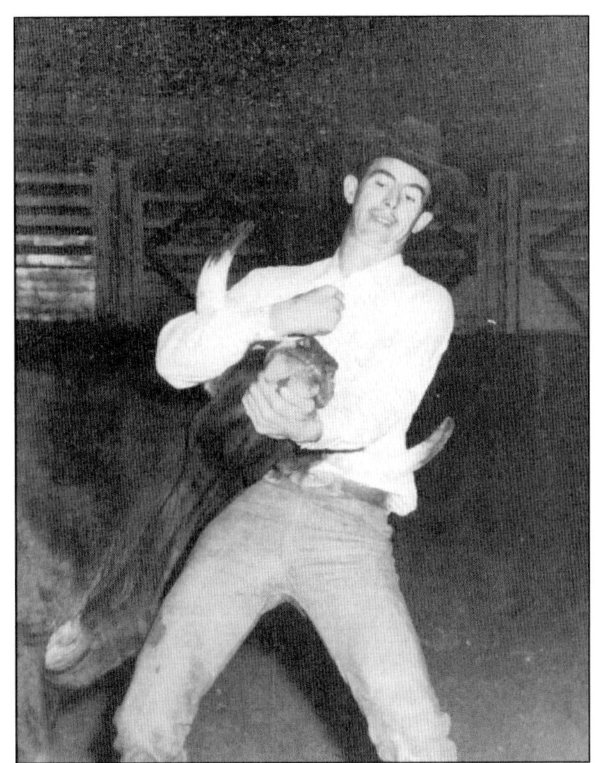

CLYDE MAY. Another outstanding rodeo talent was Clyde "Cisco" May from Luna, New Mexico. The rodeo team attracted members from across the southwestern United States, demonstrating rodeo's attraction for students and McNeese's contributions to the sport. Rodeo was a major sport at McNeese throughout the 1950s. May was selected National All-Around Champion Cowboy by the NIRA in 1957.

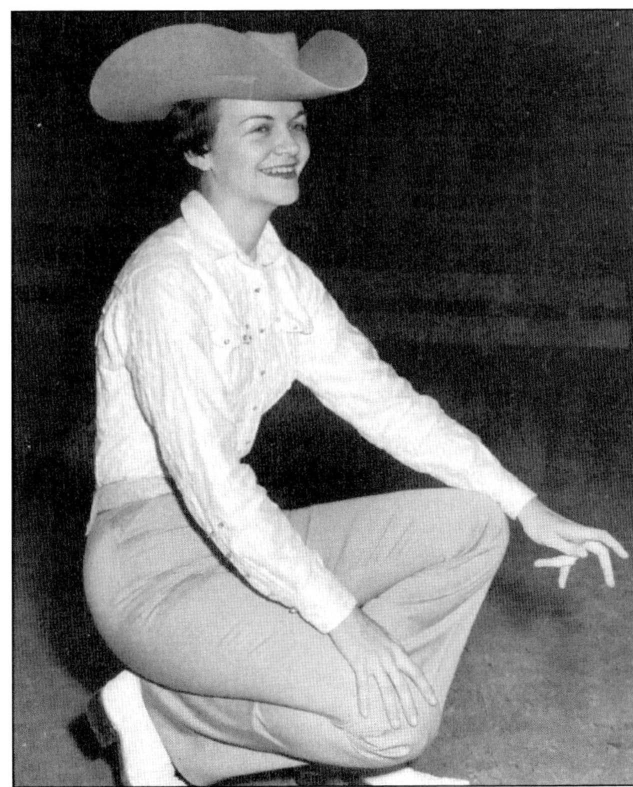

JOYCE KINNEY. Selected Rodeo Queen in 1957, Joyce "Blue Eyes" Kinney was a regular performer with the rodeo team. She participated in the barrel races and was third in the nation in 1957.

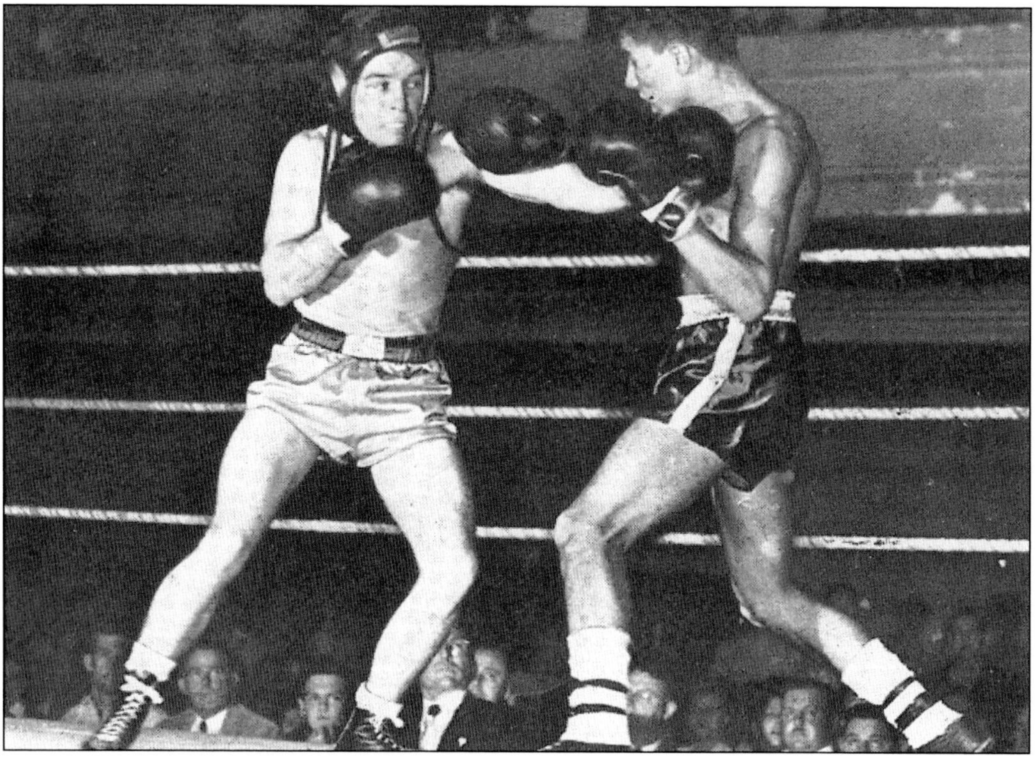

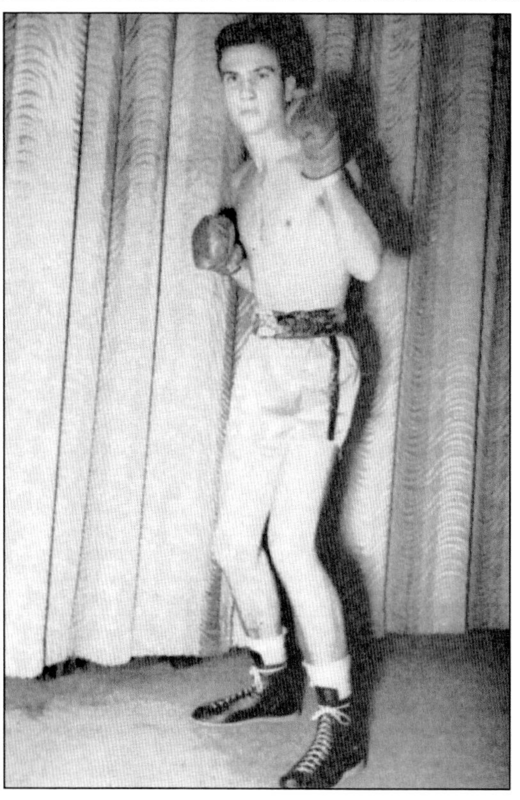

DOWELL FONTENOT. Another popular sport at McNeese during the 1940s and early 1950s was boxing. Pictured here is Dowell Fontenot, winner of the national junior college championship for 1949 and 1950, fighting Fred Flores of Allen Academy. Fontenot returned to McNeese after graduation, becoming the athletic trainer in 1956. He was appointed football trainer in 1958–1959 and remained in this position until his retirement during the 1974–1975 academic year. The Dowell "Doc" Fontenot Sports Medicine Center was named in his honor, and he was inducted into the McNeese Sports Hall of Fame in 1980.

ALBERT "RABBIT" MANUEL. Rabbit Manuel was another great favorite with boxing fans. A featherweight, Manuel was a member of McNeese's first boxing team organized in 1947. He boxed successfully for the team the two years he attended McNeese Junior College. He was inducted into the McNeese Sports Hall of Fame in 1984. The boxing team held its matches in a ring set up in the Auditorium. A.I. Ratcliff was the first coach.

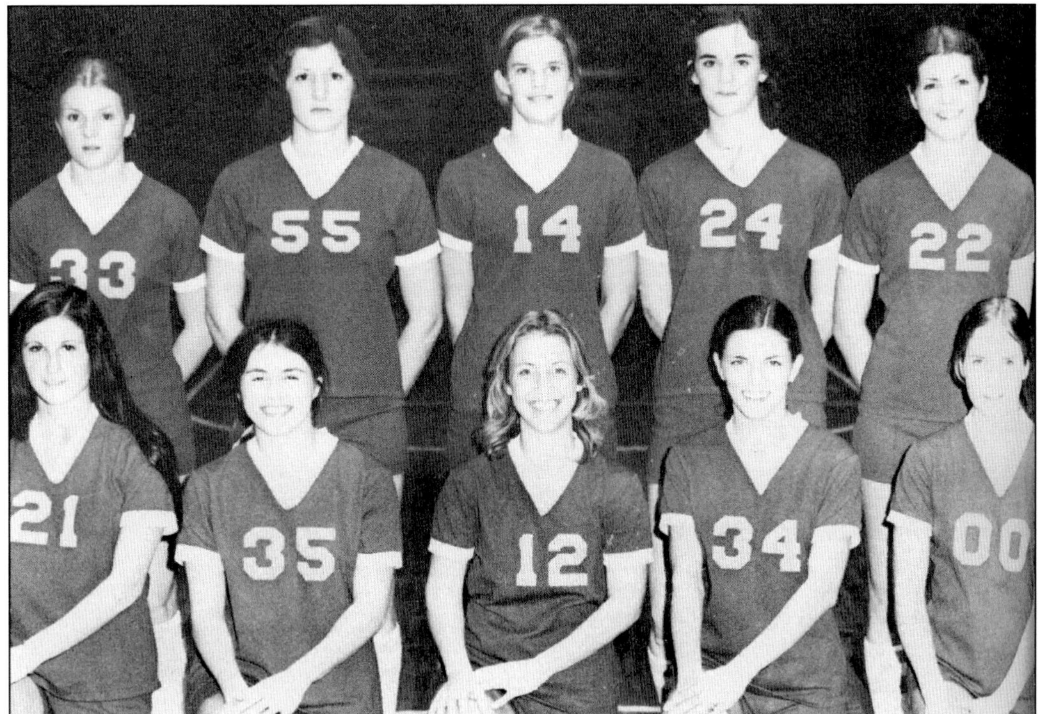

Vicki Chapman. Cowgirl athlete Vicki Chapman led the women's basketball team in scoring and rebounding during the mid-1970s. She spent the summer of 1977 playing basketball in Europe, and went on to play professionally. She was elected to the McNeese Sports Hall of Fame in 1985. The players on the 1975–1976 team seen here are, from left to right, (front row) Roxanne Allen, Kathy Cunningham, Kay Connor, Merna Miller, and Beth Oakley; (back row) Debbie Thibodeaux, Becky Dunehoo, Vicki Chapman, Beth Theriot, and Susy McKellar.

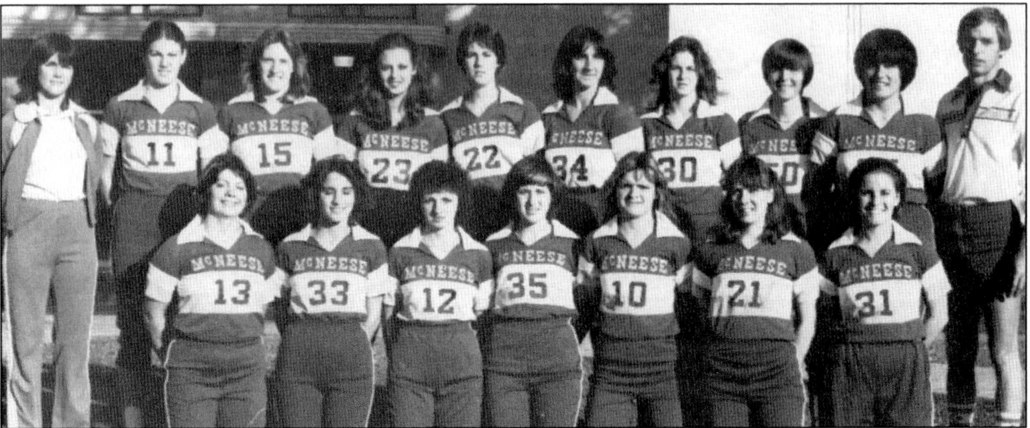

1981 Softball Team. The Cowgirl Softball Team won the State Championships in 1981. Pictured here from left to right are (front row) Kim Trahan, Cheri Mickal, Belinda Schum, Rachel Conner, Jan O'Friel, Colleen Bobbett, and Ann Roubique; (back row) assistant coach Cathy Cunningham, Olga Dupuis, Cherilyn Lantrip, Laurie Saizan, Laura Grifka, Pam Mayet, Tammy Guidry, Paula Thibodeaux, Alonda Guilbeau, and head coach Jim Draudt. Player Olga Dupuis later received an M.B.A. from McNeese and served as Internal Auditor and an instructor in the Accounting Department.

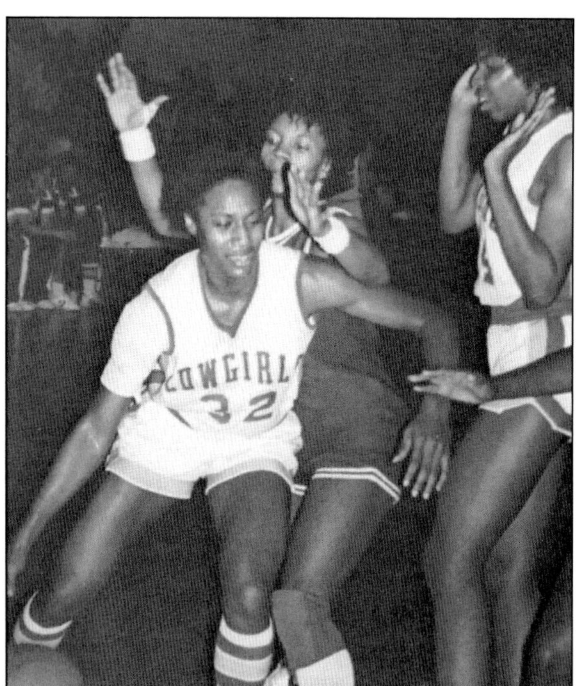

Pat "Shoney" Jean. Six-foot Pat "Shoney" Jean was a popular Cowgirl basketball player in the 1980s. She was McNeese's all time leading scorer and rebounder. She was named to the McNeese Sports Hall of Fame in 1996. Vicki Chapman, former McNeese basketball star, was the assistant coach during this time.

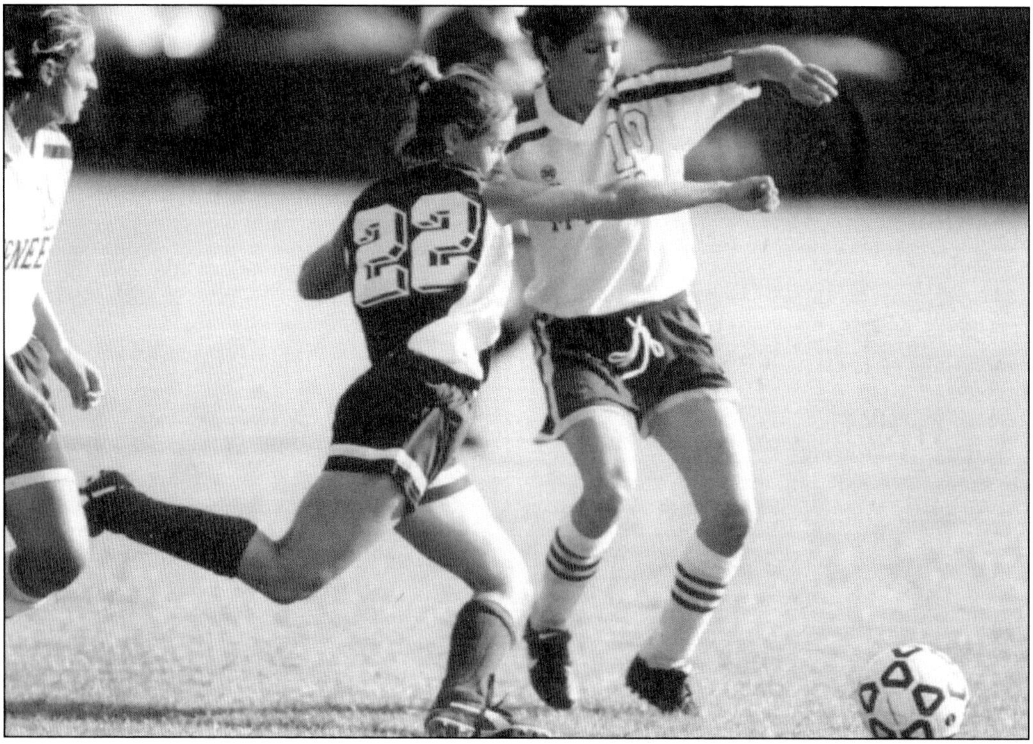

Cowgirl Soccer. Established in 1996, the Cowgirl Soccer Team finished second in the Southland Conference in 1999. Coached by Scooter Savoie, the team has improved each year. Team member Joy Keating was named the SLC Player of the Year in 1999. In this photograph, Brenna Abbitt, # 22, makes a play against an opposing team member.

Seven

ALUMNI

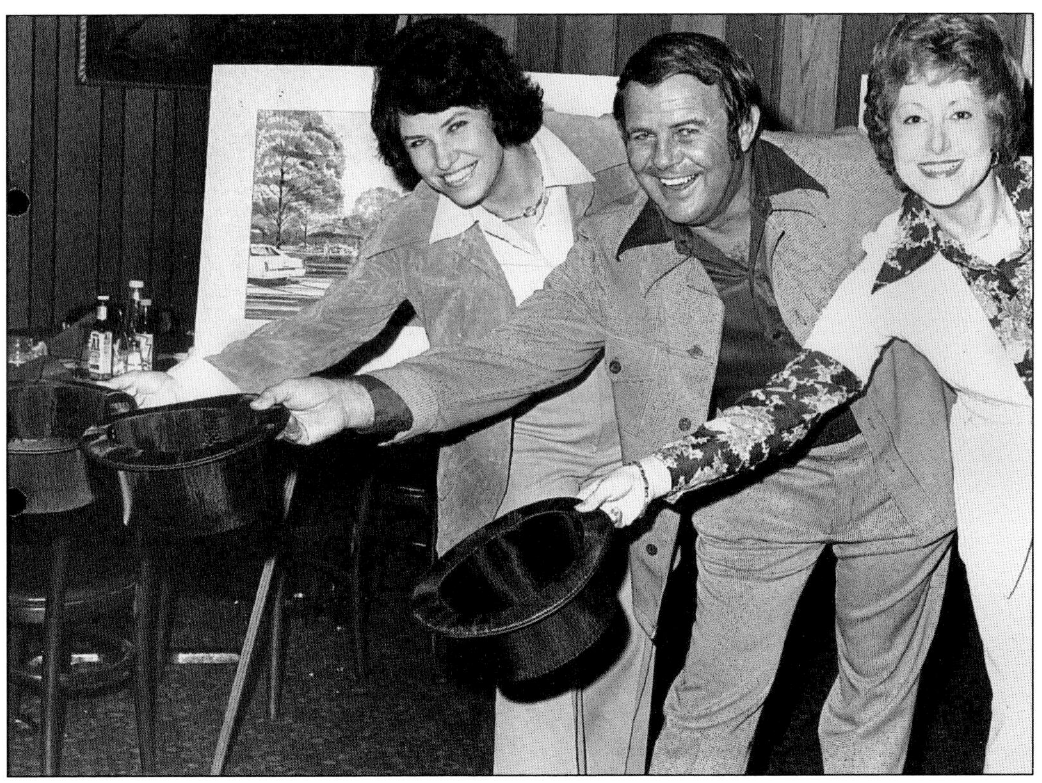

WILLIAM F. GOSSETT AND THE TOP HAT CLUB. William F. "Billy Frank" Gossett became the first full time Alumni Affairs Director in 1970–1971. A student at McNeese in the early 1950s, he served as president of the Alumni Association in 1965–1966. He was awarded the Distinguished Alumni Award in 1983 for his unselfish dedication, guidance, and work during construction of and fund raising for the Alumni Center. Gossett is pictured here with two unidentified members of the Top Hat Club, a fund-raising group organized to help raise money for the construction of the center.

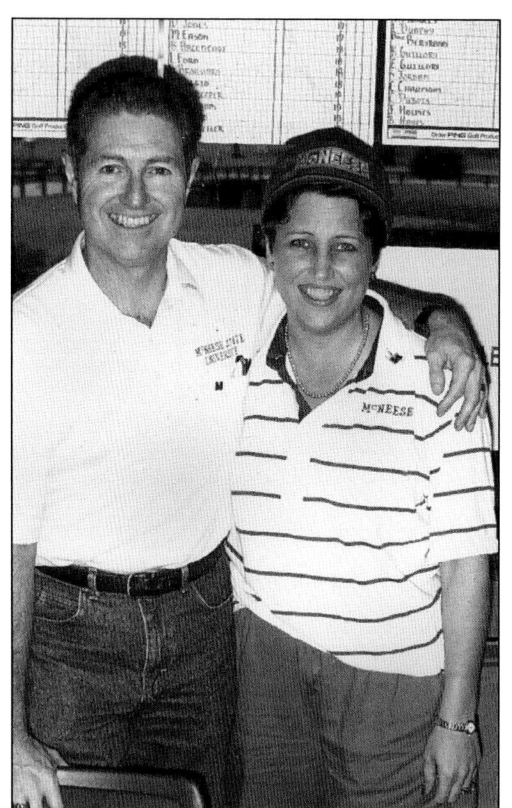

JOYCE PATTERSON. Joyce Patterson, pictured here with her husband, Dr. John C. Stubblefield, became the second Alumni Affairs Director in 1982. Patterson is responsible for many activities sponsored or hosted by the Alumni Association each year. The *Alumni News* is mailed to over 20,000 households three times a year. Approximately 1,000 graduates are added to this mailing list each year. Patterson was McNeese student body president in 1975–1976 and is a very devoted supporter of the university.

PAST PRESIDENTS. Attending the Past Presidents Dinner, sponsored by the Alumni Association during Homecoming each year, are six former presidents. All were active in their roles and accomplished a great deal for McNeese. Pictured from left to right are (seated) Richard Guillory, 1978–1979; Pat Quirk, 1976–1977; and D.C. "Chick" Green, 1975–1976; (standing) Charles Goen, 1974–1975; Dr. Lee J. Monlezun Jr., 1982–1983; and Billy Frank Gossett, 1965–1966.

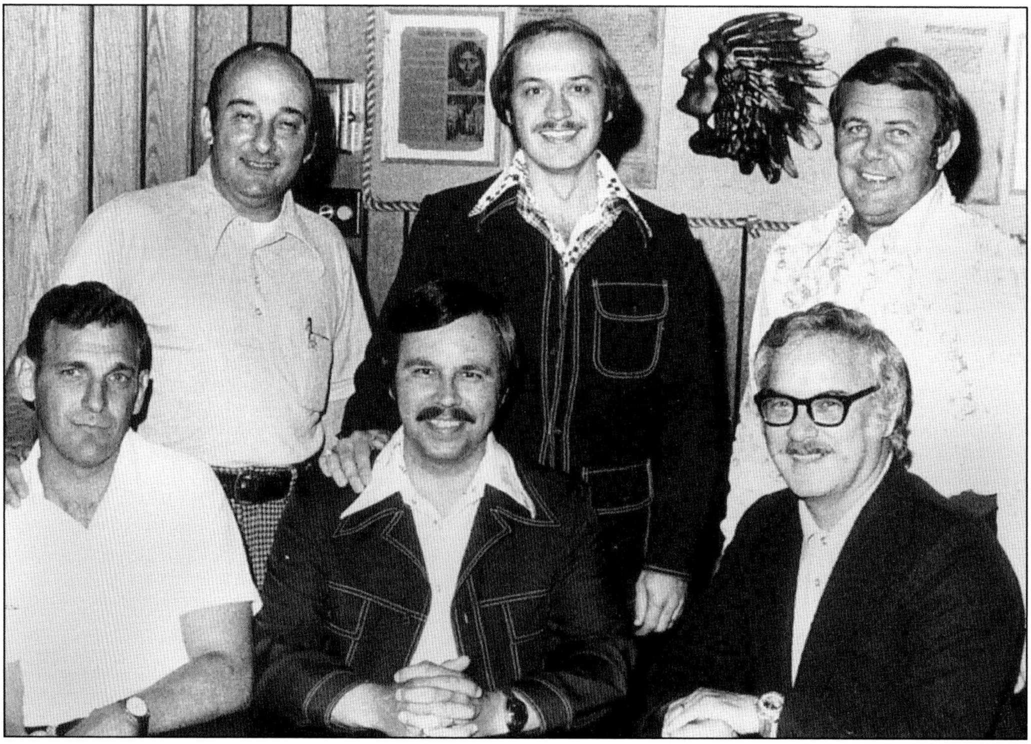

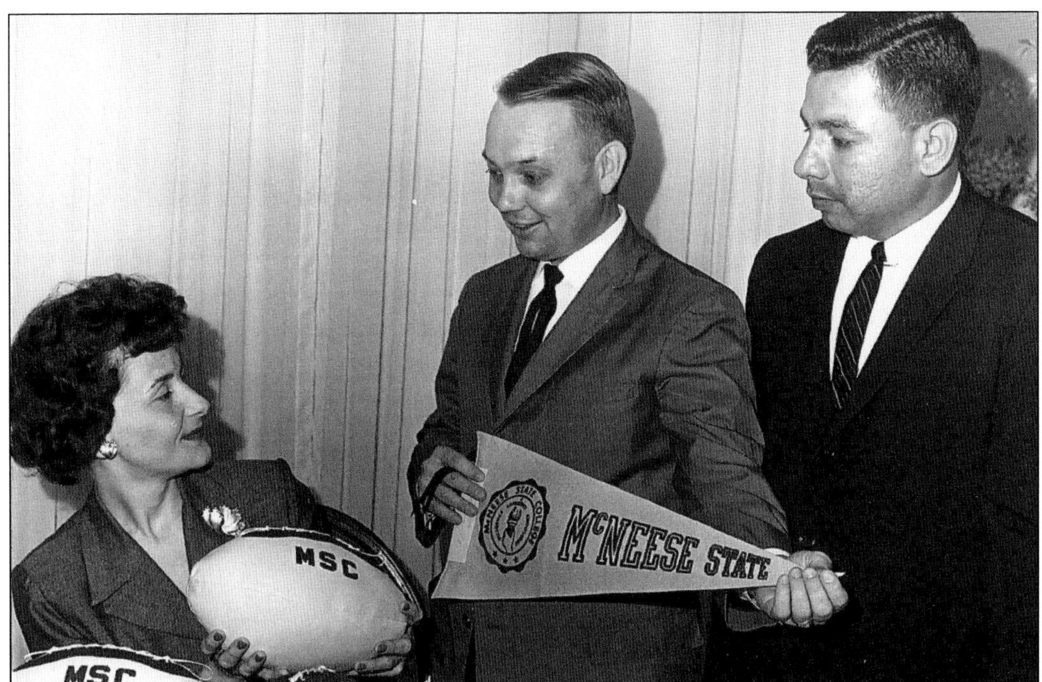

GETTING READY FOR HOMECOMING. From left to right in this 1961 photograph are Betty Lou McKellar, W.T. "Billy" Clarke, incoming president, and Alfred "Freddie" Flores, president. These officers of the Alumni Association look at decorations to be used during Homecoming festivities. The president-elect chairs the Homecoming Committee, assisted by the board members.

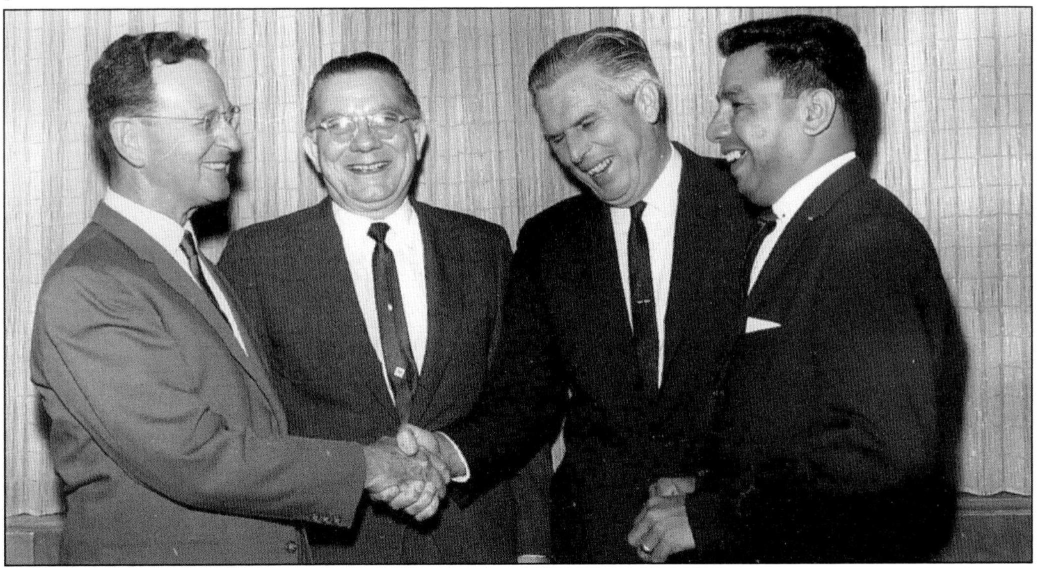

FACULTY AWARDS DINNER. Attending a 20-year award dinner at the Pioneer Club are, from left to right, Lake Charles Mayor Alfred Roberts, Dean of the College Francis G. Bulber, Pres. Wayne N. Cusic, and Alumni Affairs Pres. Alfred Flores. Traditionally, the Alumni Association awarded 20-year blue and gold lapel pins to faculty. The Association currently sponsors the Distinguished Faculty Award, originally called the President's Cup. Dr. Bulber was the second recipient of this award in 1959; Dr. Cusic was the third, the following year.

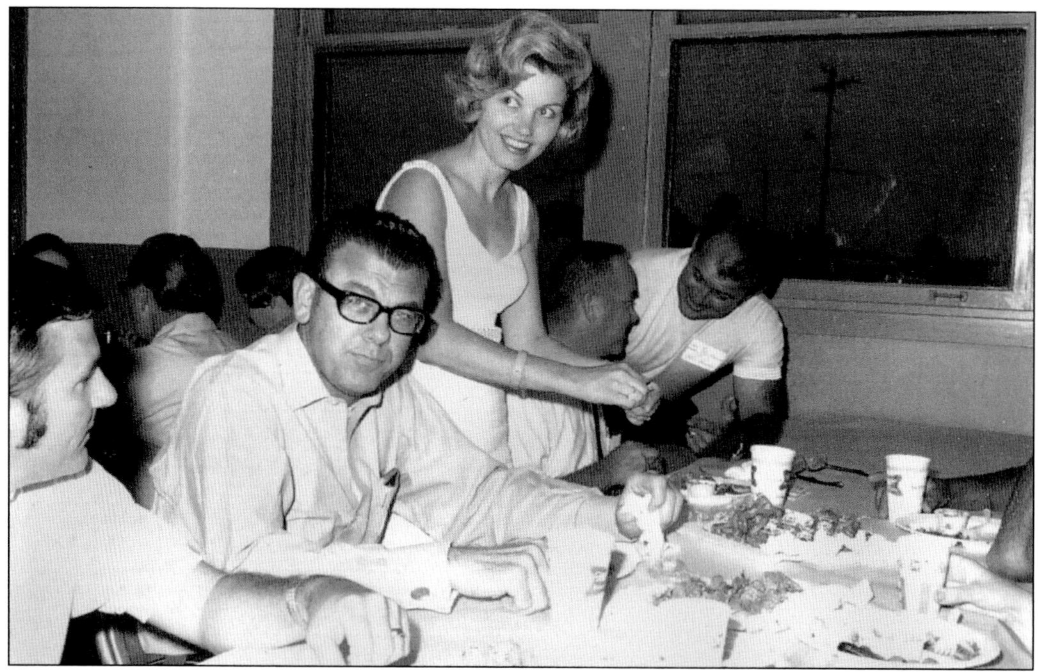

ALLEN COMMANDER. One of the most active supporters of McNeese over the years has been Allen Commander. Student body president for three years, ROTC Corp Commander, and outstanding student, Commander became active in the Alumni Association immediately following graduation. He edited the first *Alumni News* in 1954. He served in various capacities at McNeese, such as Director of Student Activities and Dean of Men, before joining the State Department during the Vietnam War. He also began the Houston Chapter of the McNeese Alumni Association. He has spent most of his academic career since the 1960s at the University of Houston and Texas A & M.

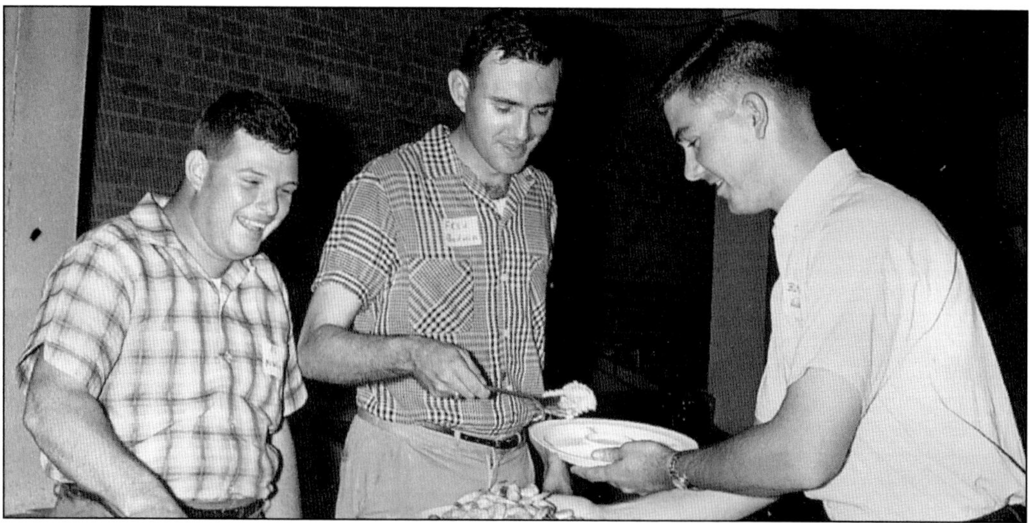

ALUMNI HONOR SENIORS. Traditionally, the spring shrimp boil was the first alumni function to which graduating seniors were invited. In this photograph, Al Newlin II, left, and Fred Godwin serve Louis "Butch" Hobbie. Newlin was Alumni Association president in 1963–1964, Godwin served as president in 1960–1961, and Hobbie was student body president in 1960. Godwin went on to practice law in Lake Charles and is currently a 14th Judicial Court Judge.

114

SHRIMP BOIL. In this 1967
photograph, Orrie Canik serves
shrimp to graduating seniors.
Today, the association sponsors
GradFest, which gives graduating
seniors the opportunity to
make final preparations for
graduation. A crawfish boil is held
in conjunction with the annual
meeting of the association each
spring. During this meeting,
donors are recognized and
officers are installed.

PENGUIN GUMBO. Joyce Patterson,
current Alumni Affairs Director,
and Hershel Bergeron have a
great time preparing gumbo
for loyal McNeese fans at the
NCAA championship game in
Chattanooga in 1997. Rival
Youngstown, Ohio, fans did not
enjoy seeing their mascot, the
penguin, hanging from a noose
in the background nor did they
appreciate the supposed main
ingredient of the gumbo.

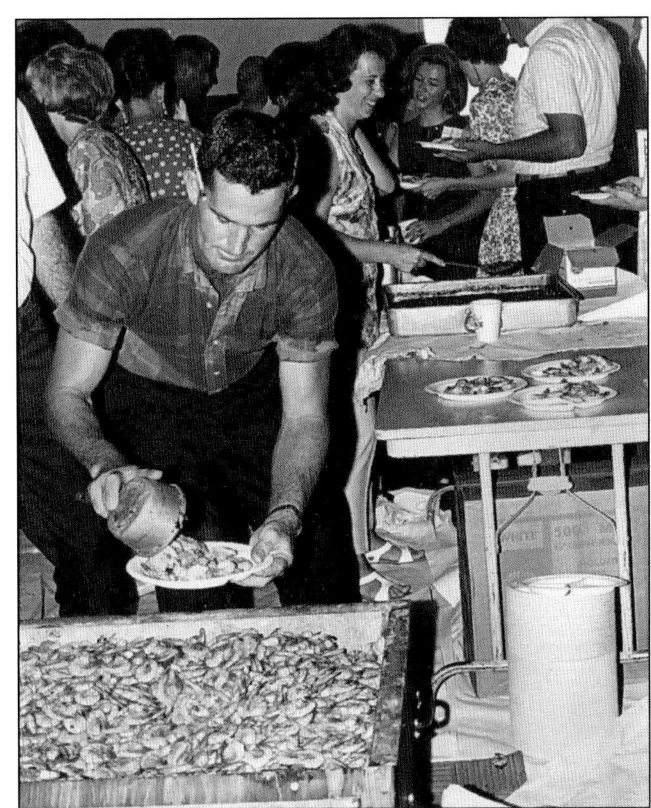

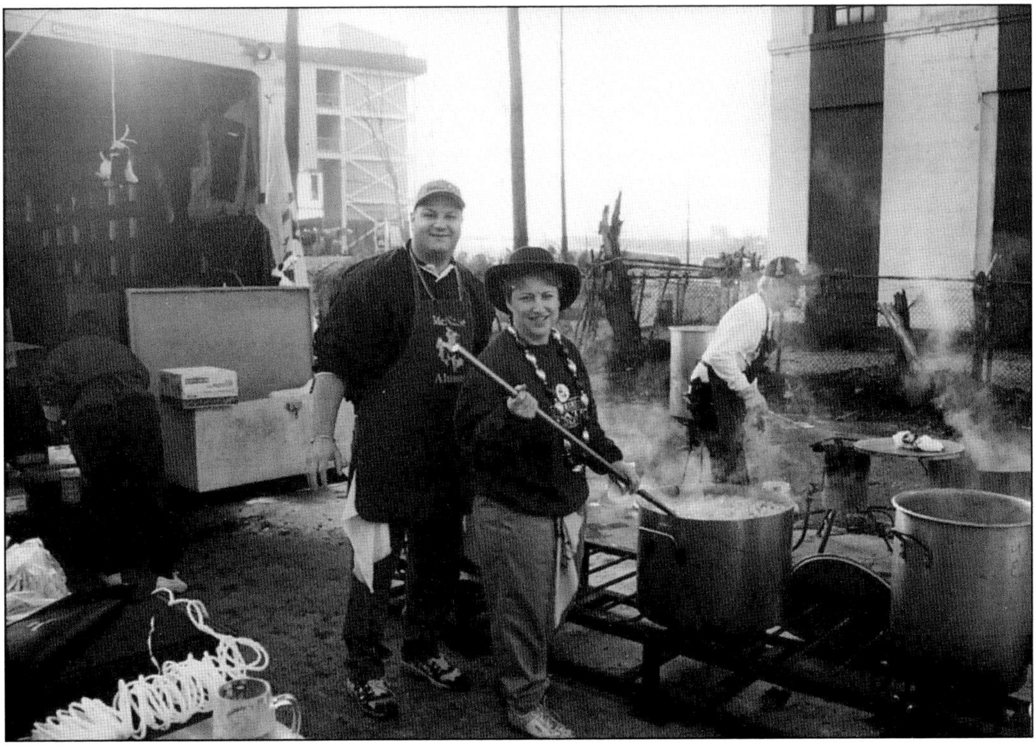

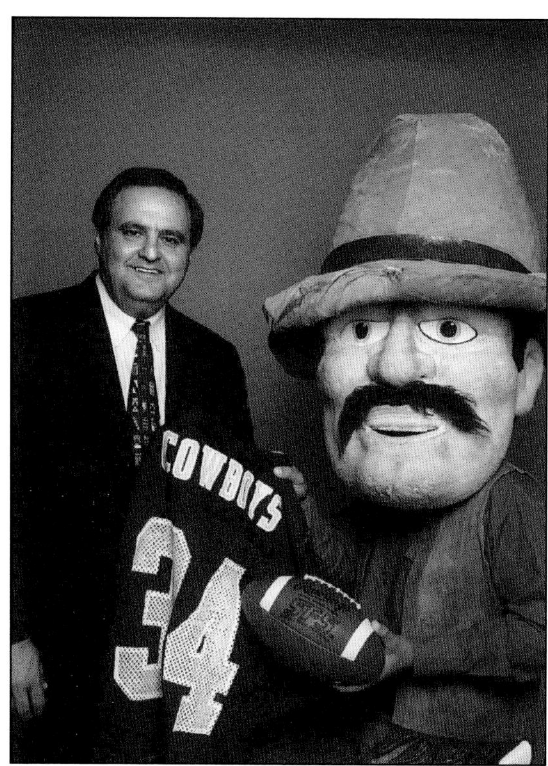

DISTINGUISHED ALUMNI AWARD. Richard Ieyoub, Louisiana Attorney General, was the recipient of the Distinguished Alumni Award in 1994. Posing here with Rowdy, McNeese's cowboy mascot, Ieyoub was awarded for his service to the legal profession and for his enthusiastic support of McNeese. Other recipients of the award include, most recently, Brigadier Gen. Joe G. Taylor, Robert F. Nash, Sheryl L. Abshire, Joe Dumars, William J. Dore, R.L. "Bubba" Nelson, Judge Earl Veron, Bessie Jean Kearns, Dr. Cecil Cyrus Vaughn, and Dr. John R. "Mickey" Royer.

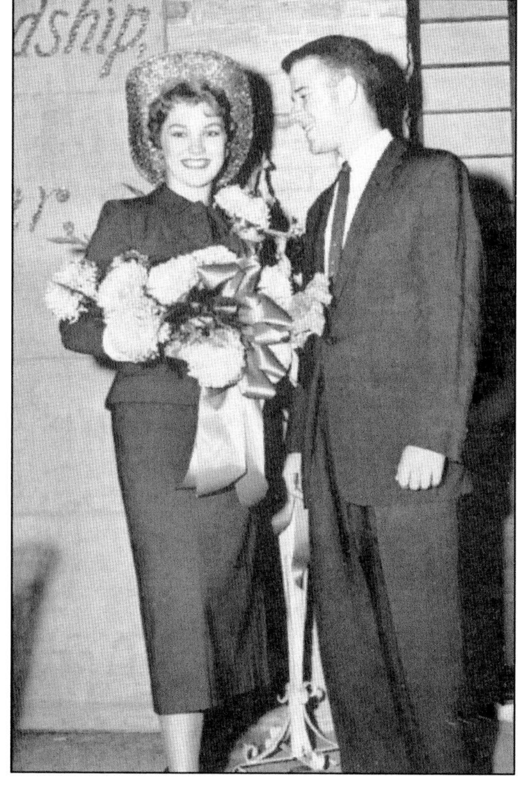

ANDRE DUBUS. As a student at McNeese in the late 1950s, Andre Dubus wrote a column in the *Contraband*, and had one of his stories included in the first *Arena*, the publication featuring works of students and alumni. Dubus went on to serve in the Marine Corps, from which experience he wrote his first novel, *The Lieutenant.* Dubus earned a master's in creative writing from the University of Iowa and taught creative writing at Bradford College for almost 20 years. He was awarded the Distinguished Alumni Award in 1996 for his accomplishments as one of America's greatest storytellers. He is pictured here escorting the Freshman Queen, Pat Lowe, who later became his wife.

116

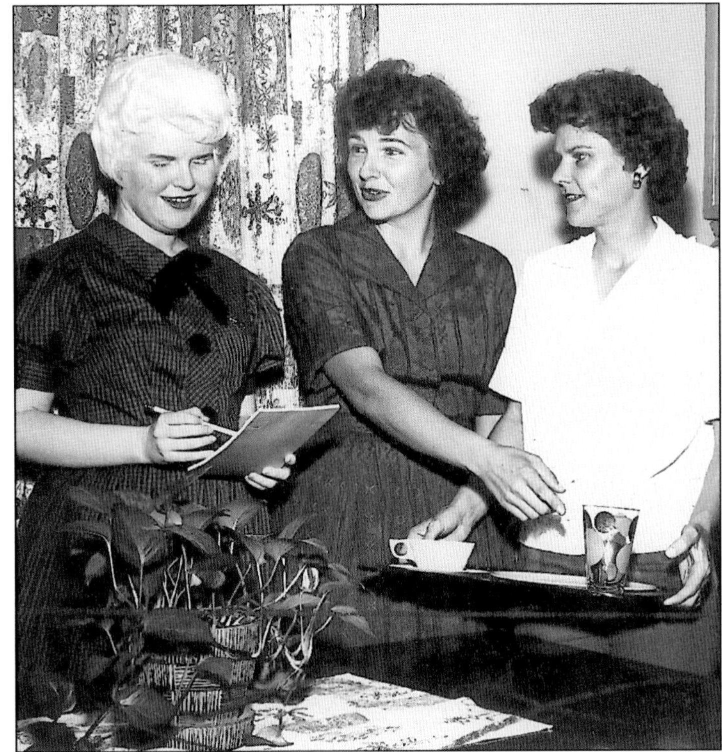

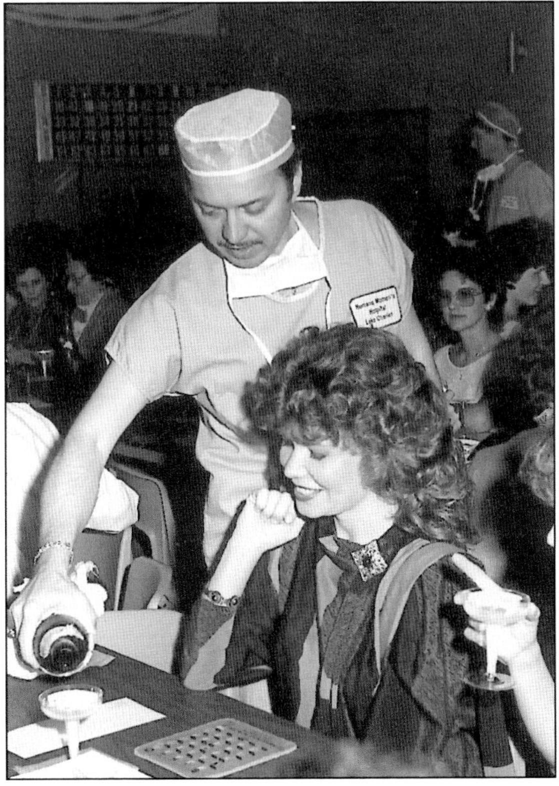

CHAMPAGNE BINGO. One of the most
popular of the Homecoming activities
planned for ladies only is Champagne
Bingo. Each year a sponsoring
organization, such as Humana Women's
Hospital in this photograph, furnishes
the champagne served to the ladies while
they play and are entertained by Master
of Ceremonies, Charlie Goen. In this
photograph, Alumni Board of Directors
member, Dr. Lee J. Monlezun Jr. pours
for bingo player, Pam Boudreaux.

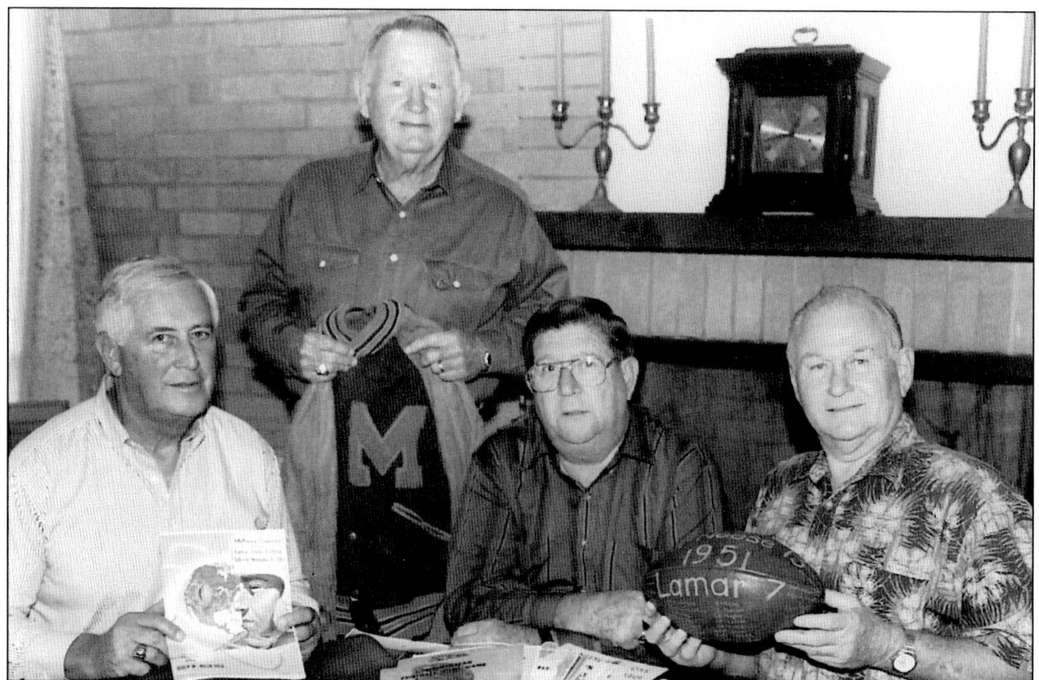

REUNIONS. Class reunions are scheduled as part of Homecoming activities. This football team reunion photograph shows Desmond Jones, standing, and seated, from left to right, Jack Salter, Jimmy Whitehead, and Jerry Chain. Jones and Whitehead were co-captains of the team in 1951. Both became active members of the Alumni Association; Whitehead served as president in 1955–1956, and Jones served as third vice president the same year. Jones went on to coach baseball and football at McNeese, and then served as Director of Financial Aid.

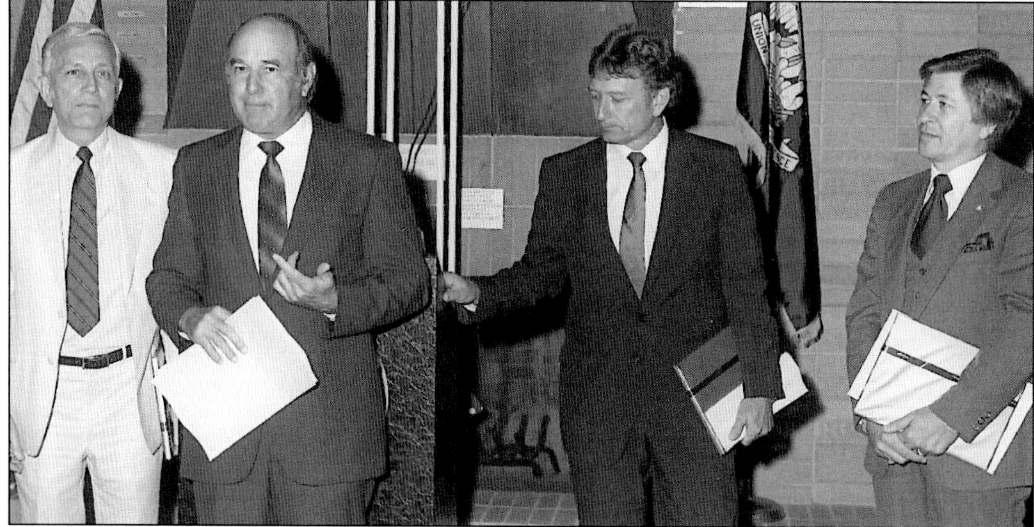

LEGISLATIVE RECEPTIONS. The Alumni Center is the scene for the Legislative Reception hosted by the McNeese administration each year before the start of the new session. University officials meet with the area legislators to discuss issues that will affect the university and seek their support for McNeese. Attending this 1985 reception are, from left to right, Sen. Bill McLeod, Pres. Jack Doland, Rep. James David Cain, and Sen. Cliff Newman.

118

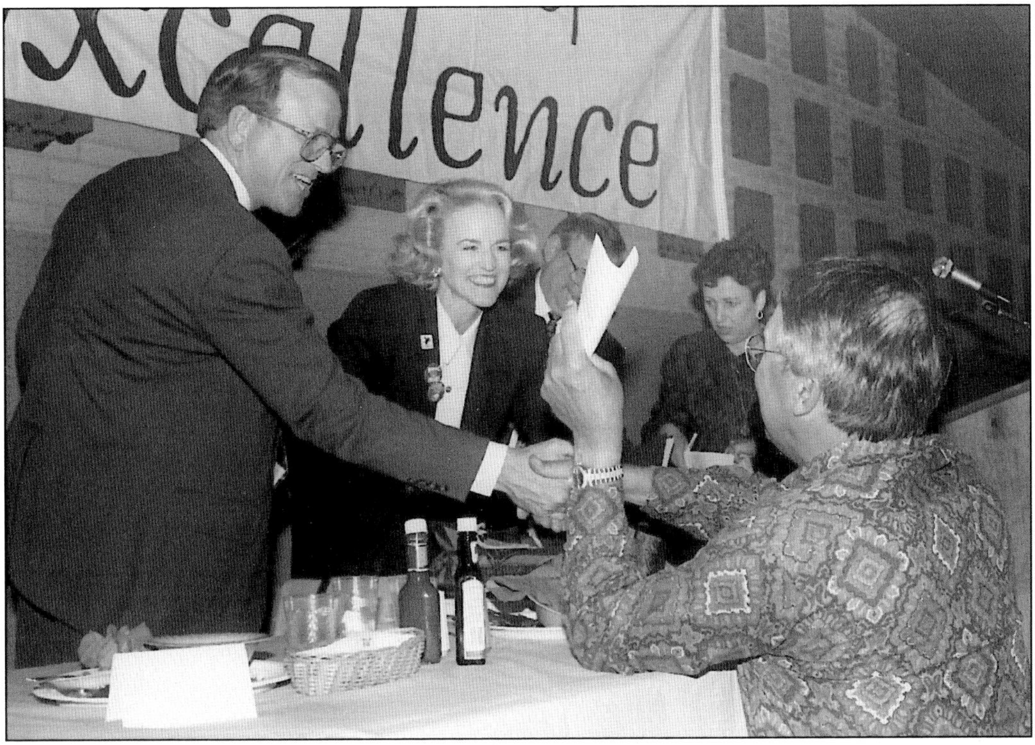

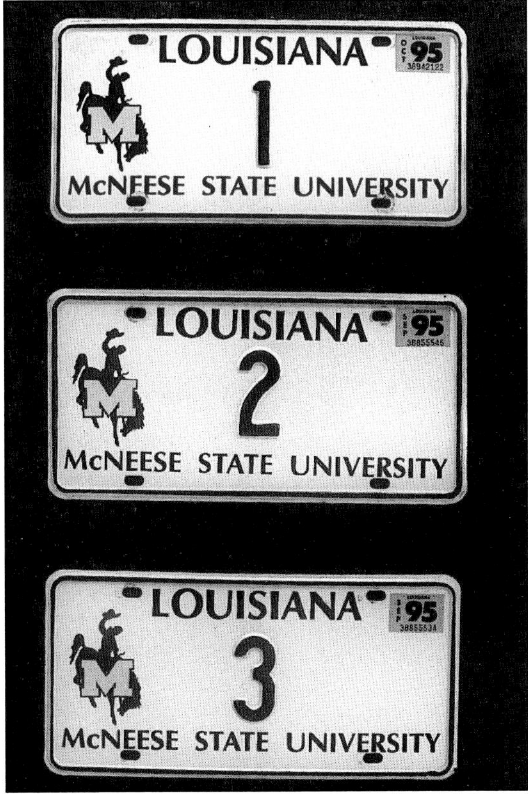

HONOR OF EXCELLENCE. The Honor of Excellence is a recruiting banquet held each year to honor outstanding high school juniors from Calcasieu Parish and their parents. In this photograph, Pres. Robert D. Hebert and Mayor Willie Mount congratulate an unidentified man. To Mount's left are Dr. Larry DeRouen and Joyce Patterson.

MCNEESE LICENSE PLATES. Initiated in 1995, the McNeese State University Plate Program raises money for scholarships for children of McNeese Alumni. The university works with the Department of Motor Vehicles to carry out what has proven to be a successful program.

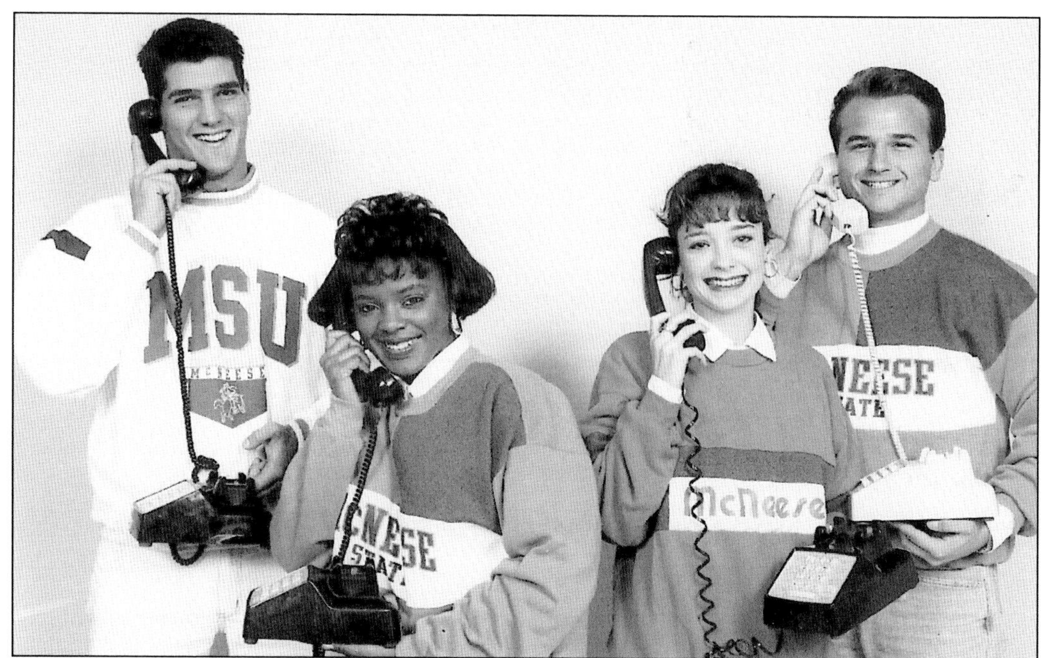

PHONATHON. The phonathon is an annual fund-raiser in which McNeese students phone prospective donors over a two-week period. The Alumni Giving Fund program generates funds for faculty development, student scholarships, and other needs. The first phonathon was held in 1993. In this publicity photograph, students John Ieyoub, Kelly ?, Stephanie Bennett, and Scott Doyle man the phones.

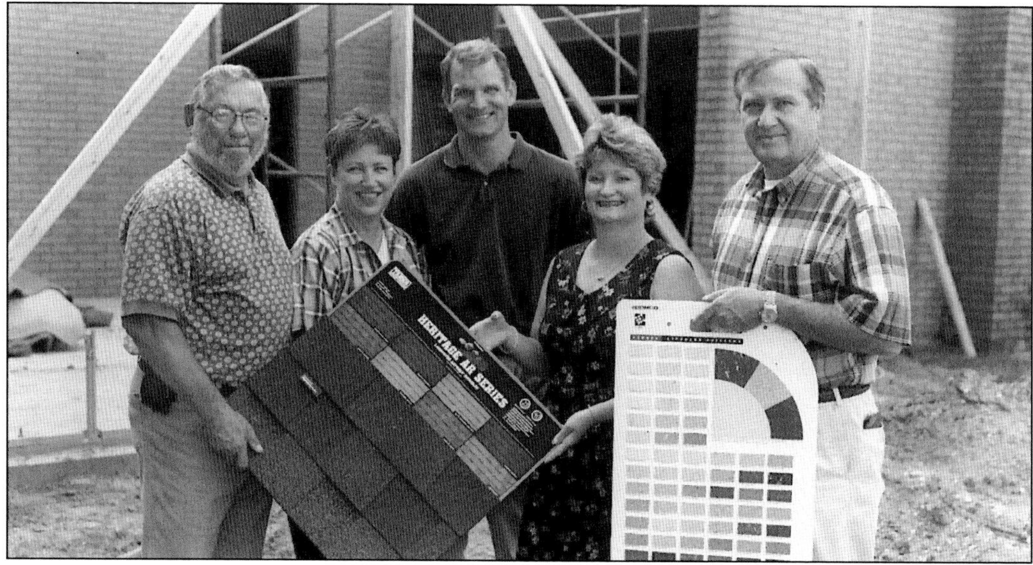

WILLIAM GRAY STREAM MEMORIAL ALUMNI CENTER. The Alumni Center was dedicated in 1978 in memory of William Gray Stream, a McNeese student who had been killed in an airplane crash. Looking over renovation plans are, from left to right, Larry DeRouen, former Director of Facilities and Planning; Joyce Patterson, Alumni Center Director; Richard Rhoden, current Director of Facilities and Plant Operations; Pam McGough, Alumni Association president and impetus for the expansion planning; and Gayle Zembower, architect.

120

Eight

MOMENTS TO REMEMBER

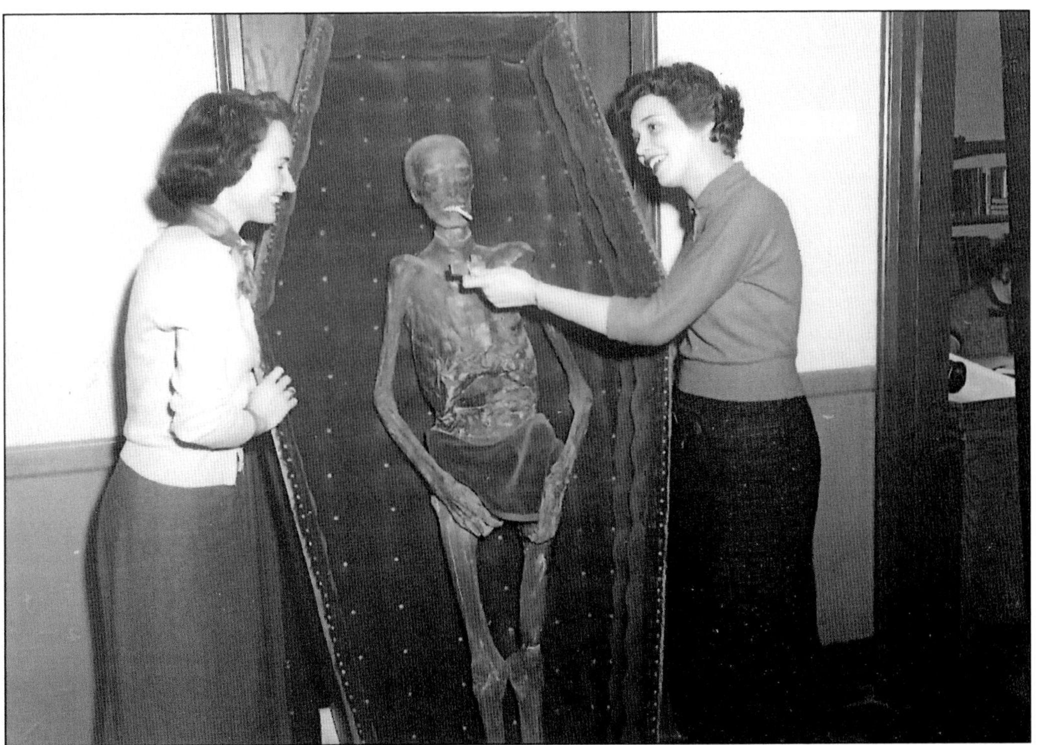

MUMMY. Patsy Harrison and Eva Jo Ward offer a cigarette to the mummy that was stored in the science building in 1955. No one knows exactly when the mummy arrived on the McNeese campus, where it came from, or who it was. Speculations are that it was the body of a transient donated to the mortuary science program that once was offered at McNeese. Efforts to give it a Christian burial have resulted in legal stalemates.

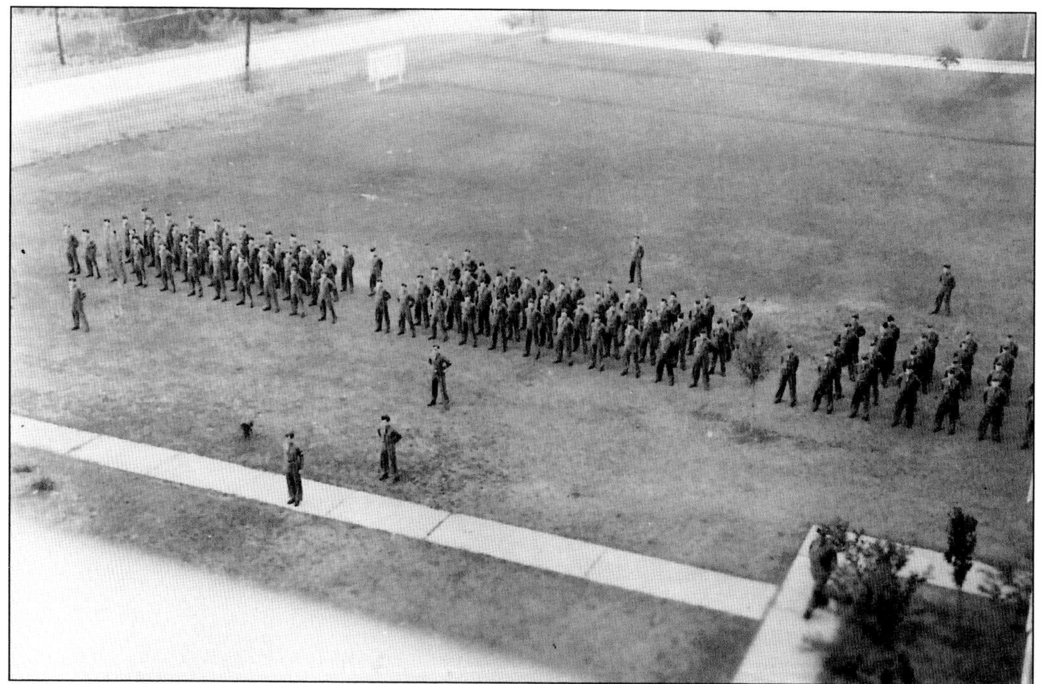

WORLD WAR II. Students assembled on December 8, 1941 to hear President Roosevelt's message to Congress asking for a declaration of war on Japan. Charles Cobb became the first student to enlist in the armed forces by signing up with the United States Marines that same day. Before long, the auditorium and the arena were filled with soldiers, military drill units had been formed, dive bombers made daily practice raids on the campus, and formations like this one were common sights on campus.

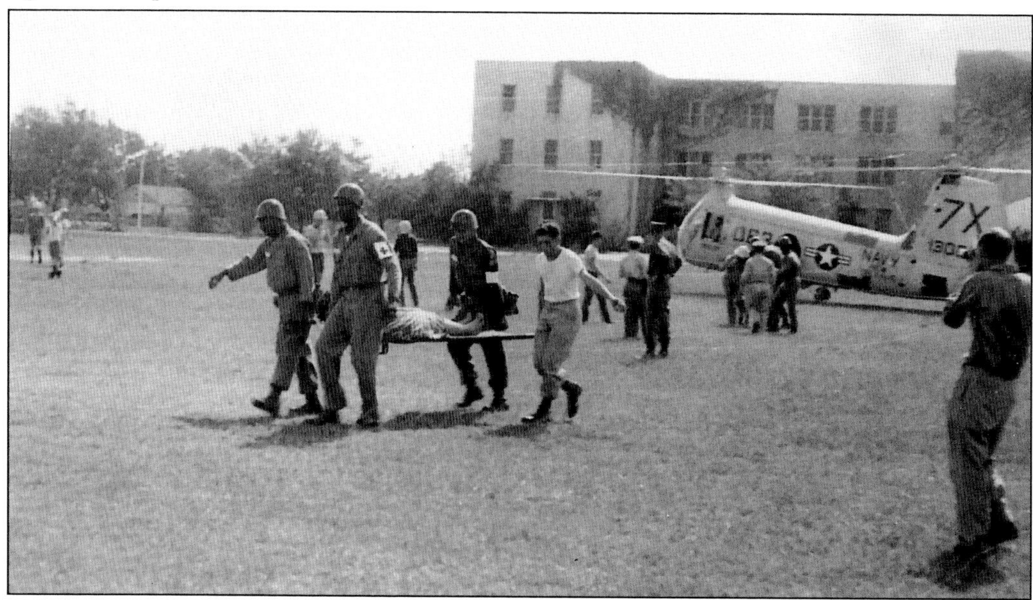

HURRICANE AUDREY. Brought in by trucks and by helicopters, evacuees from Cameron Parish found shelter on the McNeese campus after devastating Hurricane Audrey shattered their homes and their lives.

122

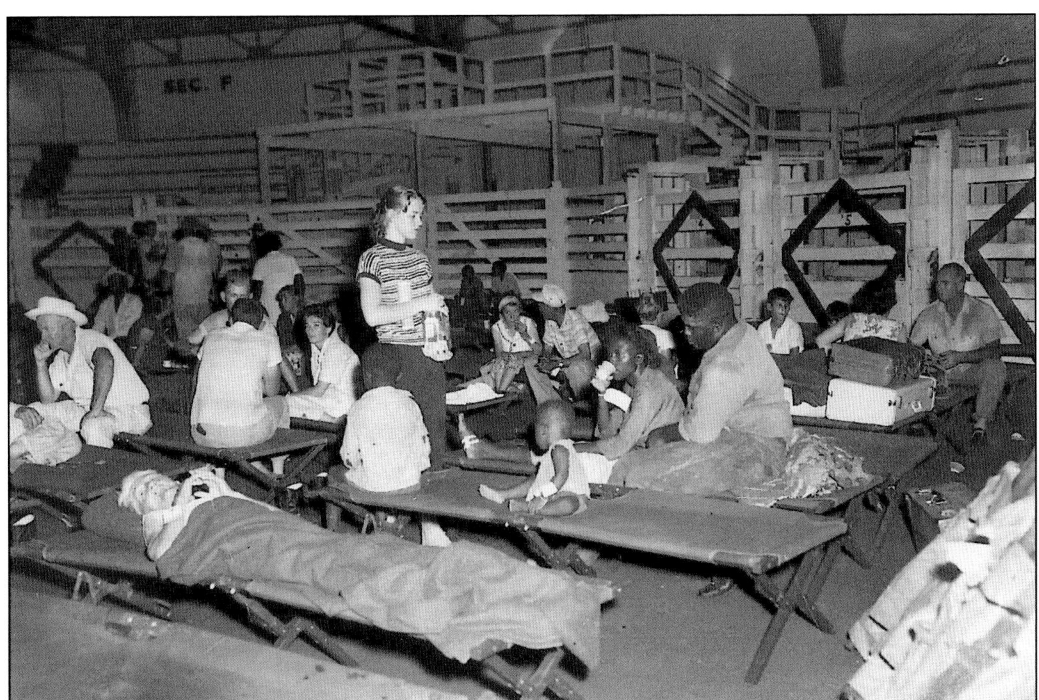

SHELTERING EVACUEES. The arena sheltered over 1,000 evacuees from Cameron Parish after Hurricane Audrey struck the area in the summer of 1957. The gymnasium served as an infirmary for those with minor injuries. College personnel, students, staff, faculty, and administration assisted in the emergency efforts.

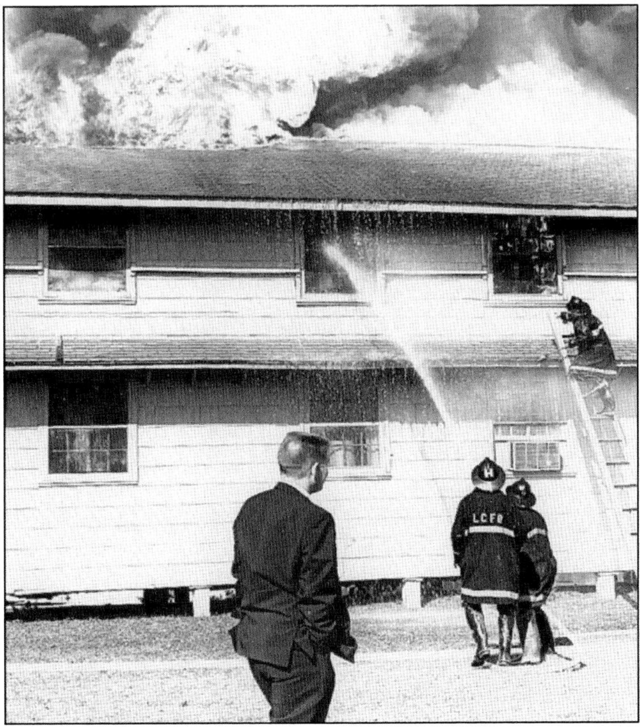

PUBLICATIONS BUILDING FIRE. In January 1966, the Publications Building burned. This was a temporary frame building that housed the campus printing room, the News Bureau, several sorority and fraternity rooms, and the offices of the student newspaper, the *Contraband*, and the student yearbook, the *Log*. The *Log*, almost ready for final editing, had to be put together again. Many records and photographs were destroyed.

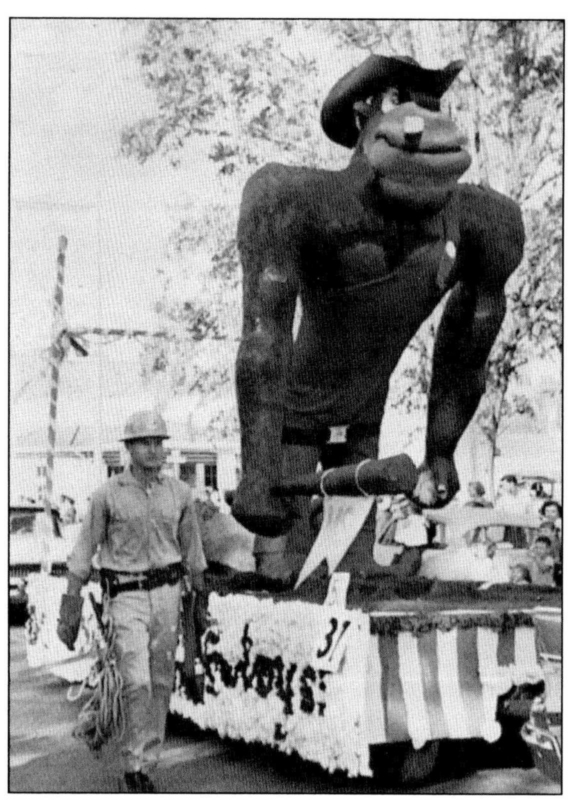

GORILLA. The first place winner in the 1957 Homecoming Parade was Delta Theta Chi's huge gorilla float. The gorilla was so tall that an electrician who walked beside the float would lift the electrical lines when the float passed under them. Other Homecoming events in addition to parades were bonfires, pep rallies, alumni activities, the Homecoming Dance, and of course, the football game.

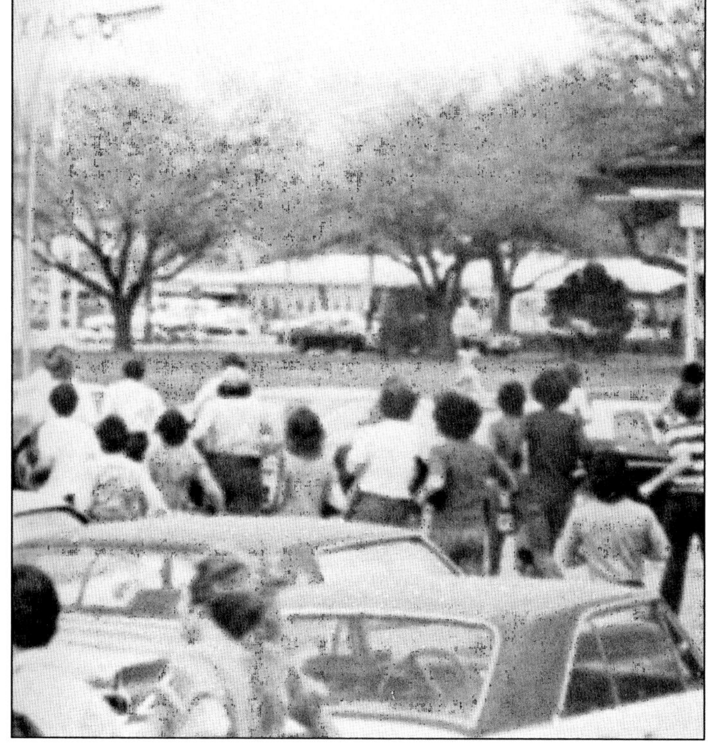

STREAKER. According to the 1974 *Log,* streaking fever hit McNeese during the spring, but was very short-lived. "It was quite a change from the more violent forms of protest prevalent in the late 1960s and early 70s. Streaking was a pleasant diversion from the usual drudgery of a spring semester—those brave enough to try their hand at it raced across campus nude, although a few found anonymity in a paper bag mask."

124

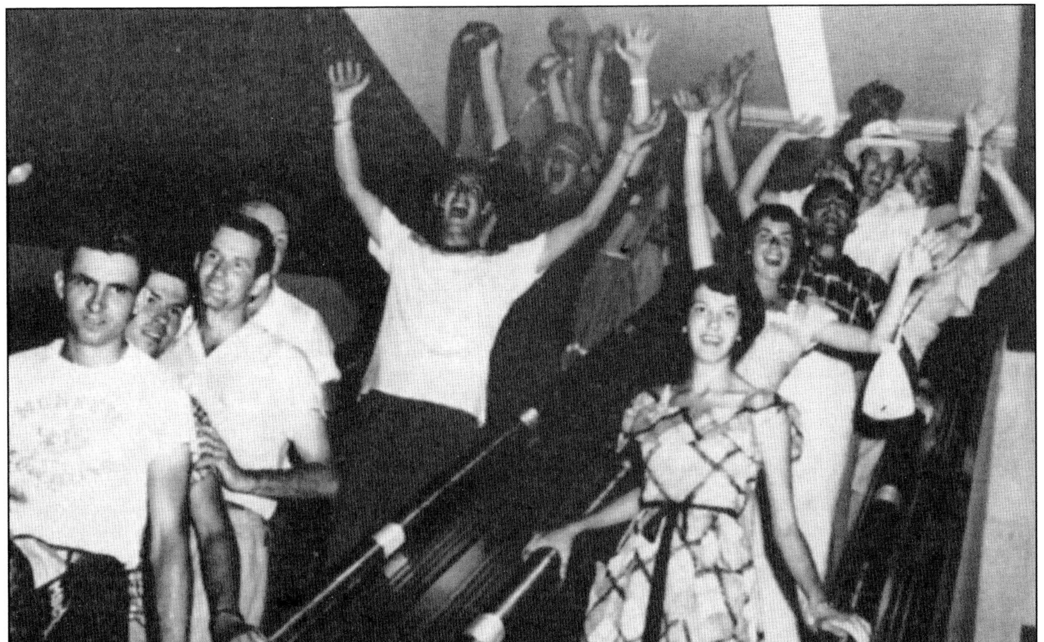

FOUR-YEAR STATUS. When President Frazar announced that the Louisiana Supreme Court had rendered their decision in favor of McNeese, the student body and faculty "went wild with joy and excitement." This 1951 picture was taken downtown where a pep rally and parade celebrated the event. Making McNeese Junior College a four-year college involved bills before the state legislature, separation from LSU, lawsuits, court testimony, and Supreme Court rulings. Appropriately, the five attorneys who handled the case were given special honors at Homecoming that year.

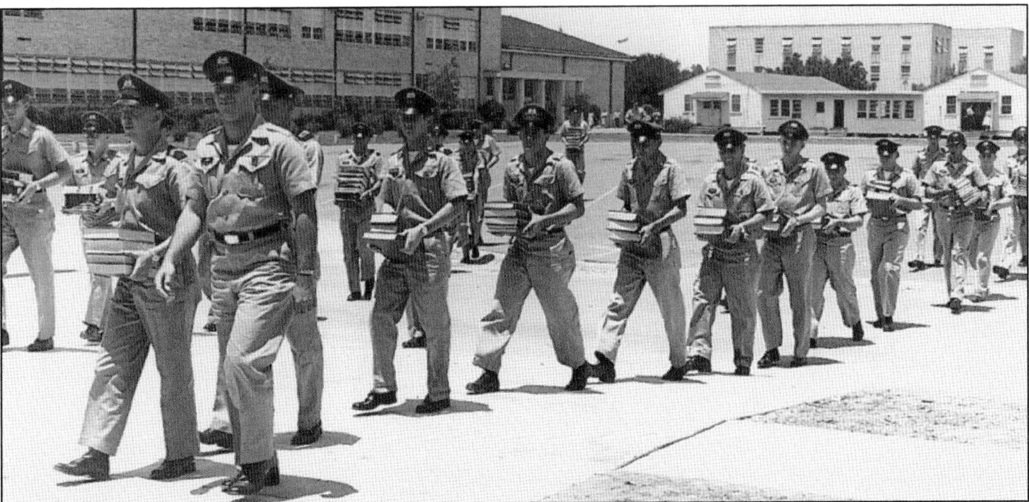

OPERATION BOOK MOVING. In an overwhelming act of cooperation and school spirit, the cadet companies of the ROTC set up the new library in 1961. Under the leadership of Cadet Colonel Reginald Fontenot, the cadets cheerfully and systematically unloaded 32,000 books from the shelves of the old library in Kaufman Hall and marched with them to the new library. The military band performed at the dedication ceremonies in November when the new building became the Lether E. Frazar Memorial Library.

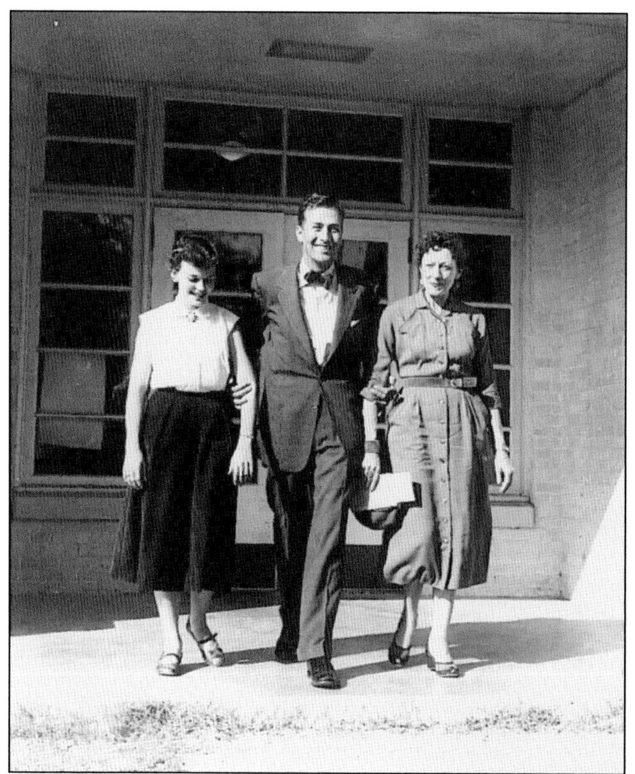

FAMOUS FACES. Throughout the years since its establishment, McNeese has played host to many famous people. The Department of Speech and Theatre has been responsible for bringing many of these people to campus. In this 1953 photograph, actor Jeffrey Lynn walks with Margery Parsons Wilson (right) and Nancy Bybee. Lynn was in town to star in a Lake Charles Little Theatre production of *Mister Roberts,* and took time out to visit the campus and talk with the Bayou Players.

COWBOYS ON CAMPUS. The Southwest Louisiana Fat Stock Show and Rodeo along with the McNeese Rodeo Team brought *Bonanza* stars Lorne Greene and Michael Landon to town. Tex Ritter, Gene Autry, and Dale Robertson were stars of the rodeo in earlier years. Other noteworthy visitors to campus included actors Vincent Price, Bette Davis, Agnes Moorehead, Edward Everett Horton, Hurd Hatfield, Charles Laughton, Broderick Crawford, Hans Conried, and Errol Flynn; writers Bennett Cerf, Harnett Kane, Andre Dubus, and Larry McMurtry; and political figures Dwight D. Eisenhower, Dan Quayle, and Barbara Bush.

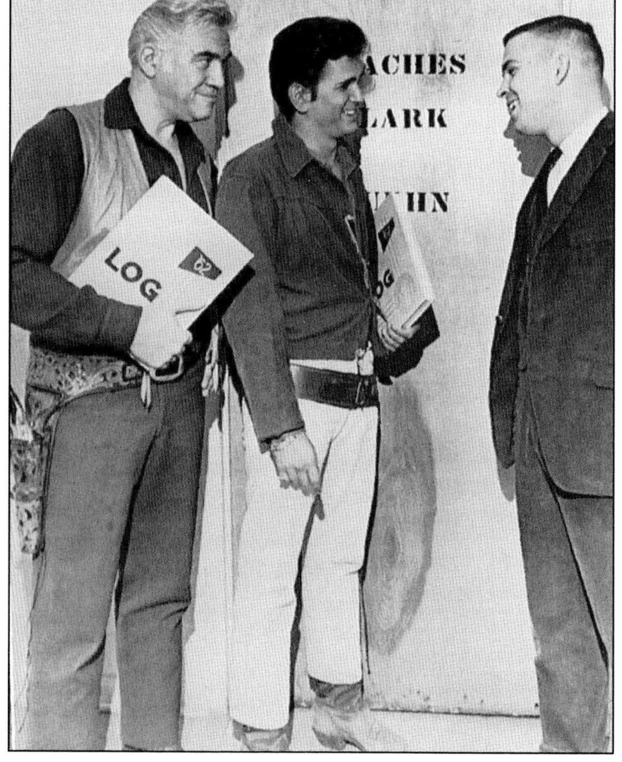

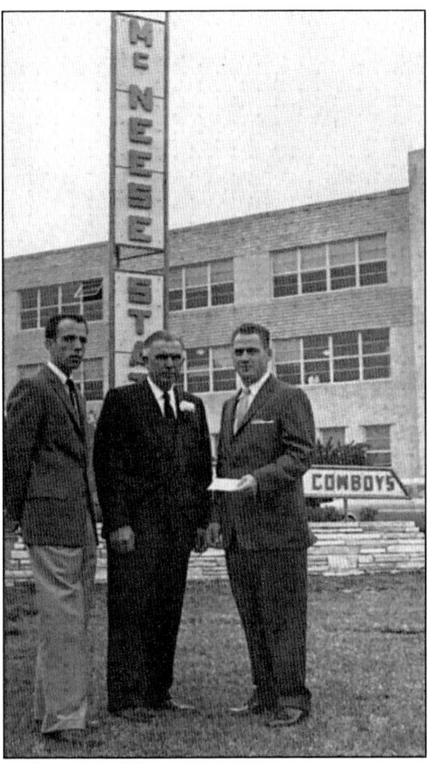

McNeese State College Sign. President Wayne N. Cusic dedicated the new college sign reading "McNeese State College–Home of the Cowboys" during the 1959 Homecoming festivities. The McNeese Alumni Association presented the sign to the college. David I. Norwood III was responsible for the design of the sign. Standing with Dr. Cusic (center) in front of Kaufman Hall are an unidentified man and Freddie LeBlanc.

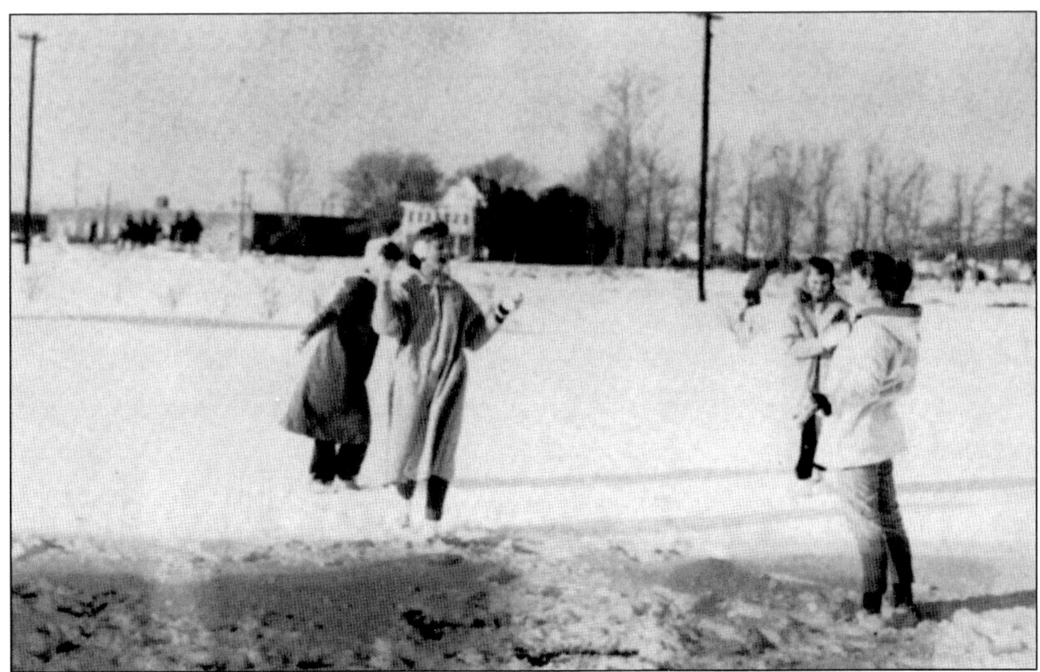

Snow! A rare occurrence in Southwest Louisiana is a snow day. Students of all ages go out to play in the snow when classes are called off. This was the scene across the McNeese campus in the winter of 1960. Two unidentified students join in the fun and frolics of a snow day.

ACKNOWLEDGMENTS

The author is greatly indebted to many people who helped make possible this photographic history of McNeese State University. I would like to acknowledge them and offer them my heartfelt thanks. Robert Benoit, Southwest Louisiana Historical Association, and Nancy Khoury, Frazar Memorial Library Director, both provided the encouragement and the support necessary for me to begin this project. Polly Fontenot, Rachel Duckham, and Lee Coyne, student workers in the Archives Department, did much of the research to find accurate information for the captions. They, with the assistance of Henry Doiron, kept the office going while I went into seclusion to bury myself in the past. I am grateful to Alan Harms, Billie Boudoin, Marianne Hartman, and Nancy Khoury for proofreading the text. My husband, Bruce Bordelon, and my children, Andrew and Jeffrey, are also to be thanked for their patience and support during the nights and weekends I worked in order to meet the publication deadline.

Three offices on campus, Alumni Affairs, Media Services, and Sports Information, provided valuable assistance and photographs. Joyce Patterson, Mary Courmier, Renee LeLeaux, John Campbell, and Louis Bonnette—thank you! Louis Bonnette merits special acknowledgement for being so patient and helpful while answering hundreds of questions from an unsports-minded author.

Most importantly, I acknowledge Dr. Joe Gray Taylor, whose book *McNeese State University 1939–1987: A Chronicle* provided so much information that preparing this book was made a much easier task.